Introduction: Reforms

1. Background

In recent years, a key challenge for Pakistan has been the revival of economic growth, job creation, and raising the standards of human development across the country. Even during the past decade, a weak position of balance of payments forced the country to resort to support from the International Monetary Fund (IMF) twice, during 2007 and 2013. While I am writing this book, the country has just completed a fund programme and there are indications that it may end up resorting again to another round of extended fund facility of the IMF. A successful graduation from IMF programmes demands Pakistan to carry out structural reforms in the areas of revenue mobilization, public expenditure management, and governance of public sector enterprises.

A related concern is the fall in (export) competitiveness despite market access provided by the European Union and the United States. While declining global commodity prices have played a role in falling value of exports in Pakistan, however, it is equally important to discuss the role of energy shortages, distortionary taxes and levies, exchange rate misalignment, and the inability of revenue authorities to clear refunds of the exporting sector. During much of the period between 2007 and 2015, the liquidity available with the private sector remained under pressure as banks were not keen to lend to the business community. This is attributed to the rising domestic bank borrowing by the government and a crowding-out effect. Besides fiscal discipline and supply-side policies, a sincere move towards bringing about export competitiveness will require a two-pronged reform focusing on: (a) a conducive and transparent regulatory environment for businesses, and (b) an infrastructure that helps generate varied forms of economies of scale.

There are reasons to believe that the state may now be willing to wholeheartedly pursue the pending reforms for inclusive growth and social justice. This optimism stems from recent diplomatic successes in the form of China-Pakistan economic cooperation (including China-Pakistan Economic Corridor—CPEC), stability in remittance inflows, low oil prices, and new trade and transit integration opportunities with Afghanistan, China, Iran, and Central Asia. While the political economy of trade with India remains uncertain, both countries have tried not to close the trade gates despite continued skirmishes at the border.

Pakistan is also trying to put together a new narrative for growth and prosperity in the wake of recent progress on trans-boundary projects such as Turkmenistan-Afghanistan-Pakistan-India

(TAPI) pipeline, Central Asia-South Asia (CASA-1000) power project, and Iran-Pakistan pipeline. There is a realization that secure energy supplies will be critical for future growth and trade expansion. Unfortunately, this realization has not been complemented with action towards improving governance of the energy sector and plugging financial and technical losses of state-owned enterprises in this sector. This continues to be a burden on the exchequer in the form of an energy-related circular debt.

The state is also trying to create a local and community-wide ownership of large infrastructure programmes, particularly in the case of CPEC, so that the chances of sabotage can be mitigated. This is particularly important in the case of gas and power supplies passing through Balochistan, and semi-autonomous tribal regions including Federally Administered Tribal Areas (FATA).

The post-18th Amendment fiscal framework has also allowed greater autonomy of provinces over spending on social sectors. The provincial growth and development strategies e.g., Punjab Growth Strategy and Khyber Pakhtunkwa Integrated Development Strategy, also provide ambitious plans and schemes to ensure local-level development including social safety nets and the equitable provision of health and education. However, even after the devolution, the greater administrative autonomy and financial flows to provincial governments have yet to result in any substantive improvement in outcome indicators such as literacy or infant mortality. In fact, infant mortality rate increased in the case of Balochistan during the period 2007–12 as per information provided by Pakistan Demographic and Health Survey (2012–13). The net primary enrolment ratio, according to Pakistan Social and Living Standards Measurement Survey (2014–15), was unchanged between 2011 and 2015 for Balochistan, Punjab, and Sindh. A gradual improvement in these outcomes will require an agenda that includes correcting governance of social sectors at provincial level and putting in place socially accountable public administration reforms. This will also require that federal government should proactively play the planning and coordination role in expediting social sector priorities across the country.

In terms of ensuring social justice, the state has yet to fully deliver on Article 34 of the constitution requiring full participation of women in national life and Article 37 providing for promotion of social justice where the state shall promote, with special care, the educational and economic interests of backward classes or areas. In this case, the shortage of resources may not be a critical issue, however, a lack of inclusive design of public sector programmes and a disregard for the voices of the community have certainly kept the achievement of these goals a distant dream.

Pakistan has made a commitment to achieve Sustainable Development Goals (SDGs), which will require an alignment of current public expenditure portfolio with (sustainable) development priorities. SDGs demand that all countries pay simultaneous attention to reforms aimed at inclusive growth, social justice, and environment. Pakistan will need to do this urgently, keeping in perspective that the country is facing environmental deterioration and recurring natural or man-made disasters, in turn imposing a burden on the exchequer. All tiers of the government will need to invest in improving adaptive capacities of the population facing these crises.

The key objective of this book is to provide a non-technical understanding of why economic growth in Pakistan has fallen behind that of peer economies. Taking a lead from recent literature on Pakistan's economy, the book explains why reform of institutions dealing with economic policy regulation and management is imperative. The book goes deeper into priority reform areas which include reform of taxation, public expenditure management, energy governance, trade, transit, and the labour market.

The book aims to maintain a non-technical language (to the extent possible); therefore, it will be an important resource for readers wishing to have an understanding of economic challenges and reform options. This book can specifically support the work performed by academia, policymakers, journalists, and civil society organizations interested in carrying out research and advocacy work as part of their social accountability efforts and improving economic governance in the country.

More specifically, the intended audience includes:

- The policy formulation community in Pakistan dealing with reforms in agriculture, industry, services sectors, trade,

labour market, and infrastructure. Key issues of economic governance constraining growth, poverty reduction, and inequality mitigation targets will be of interest to this community.
- The policy practice community in Pakistan, particularly those related to federal ministries and provincial departments of finance, planning, revenue, foreign affairs, commerce, industries, and agriculture.
- Development partner organizations which design and implement their foreign assistance packages for improved socio-economic outcomes.
- The academic community particularly those carrying out research on productive sectors of the economy and areas of (socio-economic) reform.
- The business community interested in possible options for kick starting an evidence-based public-private dialogue and possibly looking into ways to self-organize or influence policy formulation in a socially favourable manner.
- Journalists covering issues of economic governance, macroeconomic stability, and inclusive growth prospects for Pakistan.
- Civil society organizations including independent think tanks carrying out policy research and advocacy work on reform of public sector institutions in Pakistan.

The approach for structuring each chapter and explaining key arguments includes: (a) in-depth desk and literature review for each topic, (b) statistical analysis of data that have been collected by others, including analysis of official statistics,

(c) primary research conducted by the author on selected themes of Pakistan's economy provided in this book, and (d) qualitative analysis using key informant interviews and focus group meetings to discuss future reform options.

2. A Brief Summary

This section provides a brief insight into the chapters which will follow. The next chapter focuses on explaining the fragmented structure of economic governance often responsible for less than effective implementation of already approved laws and policies. The need for early finalization of post-18th Amendment laws, and institutions which can strengthen federal-provincial and inter-provincial economic coordination has been discussed. The need for improving rankings in global governance and related indicators is termed important from the viewpoint of domestic and foreign investors.

This ranking can be improved through:

- reform of public administration for improved service delivery,
- strengthening the working relationship between the Council of Common Interests, the federal and provincial governments,
- decentralizing non-relevant tasks managed by the Ministry of Finance (MoF),
- restructuring and enhancing the role of the Ministry of

Commerce (MoC) in implementing policies for (export) competitiveness,
- management reforms at energy sector generation and distribution companies,
- administrative reforms at the Federal Board of Revenue (FBR)[1],
- a more strengthened relationship between the Planning Commission (PC) and provincial Planning and Development Departments[2],
- deepening of administrative decentralization at sub-province level,
- economy-wide regulatory impact assessment to rationalize (regulatory) burden on businesses, and
- judicial reforms that facilitate businesses and dispute resolution.

While this chapter benefited from our recent interviews with relevant parliamentarians, officials at the Competition Commission of Pakistan, Securities and Exchange Commission of Pakistan, National Accountability Bureau, State Bank of Pakistan, Planning Commission of Pakistan, Ministry of Finance, Ministry of Commerce, and Federal Board of Revenue, our analysis on economic governance has several limitations. Perhaps a future effort needs to go deeper into reform of institutions responsible for economic governance at the provincial and sub-province levels.

In chapter three, we offer a detailed discussion on necessary reforms to make the tax regime fair and just. The chapter also highlights the need for a change in the public sector's view towards the entire tax collection exercise. Instead of being only an instrument to fund government expenditures, taxes need to be viewed as instruments that can support inclusive growth through job creation and incomes, and wealth redistribution.

To enhance the efficiency of direct taxes in Pakistan, we recommend doing away with various obsolete and untargeted concessions in the federal and provincial tax schedules. No future concessions should be allowed without a scientifically conducted economy-wide tax incidence analysis and approval of the National Assembly's Senate and Standing Committees on Finance and Revenue. Alongside improved tax policy, administration reforms including measures that strengthen audit capacities of revenue authorities will be required.

With enhanced powers now vested with the provinces to collect provincial taxes, all sub-national governments will need to conduct a baseline census of tax bases under their jurisdiction. Equally important is to connect, through cloud-based services, these provincial revenue authorities with the federal government's Risk Assessment and Management System (RAMS) being developed by FBR and Pakistan Revenue Automation Limited (PRAL). This step will be critical to curtail future tax evasion. This outcome can be further helped by allowing tax authorities' access to NADRA databases for validation of tax returns. The provincial authorities may pursue GIS-based validation of real estate holdings and commercial activity to help the audit exercise. On the outreach side, efforts will be required to improve taxpayers' information regarding provincial taxes, ideally through effective one-window operations. The low-yielding taxes such as cotton fee, entertainment tax, and tax on property transfers may be merged or abolished in order to bring down the compliance costs faced by taxpayers.

In chapter four, our focus is on looking into measures that could improve efficiency and effectiveness of public expenditure in Pakistan. We argue that the current composition of public spending is unable to help SDGs as: (a) little room is left for pro-welfare expenditures after disbursing for debt servicing, public administration, spending on law and order, and defence; and (b) low levels of development spending have weak outcomes due to poor portfolio management, lack of transparent monitoring of development schemes, and unchecked multiplicity of similar programmes initiated at different tiers of the government.

We propose that more effective laws are required to prevent governments from initiating politically motivated development schemes. The provision of subsidies even for pro-poor reasons should be first subject to scientifically conducted benefit incidence analysis and approval by Parliament. The liabilities of loss-making public sector enterprises need to be restructured so that these can be made attractive for private participation, public-private partnerships, or privatization, if need be. We also recommend a revision of Fiscal Responsibility and Debt Limitation Act to keep the growing debt burden under check and also protect the disbursements for SDGs. Finally, most public finance management reforms aiming at results-based management will require reform of the civil service which remains the only instrument to implement government programmes and projects.

In chapter five, we explain reasons for relatively low levels of export performance of Pakistan vis-à-vis peer economies. We argue that the focus of Strategic Trade Policy Framework should be on putting in place policies of competitiveness rather than only export promotion. Similarly, comprehensive trade facilitation reforms that bring down the logistics costs and overall cost of doing business are overdue. This goal in the long run can be addressed through timely implementation of CPEC projects.

A review of existing export promotion measures at federal and provincial government levels may be conducted. There is no compendium which provides information on all fiscal or otherwise incentives provided to exporters by various governments at different administrative tiers. Several such incentives are now obsolete and in fact a hurdle in the promotion of fair competition. A working group should be convened by MoC to look into ways through which reasons may be evaluated for Pakistan's less than optimal benefit from Generalized System of Preferences (GSP) market access facility. The same working group may advise on how best the government can help businesses in ensuring compliance with Sanitary and Phytosanitary (SPS) agreements and dealing with Technical Barriers to Trade (TBT), strengthening dispute resolution mechanism, and putting in place policies and measures which can help Pakistani firms to become part of regional supply chains. Specific mechanisms are also required within MoC to institutionalize internal monitoring and evaluation of its operations and shedding non-core tasks under this ministry. Similarly, a research unit capable of conducting quantitative analysis required in negotiation of trade agreements should be established on a permanent basis.

Finally, the business associations will also need to be better equipped with new knowledge and to organize their roles and responsibilities so that better public-private dialogue necessary to reach a consensus around reforms is reached. The more experienced players within the larger Chambers of Commerce and Industries and other business associations can provide mentoring for micro, small, and medium enterprises and help them in their participation in trade.

Chapter six focuses on improving Pakistan's physical connectivity with neighbours which in turn may also help the regional integration process as a whole, including trade and investment cooperation. We argue that Pakistan's economies of location allow the country to position itself as a conduit of trade, transport, and energy. Over time, physical connectivity can allow for improved business to business and people to people interaction. We also explain the pro-poor advantages of connectivity-related infrastructure and provide evidence of, for example, welfare gains to Balochistan and Khyber Pakhtunkhwa provinces of Pakistan as a result of transit trade with Afghanistan.

A key element in Pakistan's foreign and trade policies should be to offer benefits of CPEC to neighbouring countries. In this regard, Iran has already approached the government of Pakistan and shown willingness for energy and transport linkages with the CPEC network. Pakistan should also push for an early implementation of Quadrilateral Traffic in Transit Agreement (QTTA) among Pakistan, China, Kazakhstan, and Kyrgyz Republic. The operationalization of this agreement will also require implementation of uniform customs transit procedures, modern border trade infrastructure such as installation and operationalization of electronically integrated scanning system, and implementation of TIR and multi-modal transit. Pakistan's role in Central Asia Regional Economic Cooperation (CAREC) programme can also be enhanced through timely implementation of QTTA.

The final chapter focuses on reforms which can help in the implementation of SDG-8 i.e., to 'promote sustained, inclusive, and sustainable economic growth; full and productive employment, and decent work for all.' Targeted public sector interventions will be required to help participation of women and youth in the labour market and ease the constraints to (labour) mobility.

To help increase women's wage and self-employment, supply-side measures may include a more inclusive education at all levels of schooling, promotion of technical and vocational education and training, and social mobilization efforts through local community-based organizations to ease discriminatory cultural norms, allowing more inclusive access to finance that in turn can help women's entrepreneurship.

Reforms to address underemployment and unemployment of youth will need to be grounded in the overall framework for youth and community engagement at provincial government levels. We recommend using fiscal policy tools, including public investment in active and passive labour market schemes, for supporting sustainable jobs for youth. In cases where fiscal policy fails, it is important to reform labour market institutions including strengthening of employer and employee relations in both private and public sectors and workers mobility. Finally, we recommend that for specific cases of prolonged unemployment, well-designed social safety nets can help in enhancing the prospects of decent and productive work.

3. Conclusion: Why this book was attempted?

During most of my career the focus of public institutions that I served was around: (a) Pakistan's relatively lower economic growth vis-à-vis its own potential growth rate and most peer economies, and (b) reinvigorating existing and finding new sources of inclusive economic growth. As Box 1 indicates, since 1993 Pakistan witnessed a lower expansion in national output compared to, for example, Bangladesh, India, and Vietnam. A key reason for continued sluggish growth since the early-1990s was the inability of the country to attract local and foreign investment. For example, in 2015, the fixed investment to GDP ratio for Pakistan stood at 13.8 per cent compared to Vietnam at 23.8 per cent, and Bangladesh and India close to 30 per cent. The stagnant growth in case of Pakistan also resulted in an almost flat exports to GDP ratio during this period. Pakistan's fiscal discipline was also a concern given that a failure to cut down the government's current expenditures, untargeted subsidies, and losses of public sector enterprises resulted in higher levels of budget deficits.

At the time of writing this book I have already spent over fifteen years of my professional career studying Pakistan's socio-economic issues through varied lens. I started my career from the private sector and later spent a decade in public service before joining the think tank community of which I have now been a part for around six years. In all my roles I have remained a researcher and an advocate for reform of economic policy in Pakistan. I was also fortunate to have worked with some of the best resource persons who had a very positive vision of Pakistan's economic future.

At some point in the recent past I felt that the knowledge and experience accumulated during these years needed to be documented before it gets too late and lessons may become obsolete; no better year to attempt this work than the country's celebration of its seventieth independence day. In a recent publication my co-authors and I attempted to identify the emerging mega trends that the country may experience at this juncture. These include: first, emerging examples of individual

Box 1: Pakistan's Macroeconomic Performance

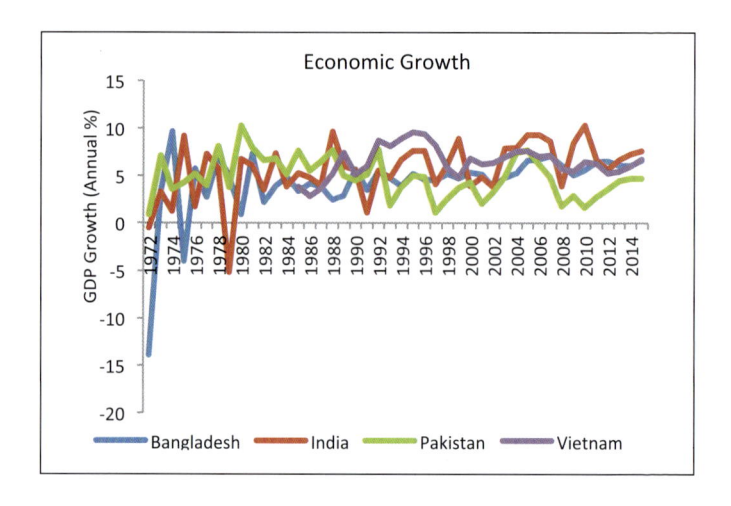

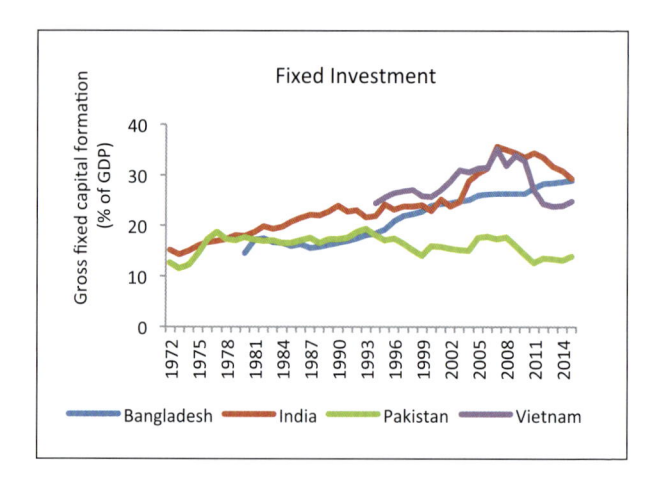

INTRODUCTION: A CASE FOR REFORMS   17

Exports of Goods and Services

(chart showing Exports % of GDP for Bangladesh, India, Pakistan, Vietnam from 1972 to 2014)

Budget Deficit

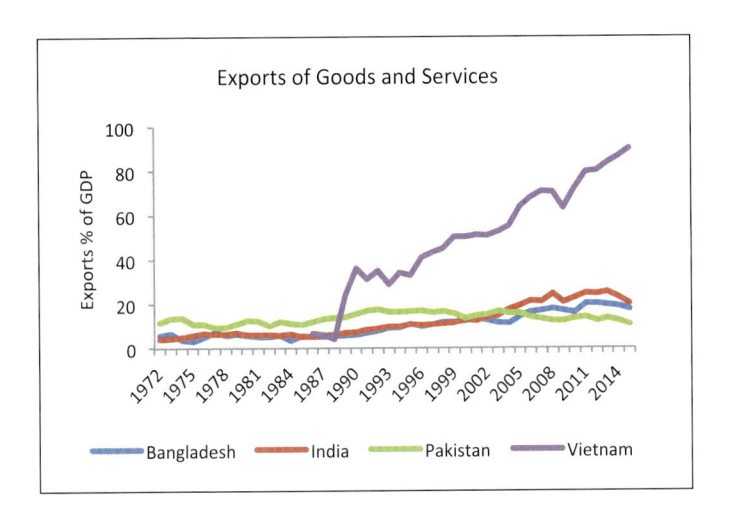

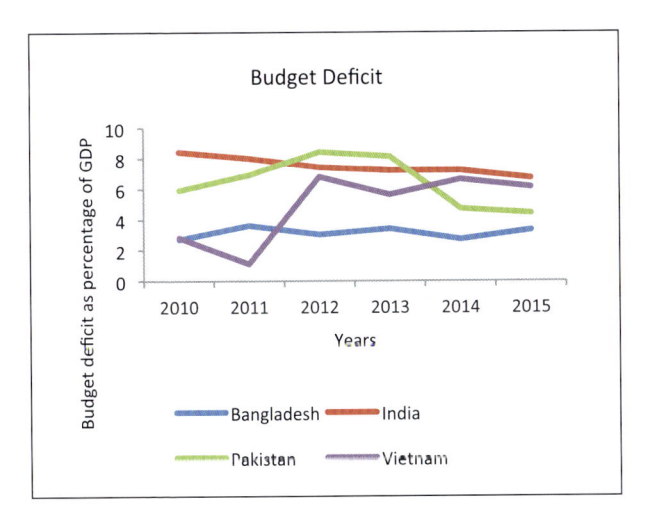

(chart showing Budget deficit as percentage of GDP for Bangladesh, India, Pakistan, Vietnam from 2010 to 2015)

Source: Data on economic growth, investment, and exports is from World Development Indicators. Data on budget deficit is from IMF's Global Finance Survey[3].

empowerment which take the form of a rising middle class, access to information and communication technologies, pro-poor and pro-women legislation, right to information laws, and a relatively independent media (in comparison to past decades). Second, Pakistan's demographic dividend will be of potential benefit if harnessed and will be complemented by the development of new cities, increased mobility of skilled and semi-skilled workers, knowledge spillovers (across regions and income cohorts), and a Diaspora which is continuously contributing to skills and technology transfer to Pakistan. Third, there has been an emergence of new power centres in Pakistan. The space in the power canvas is now shared by parliamentary forces, judiciary, civil society organizations, the corporate sector, and the media.

While the country experiences the above long-term trends, it is important to see how the citizens, policymakers, and new power centres will respond to the prevalent threats to inclusive economic growth, social justice, and environmental upgradation. Such threats may include violent conflicts, man-made and natural disasters, corruption, and a general failure of the public sector to invest in human resource development. It is in this context that the analysis which follows can provide some entry points for future reform of Pakistan's economy.

This book is also important to me as one would like to document the tested ideas and perhaps lessons from failures from which future researchers and policy entrepreneurs can derive lessons and try to design better programmes for economic uplift. Therefore, in many respects the lapses in economic policy management highlighted in this book may be seen as an exercise of confession. One would of course also like to indicate towards new directions in (policy) reforms which the current and future policymakers and practitioners could pursue.

As Pakistanis we are also mindful that upon travelling abroad one realizes the image and perception which people from other parts of the world carry about Pakistan. While the young generation of the developed world may not even know about this country on the map, the older generation would view this country unsafe for travel and known for militancy, insurgency, and terrorism. Perhaps, for people like me who will continue to live in Pakistan for the foreseeable future it is the need of the hour to exhibit with evidence that there is another side of Pakistan. I bear in mind that the youth, rising middle class, decent infrastructure, and economies of location will remain potential benefits unless the state makes itself relevant to its own people, its neighbours, and the world. Making Pakistan relevant should be the single most important goal for any government in office. While branding the small everyday successes of this country are important for image-building; however, a longer term commitment to a Pakistan free of violent conflicts has to be demonstrated by urgent reforms related to security and law enforcement. The internal and external threats to Pakistan will require a collective response from the armed forces, police, and citizens.

Let me also state that I have had the chance to observe brain drain at its peak during the past decade and a half. Currently,

Pakistan may not be the most attractive place to live for its own youth. They dream of a different world which is now possible to achieve given a more physically and virtually connected globe. The ultimate disadvantage in this flight of human resource is for a country which continues to lose the best minds. Therefore, a key motivation for writing this book was also to see how Pakistan can become a more attractive place to live for its youth, where they could be more creative with their thinking, implement new ideas, and over time become part of a dynamic global entrepreneurial class. For this to happen, a related goal has to be a more inclusive Pakistan. It is only equality of opportunity which will allow a level playing field to all other segments of population alike.

Notes

1. There is a need to build social capital between taxpayer and collection authorities at various levels of (tax) administration.
2. This will render effective coordination across federal government's Public Sector Development Programme and provincial Annual Development Plans.
3. Global Finance., 'Percentage of Public Deficit/Surplus in GDP Around the World' from https://www.gfmag.com/global-data/economic-data/public-deficit-percentage-gdp?page=2.

Chapter 2

Macroeconomic Policy Governance

1. Background

According to Dixit (2008), economic governance 'consists of the processes that support economic activity and economic transactions by protecting property rights, enforcing contracts, and taking collective action to provide appropriate physical and organizational infrastructure. These processes are carried out within formal and informal institutions. The study of economic governance involves the analysis and comparison of the performance of different institutions under varied conditions, the evolution of these institutions, and the transitions from one set of institutions to another.' There is a growing body of literature that explains economic governance and its payoffs. We also see that the study of governance and government have similar yet different domains. For example, the former may also include non-governmental governance arrangements as well (Dixit 2009). We also observe that individual and collective commitment problems can affect formation of institutions and their governance (Sanchez-Pages and Straub 2010). There is also a large body of Pakistan-specific literature on this subject which brings out the following key themes discussed in this section.

Lack of governance hampers long-term economic growth and exacerbates poverty. Haq R and Zia U (2009) observed for the period 1996–2005 that the poorest segment of the population could not benefit from short phases of economic growth. Poverty and inequality in fact, has increased due to a lack of systems that bring about accountability, rule of law, and elimination of corruption. Qayyum, A, and Khawaja I (2008) demonstrate that the prevalence of corruption and lack of effective human resources (HR) and labour market institutions are significant elements hampering economic growth (see also Shahbaz M et al. 2011, Amin M et al. 2013). The authors also point towards the weaknesses of regulatory institutions such as the State Bank of Pakistan (SBP) and Securities and Exchange Commission of Pakistan (SECP) in not delivering their oversight role (see also Ahmad N 2005).

Delays in legal and judicial reforms accentuate governance challenges, in turn worsening poverty and inequality. Lack of justice results in increased inequality of opportunities. Hussain A (2013) explains how the trio of power, land occupancy, and labour market rigidities worsens the living conditions of labour in the agriculture sector. Lack of information and costly access to justice are important factors that push poverty and inequality to higher levels. This situation is not helped by the weak democratic institutions either which may have a vested interest in not demanding the judicial reforms. Zakaria M and

Fida B A (2009) exhibit a negative relation between democracy and per capita income in Pakistan for the period 1947–2006, indicating that the fruits of democratic transition are still not translating into public welfare. While Pakistan has embarked on an agenda of devolution and fiscal decentralization, however the true empowerment of local governments has still not been achieved. For democracy and judicial reforms to deliver, the promotion of social accountability is also essential (Yaseen 2013).

Interventions by the military may have an unfavourable impact on the working of democratic governments. Hussain A (2008) elaborates how the military, a major power centre in the country, may have hindered the development and working of democratic institutions. This power centre also had support from elements from within the bureaucracy, the judiciary, and local elites. Even after prolonged periods of military rule, which promised prosperity, the outcomes indicators in education, health, clean water, and sanitation did not see substantial improvement. A greater concern of course was that the process of constitutional development was stalled. The political elite who were groomed by the military rulers proved to be oligarchs by the time they reached an office of public service. The military also significantly engineered the structure and performance of civil service to their advantage, which in turn weakened the quality of the bureaucracy and led to a brain drain (ICG 2010, Chaudry 2011).

Lack of civil service reforms decreases efficiency and effectiveness of public expenditure. Husain I (1999, 2012) explains that weak bureaucratic quality and culture is hampering public service delivery. This results in issues of access to basic needs, as regulations in terms of education, health, environment standards, food and drug quality control, and consumer protection are not fully implemented to protect the poorest of the poor (see also Ahmed and Ahmed 2014). Civil service reform is closely related to the reform of key institutions in Pakistan. For example Khawaja M I and Khan S (2009) explain how divergent interests of people involved in operations of the public sector hinder the institutional performance. While micro-level governance reform (focusing on select sectors) in the delivery of, for example, education and health are necessary, however these cannot be sustained over a longer period without macro-level reform of public sector management and enforcement of accountability of public servants.

A corrupt civil service also affects businesses, tax revenues, and the exchequer's performance. Haider A et al. (2011) explain for the period 1950–2011 how a high incidence of corruption reduced economic growth. Furthermore, as a result of corruption, rampant misuse of public revenues becomes a common practice thus leaving the government with no option but to increase fiscal deficit (at times up to unsustainable limits) to meet government expenditures. This increase in fiscal deficit, often through borrowing or printing of money in turn has implications for inflation.

Javaid U (2010) describes how corruption is directly hurting the investment flows into the country. The author explains that the reform of civil service during the military era largely failed as they were not accompanied by the reform of the judiciary which could independently dispense justice and act against the misdoings of public officials. This strengthened the cartel between civil and military elites (Aziz 2001, Akhtar et al. 2006). The weakening of civil society (groups) during the Zia regime also proved detrimental to the cause as the voices of dissent were silenced (Candland 2009). The elite capture of resources has the tendency to further consolidate gains for the dominant class. Ahmad R E et al. (2014) explain for the period 2008–2013 that political institutions continue to benefit a small number of corporate sector families and religious groups at the expense of the majority.

Civil service reforms will require complementary correction of an accountability regime. Haq N and Khawaja I (2007) have explained how the prevalent corruption in the civil service, in the absence of an appropriate accountability process, erodes public trust (also see Farooq A et al. 2013). This has also negatively impacted the morale of officials having the willingness and ability to deliver. It is this segment of public servants who remain of the view that military and political interference in their official work will never allow them the autonomy to perform well and achieve desired targets. Some have gone to the extent of arguing that existing accountability-related institutions such as the National Accountability Bureau (NAB) also require a reform. NAB is currently perceived as an institution which is prone to misuse against civil servants and the political community (Shah 2012).

Demand-side and supply-side accountability mechanisms can help sustainable development. For this to happen Samad S (2008) discusses how NAB needs to be insulated from political pressure and corruption (see also PILDAT 2015). Kirk T (2014) highlights that citizen-led accountability programmes proved effective in both peaceful and conflict-affected constituencies of Pakistan, where the programmes help volunteer groups to raise an organized voice at appropriate platforms. Abbas M H and Ahmed V (2014), using data from a national survey, observed that people are aware of the gaps in public service delivery of essential services. On most occasions, such gaps are not reported due to a lack of social capital between service users and government institutions (Khan et al. 2013). The social accountability instruments can be particularly useful for a population not having formal education or knowledge of registering grievances. In this regard, the civil society organizations which have the mandate to mobilize local communities can play an effective role. Yaseen (2013) also suggests a stronger role of such organizations in mobilizing communities, and recommends effective implementation of the Right to Information Act which can further augment social accountability mechanisms at the grass roots level.

Regulatory reform and transparency can help the government to exit from non-essential services. Such an environment will also imply a more enabling business climate in which business initiatives can flourish and the private sector can become the engine of economic growth and job creation (GoP 2011). Akhtar S (2007) indicates the success of the regulatory framework implemented by SBP which helped the financial sector to support economic growth during early and mid-2000s. Effective and autonomous management at SBP was a key factor in deregulation of the financial sector and in urging the privatized banks to comply with the international accounting and disclosure standards.

The reform of regulatory bodies is particularly more important as Pakistan moves towards privatization of some large public sector enterprises (PSEs) in electricity, gas, and transport sectors.[1] Kemal A R (2002) explained that the overall process of privatizing PSEs such as public utilities led to the improvement of the regulatory framework in Pakistan. This helped the government to limit its role in the economy and the private sector flourished. The author also stresses that regulatory authorities need to be sheltered from vested groups so that a competitive environment can be ensured. Improved perceptions regarding political stability, freedom of expression, and accountability help in sustaining economic growth over longer periods (see Zubair S S and Khan M A 2014, Haq R, and Zia U 2006).

Transparency in fiscal policy under the parliament's watch can help prioritize government operations. The reasons for prolonged and large budget deficits ought to be scrutinized by the parliament. Qasim A W et al. (2015) observed for the period 1976–2014 that budget deficit, particularly debt servicing, negatively affects the growth process. A sustained effort to restructure the tax system and plug leakages in the public expenditure supply chain can help in narrowing down the gap between revenues and spending. Nabi I (2008) explained that tax burden can be reduced over time by using public resources effectively and by promoting public and private partnership in social investments and infrastructure. Monitoring and evaluation, along with further access to information, can also strengthen the effectiveness of public programmes. Ahmed V et al. (2013) indicated that targeted investments in public infrastructure provide momentum to the growth process. However, it is important to prioritize which type of infrastructure investment, under market failure, may be taken up by the public sector.

The next section provides a brief discussion on the legal framework of economic governance in the country. Section three explains how Pakistan performs, in terms of economic governance, across a cross-section of countries, and also points towards some issues curtailing efficient (institutional) management of the economy. Section four then proposes some remedial actions based on the author's recent research. These measures cannot be termed as a comprehensive strategy for reforming economic governance, rather only the low hanging fruits that may act as an entry point. Our policy recommendations in this chapter are confined to the federal government and it is suggested that a future effort should extend the discussion on province-specific improvements. We conclude this chapter with a brief discussion on the gaps in our methodology which could be bridged through future research.

2. Legal Framework of Economic Governance

The Constitution of Pakistan provides for a comprehensive set of rules under which free and fair markets can function. Article 18 ensures freedom of trade, business, and professions. The state is however allowed to step in if the rules of competition are being violated. In Article 38, the state has the responsibility to promote social and economic well-being of the people. This is sometimes narrowly interpreted in terms of the state's responsibility to provide social protection and social safety nets. However, economic wellbeing is a much broader concept and also allows for the people's right to own and formalize businesses. In this context it becomes the government's responsibility to design rules, policies, and programmes that promote entrepreneurship, and attract domestic and foreign investment. A broader interpretation also includes the state's responsibility to ensure that assistance programmes, including those involved in the support of multilateral and bilateral development partners, have a longer term favourable impact on welfare. Similarly, the incidence of monetary and fiscal policies needs to be pro-welfare.

To regulate the government's revenues and spending, Article 73 provides procedures with respect to the Money Bill.[2] This also has linkages with Article 77 which ensures that taxes can only be levied by law. Both these provisions imply that any changes in taxes and borrowing by the government will need approval of the National Assembly, which in turn will take advice of the Senate. Any Statutory Regulatory Order (SRO) by the Federal Board of Revenue (FBR) or directives of the Economic Coordination Committee (ECC) related to taxes, spending, and borrowing which do not have a parliamentary cover can be termed irregular.

To provide the parliament dominance over the spending priorities, Article 74 provides rules for expenditure from the federal consolidated fund or withdrawal from the public account of the federation. These expenditures and withdrawals have to be part of the Money Bill and need the approval of the parliament. Similarly Article 84 provides for the rules regarding supplementary and excess grants. Again, these grants can only be allowed through a National Assembly Supplementary Budget Statement and certainly require a debate at the floor of the parliament.

The above-mentioned provisions in the constitution are further strengthened by the recent legislative efforts. For example, The Competition Act, 2010 gives the Competition Commission of Pakistan (CCP) investigative powers to ensure free competition across all commercial activities (including those undertaken by the public sector). CCP works to enhance economic efficiency, and also to protect consumers from anti-competitive practices. Some recent legislative efforts initiated by SECP and SBP are also discussed later in this chapter.

The 18th Constitutional Amendment brought with it some changes in the structure of economic governance. Article-154(1) states that 'The Council shall formulate and regulate policies in relation to matters in Part II of the Federal Legislative List and shall exercise supervision and control over related institutions.' Article-156(2) states that 'The National Economic Council (NEC) shall review the overall economic condition of the country and shall, for advising the Federal Government and the Provincial Governments, formulate plans in respect of financial, commercial, social, and economic policies; and in formulating such plans it shall, amongst other factors, ensure balanced development and regional equity and shall also be guided by the Principles of Policy set out in Chapter 2 of Part-II.'

Tahir and Tahir (2013) explain that while NEC has the mandate of formulating plans 'for advising' the government including the provinces, this advice requires a legal approval forum for operationalization. The economic planning which is on part-II of the federal list implies that this is the domain of the Council of Common Interests (CCI). CCI perhaps cannot perform its duties unless it has supervisory control over NEC and all other economic planning institutions. If this process is allowed to happen, it will imply a shift from centralized planning of development budget to a more federalized planning.

The process of devolution was also accompanied by fiscal decentralization. While the 18th Amendment provided the provinces with administrative and financial control over social and production sectors, including a larger role in public utilities, water resource management, natural resources and ports, the seventh National Finance Commission (NFC) award enabled the provinces to collectively have a larger annual development programme in comparison to the federal government's public sector development programme (PSDP). The Seventh Award increased the share of the provinces in federal tax revenues from 46.5% to 57.5%. The provinces can now also impose provincial taxes (not having overlaps with federal or local taxes), and also engage development partners in procuring assistance (including grants and debt). Article 160(3A, B) requires that an NFC award has parliamentary oversight and is regularly updated keeping in view changing province-specific circumstances.

The tenth review under the Extended Fund Facility (EFF) for Pakistan by the International Monetary Fund (IMF) points towards the need for deepening the post-18th Amendment economic governance legislation in order to bring greater efficiency in fiscal, monetary, and trade policies. Foremost among these legislative changes is the planned amendment to the Fiscal Responsibility and Debt Limitation (FRDL) Act, which has the potential to bind the federal government to its commitment towards plugging leakages in the public expenditure supply chain, limiting fiscal deficit, and protecting social sector spending.

Second, further strengthening of policy coordination between federal and provincial governments is desired. For this, the existing law needs to be amended to empower NFC, and a Fiscal Coordination Committee, comprising of federal and provincial financial and planning secretaries may be constituted.

The Committee may meet on a quarterly basis to follow up the decisions under CCI, NEC, NFC, and ECC.

Third, the commitment with IMF also demands amendments to SBP law to strengthen the central bank's autonomy. The membership of the independent monetary policy committee will require expansion. The terms of reference given to the committee should also be regularly updated in the light of ongoing challenges facing the national economy.

An important forum for strengthening policy coordination is the monetary and fiscal policies coordination board. This board currently lacks independence and has a narrow membership. The board is chaired by the Finance Minister, whereas ideally an independent head should chair this forum. Second, the representation of several federal economic ministries and departments is missing. Similarly, the representation of provincial governments is also missing. Provinces now have responsibilities, after the 18th Amendment, to play their role in fiscal reform. It is therefore important to provide them with a voice at this forum. Third, the board lacks representation of capital and money market bodies. Finally, the number of independent economists on the board needs to be increased. Ideally independent economists from all provinces should be a part of this board. Pakistan's experience of monetary and fiscal policies coordination may be seen in Arby and Hanif (2010) and Andlib et al. (2012). These studies explain that fiscal policy continues to dominate the monetary policy which in turn undermines the autonomy of central bank operations.

The discussion on economic governance will not be complete without the mention of weak administration of public sector development programmes in Pakistan. Figure 1 illustrates the various levels of decision-making forums and corresponding approval authorities. The approval limit of each tier is associated with the monetary value of the public sector project. For example the project manuals of federal and provincial planning departments allow that District Development Committee can approve projects up to PKR 50 million. The approval limits will increase as we move upwards e.g., Divisional Development Working Party (PKR 100 million), Departmental Development Sub-Committee (200 million), and Provincial Development Working Party (PKR 10,000 million). At the federal level there are three forums namely, Departmental Development Working Party (PKR 60 million), Central Development Working Party (PKR 3,000 million), and Executive Committee of NEC (above PKR 3,000 million).

The key governance issues facing the development administration are discussed in greater detail in Chapter 4, which include: a lack of technical expertise to implement mega projects having multi-year financial cycles, duplication of development programmes across federal and provincial domain, and weak capacity to physically monitor projects under ADP and PSDP.

Figure 1: Administration of Development Policy, Programmes, and Projects*

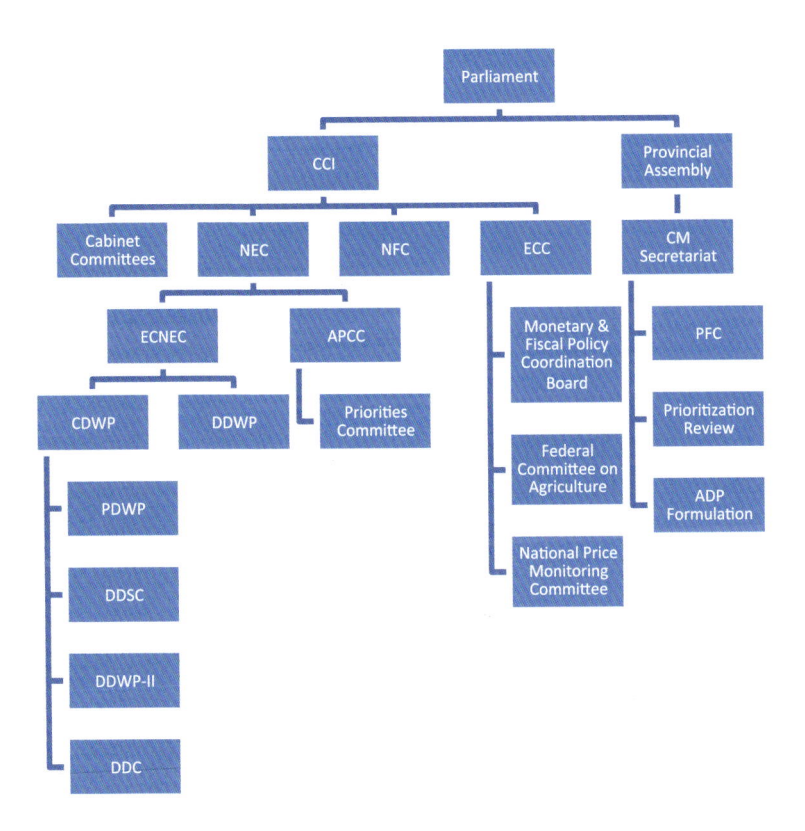

*CCI: Council of Common Interests, NEC: National Economic Council, NFC: National Finance Commission, ECC: Economic Coordination Committee, ECNEC: Executive Committee of NEC, APCC: Annual Plan Coordination Committee, CDWP: Central Development Working Party, DDWP: Departmental Development Working Party, PDWP: Provincial Development Working Party, DDSC: Departmental Development Sub-Committee, DDWP-II: Divisional Departmental Working Party, DDC: District Development Committee, PFC: Provincial Finance Commission, ADP: Annual Development Programme.

3. Institutions and Regulatory Environment: Situation Analysis

Pakistan remains in the list of economies which had to resort to IMF support on a recurrent basis. During the past three decades, Pakistan has faced several balance of payment crises and had to bank upon external assistance. An incomplete and unsuccessful nationalization attempt during the 1970s and a war economy of 1980s left behind a weak private sector, whose growth was stifled by distortive regulation. The 1990s also saw political instability ultimately resulting in another episode of military takeover. During the early 2000s, a pickup in growth was not accompanied by reforms in the rule of law and civil service. Similarly, structural improvements in the taxation and energy sector were not carried out. Weak economic fundamentals could not sustain the food and fuel price shocks between 2006 and 2008, and an uneasy transition towards a democratic setup. This ultimately resulted in subdued economic growth after 2010.

There are six main consequences of poor economic governance and lack of timely reforms. First, the public sector is now producing and managing goods and services that can be more effectively provided by competitive markets. Second, excessive and distortive regulation is hurting entry and exit of the private sector. Third, weak regulators are unable to check market imperfections and existence of monopolies. Fourth, inability to bring management reforms in PSEs is resulting in losses, which in turn add to the fiscal deficit. Fifth, even after large social security programmes at the federal and provincial levels (e.g.,

Benazir Income Support Programme), untargeted subsidies continue to exist. These subsidies are allowed to power and gas entities, textile sector, wheat, fertiliser, and railways. Sixth, due to a lack of reform in public sector HR management, there is continued decline in professionalism and service delivery by the civil service (GoP 2011).

The above-mentioned has clearly resulted in Pakistan's low performance across various governance indicators, e.g., control of corruption, government effectiveness, and regulatory quality (Box 1). The political instability during the 1990s and the increase in violence during later years prevented the implementation of key economic governance reforms. The reach of these desired changes in several geographical areas of the country was also weak due to the ongoing war against terror. A cross-country comparison of governance indicators across countries is provided in correlation with their income levels (see Annex-I). Pakistan does better than several other countries in the sample, in voice and accountability (V&A) measure. However, it is lagging in all other governance indicators. Perhaps the improvement in V&A measure can be explained by the rise of civil society organizations, access to information through right to information legislation, and improved responsiveness of superior judiciary and private media entities.

The low ranking in the economic governance indicators may differ across provinces. For example, in the case of Sindh, weak fiscal governance can be attributed to, among other factors, delays in implementing reforms of revenue collection, financial

Box 1: Worldwide Governance Indicators— Pakistan and Peer Economies

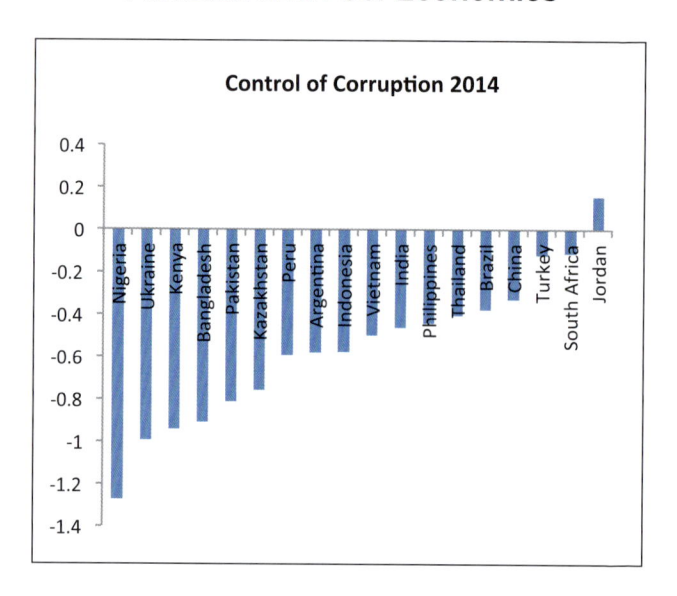

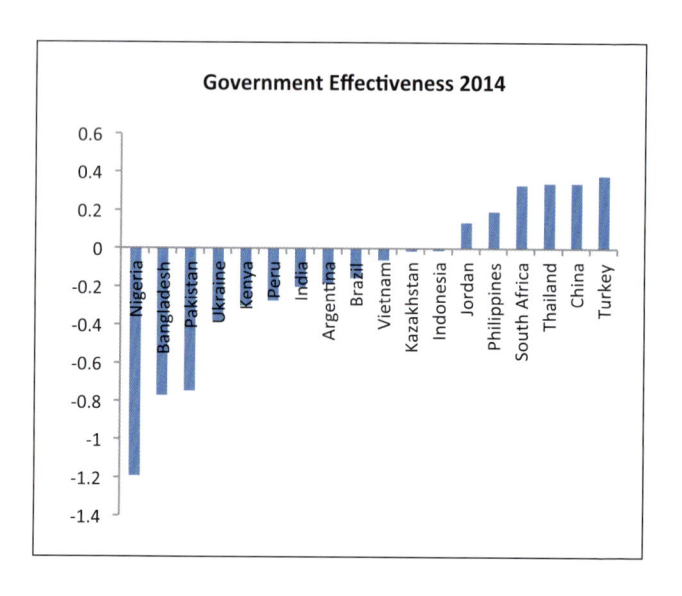

Control of Corruption 2014

Government Effectiveness 2014

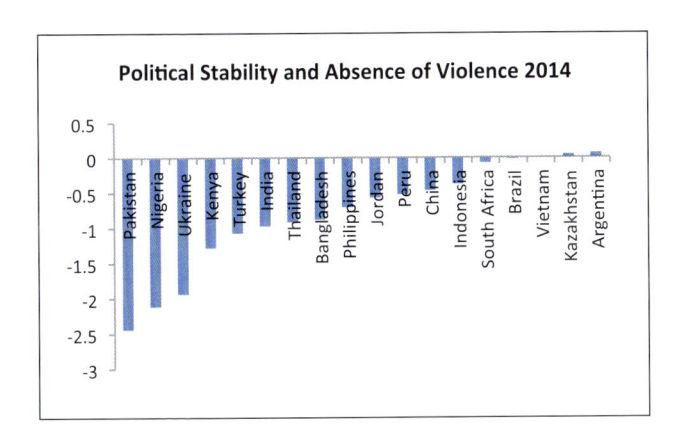

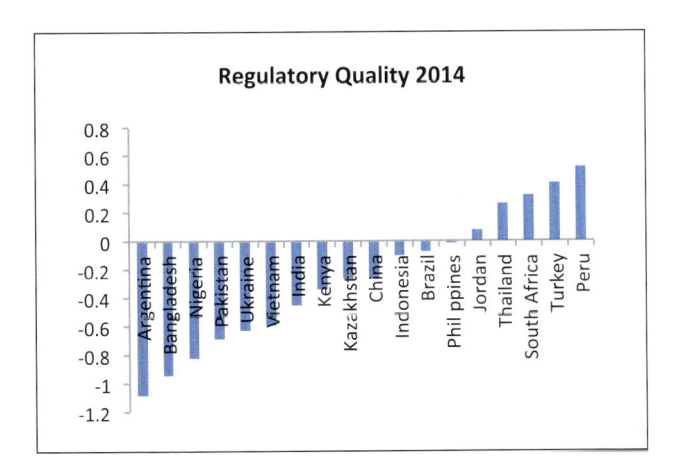

MACROECONOMIC POLICY GOVERNANCE 39

Political Stability and Absence of Violence 2014

Regulatory Quality 2014

Source: Worldwide Governance Indicators, www.govindicators.org.

Note: The standard normal units range from -2.5 to 2.5 with higher values corresponding to an improvement.

management, civil service, and decentralization (Ahmed 2016). In the case of Punjab's fiscal management, it is observed that budgets are not aligned with the overall growth strategy at the provincial level. In almost all provinces, a limited budget monitoring along with weak internal (financial) controls hurt the development objectives. Lack of monitoring is also due to obsolete accounting and audit systems in the public sector. Most of these are financial administration reforms and certainly need to be complemented with province-specific resource mobilization strategy (see Ahmed 2015c) and prudent measures to expand public spending where the market fails.

In March 2016, Pakistan while requesting the eleventh tranche of 36 months-EFF provided by the IMF, committed to the Executive Board of the IMF that it would amend the fiscal responsibility legislation, introduce new measures in tax administration, strengthen central bank autonomy, and contain losses of PSEs that could not be restructured or privatized.

More specifically, towards the above-mentioned goals it was committed that tax-to-GDP ratio would be increased to 14.5 per cent by 2019–20 through rationalization of tax concessions and exemptions, the general sales tax (GST) regime on goods and services would be reformed in coordination with provincial governments, and processing of GST and other refunds would be expedited. Moreover, Pakistan also committed that it would introduce risk-based auditing, initiate income tax audits for high net worth individuals, minimize under-declaration in customs, introduce market value-based real estate tax at the provincial level, and ratify the legislation against 'benami' transactions. While some of these will require a legislative change, other goals can be achieved through introducing IT-enabled tax compliance within the federal and provincial tax administration.

It was also committed that amendments will be made to FRDL Act to ensure debt sustainability. These amendments will focus on setting a limit on the federal government budget deficit of 4 per cent to GDP during the period 2017–18 and 2019–20 and 3.5 per cent thereafter; continuation of the limit on public debt of 60 per cent of GDP until 2017–18 and subsequent downward move towards 50 per cent during a 15-year time horizon. Again, this will require institutional changes at the federal level so that leakages such as the circular debt, untargeted subsidies, and recurrent expenditures of a large government can be rationalized. Similarly, fiscal incentives need to be ensured by law so that provinces have the motivation to achieve surplus (or reduction in deficits) in their annual budgets.

It was mentioned in a letter by the Finance Minister to IMF that Pakistan will further strengthen policy coordination between federal and provincial governments. The NFC meeting was delayed and it was promised that during the next round, representatives from federal and provincial governments will aim to balance devolution of revenue and expenditure responsibilities. Provinces will be encouraged to improve their revenue collection, specifically through improved taxation of agriculture, enhancing taxpayer compliance, and identifying misdeclarations. A Fiscal Coordination Committee, comprising federal and provincial finance secretaries, will meet on a quarterly basis with the aim to improve national level coordination of the fiscal policy.

Apart from the above-mentioned, there were also commitments towards reinforcing the regulatory and supervisory framework. These included revision to the SECP Act, Futures Trading Bill, strengthening of joint task force of SBP-SECP for assessment of banking sector, improved recovery of non-performing loans through amendments to Financial Institutions Ordinance, Corporate Restructuring Companies Act, Corporate Rehabilitation Act, developing a contingency planning framework at SBP, and strengthening the anti-money laundering framework. Furthermore, governance, regulatory, and transparency improvements were also committed for gas, oil, and power sectors. While these legal changes are important, a key issue currently is the lack of coordination between various regulatory bodies responsible for ensuring a level-playing field for the private sector and also safeguarding consumer rights.

The letter to the IMF also mentioned that quick interventions and medium-term reform measures will be required to improve the business climate, liberalizing trade, and reforming public enterprises. The current business climate is a barrier to the entry of new firms and investment. There exist weaknesses in the legal framework for creditors' rights and contract enforcement. A future strategy to improve the business climate will aim to streamline business procedures and regulatory framework through ease in starting business, getting construction permits, elimination or streamlining of already identified 39 income and sales tax processes, registering property (through greater transparency in land management systems), changing bankruptcy regime to support the rehabilitation of weak but promising enterprises, improving access to formal credit through implementation of National Financial Inclusion Strategy, getting access to utilities like electricity and gas, and resolving insolvencies. Furthermore, the complex regime faced by exporters and importers will be revisited so that there is faster processing of trade documentation.

The above-mentioned commitments by the government, while pointing to the right direction, ignored a key element in reform execution i.e., identification and role of HR that can act as a change agent. For example, why are we expecting a different outcome of reforms with the same administrative machinery at FBR which has been around for decades? Similarly, reform of PSEs is being committed without any fundamental change in recruitment, reward, and accountability structure for the management and their teams. Several aspects of governance, other than HR management, have also been ignored in this prescription. For example, the weak financial position of select PSEs (given in Annex-II) itself is a disincentive for well-qualified candidates to join top positions in these entities. Improved balance sheets of generation and distribution companies in the power sector are being promised without a crackdown on power and gas theft, and adulteration in petroleum products. Better results from Pakistan International Airlines, Pakistan Steel Mills, and Pakistan Railways are being expected without addressing aging and shortage of equipment, large circular debt, ability to monopolize the market, overstaffing, and union issues.

The above-mentioned issues become harder to address when the economic ministries and departments lack specialized fiscal and financial management cadre that has the institutional memory and ability to shape political will for difficult adjustments, and perform the necessary task of change management. The bottom line is that successive governments have never committed to targets that can improve the efficiency and effectiveness of civil service in government, semi-government, and autonomous bodies. Yet the civil service remains the only instrument for implementing fundamental changes in the public sector.

This lack of civil service and accountability reforms and the resultant poor service delivery partially explains why the key governance indicators have seen less than desired improvement over time (Box 2). The control of corruption indicator 'captures perceptions of the extent to which public power is exercised for private gain, including both petty and grand forms of corruption, as well as "capture" of the state by elites and private interests'.[3] The standard normal units range from -2.5 to 2.5 with higher values corresponding to improved outlook. Since 1996 this indicator has remained negative for Pakistan, hovering between -1.1 and -0.7. This is despite three large programmes (in the recent past) to bring about improvements in the capacity of civil services.[4] The evaluations of these past efforts may be carefully studied to gauge reasons for weak outcomes.

Box 2: Worldwide Governance Indicators—Pakistan's Performance 1996–2014

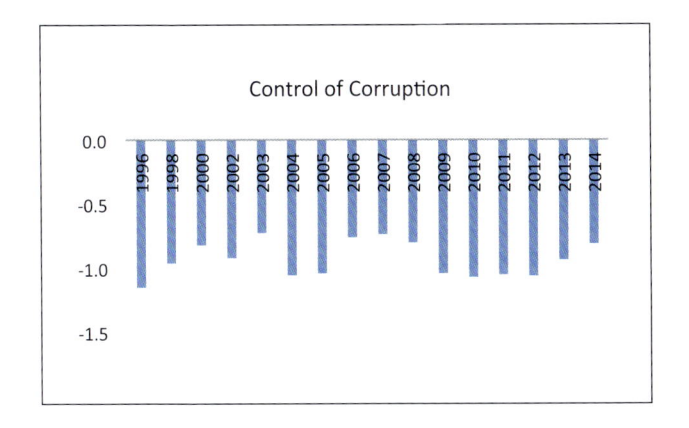

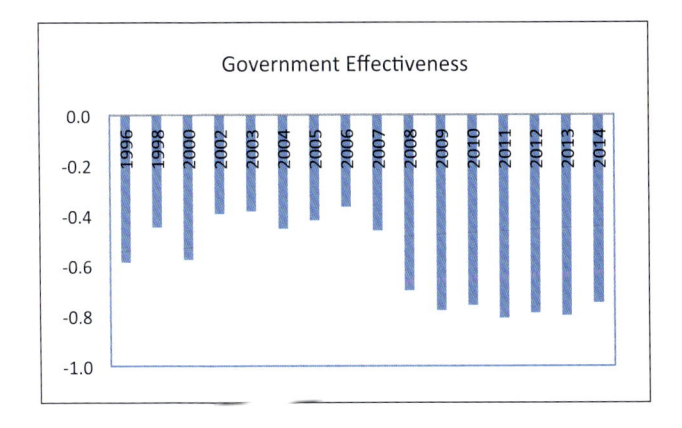

Political Stability and Absence of Violence

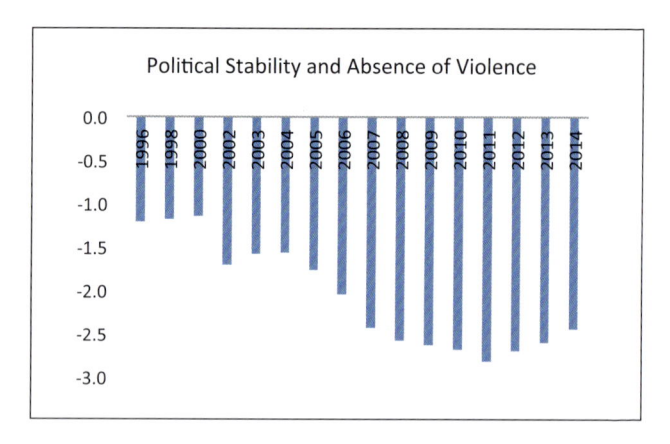

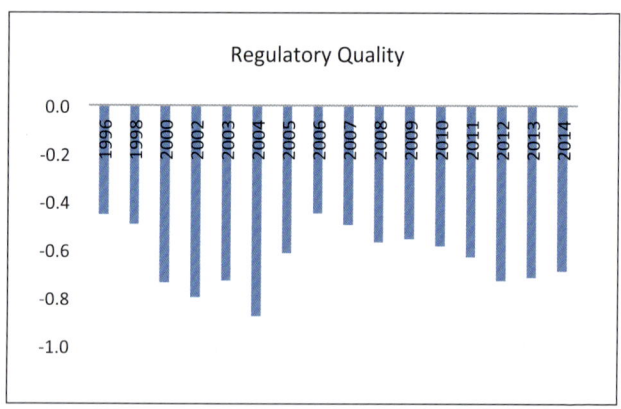

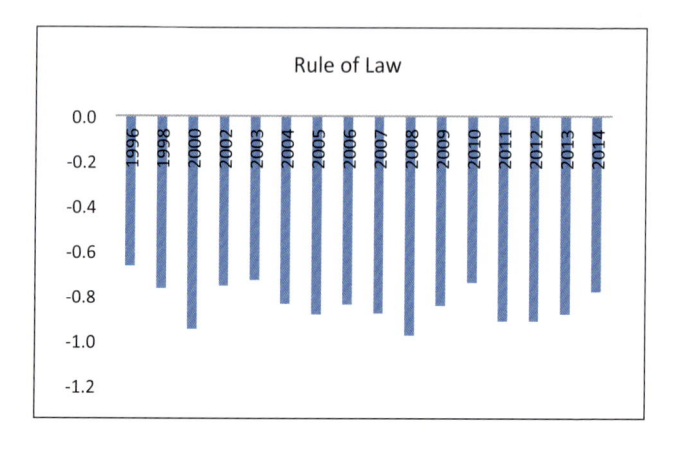

Regulatory Quality

Rule of Law

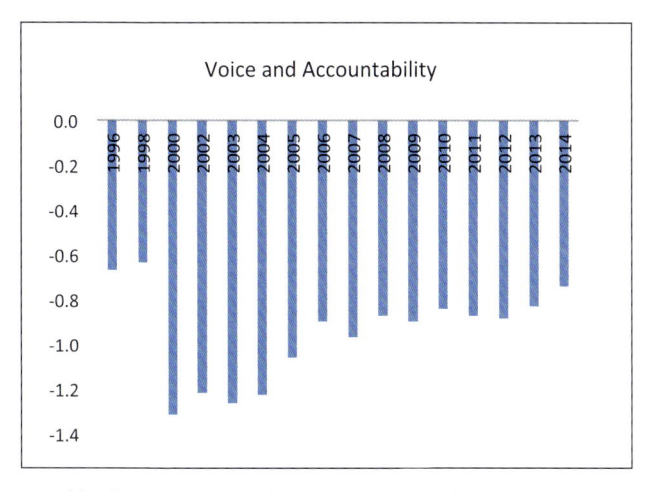

[Chart: Voice and Accountability, 1996–2014, values ranging approximately from -0.6 to -1.3]

Source: Worldwide Governance Indicators, www.govindicators.org.

Note: The standard normal units range from -2.5 to 2.5 with higher values corresponding to an improvement.

The government effectiveness indicator, exhibited in Box 2, captures 'perceptions of the quality of public services, the quality of the civil service and the degree of its independence from political pressures, the quality of policy formulation and implementation, and the credibility of the government's commitment to such policies'. The period since 2009 has witnessed a stubborn degree of government ineffectiveness with the value increasing from -0.4 in 2002 to -0.7 in 2014. Government effectiveness is closely linked or impacted by political stability in the country. The indicator on political stability and absence of violence measures 'perceptions of the likelihood of political instability and politically-motivated violence, including terrorism'. Some important components of this measure include armed conflict, social unrest, and international tensions faced by the country. After a peak of -2.8 in 2011, this measure is now slowly tapering down and was -2.4 in 2014. This small improvement may have been due to perceptions of improved political stability after Zarb-e-Azab military operation, and management of law and order in Karachi being handed over to Rangers. Over the longer run, Pakistan remains a poor performer in this area. Since 1996, this indicator rose from -1.2 to -2.4 in 2014. This of course had implications for the business climate and difficulties in attracting investors' interest.

The 'rule of law' measure captures perceptions of the extent to which there is confidence in the rules of the society. These rules deal with contract enforcement, property rights, police, and civil courts. Despite several reforms to streamline the regulatory regime faced by businesses, and legal and judicial processes, this measure ranges between -0.7 and -0.9 since 1996. An improvement in this score is not possible unless courts reduce the backlog, and expedite the disposal of outstanding cases.

Our next measure deals with regulatory quality in Pakistan. What to regulate and how to regulate remains an important consideration across most mixed economic systems. The measure of 'regulatory quality' here captures perceptions of the ability of the government to formulate and implement policies and regulations that permit and promote private sector development. Excessive regulatory burden can increase cost of doing business and rent-seeking. This in turn hurts efficiency and competitiveness. From -0.4 in 2006 this measure has deteriorated to -0.7 in 2014. CCP has conducted sectoral competition assessment studies for key sectors, which reveal that the ability of existing firms in keeping monopolistic powers may have strengthened.[5]

Voice and accountability is an important element for ensuring demand-side accountability. Reforms that allow 'right to information', transparency in public procurement, deregulation of media, observer status for non-governmental and civil society organizations, enhance the ability of the private sector and citizens to hold government institutions and functionaries accountable. The 'voice and accountability' measure captures perceptions of the extent to which a country's citizens are able to participate in selecting their government, as well as freedom of expression, freedom of association, and free media. Pakistan has made considerable effort towards bringing reforms in this area. From as high as -1.3 during 2000 (during military rule), the country has had a successful democratic transition and the index has improved to -0.7 in 2014.

The lack of government effectiveness and poor regulatory quality at the macro and micro level landed the country in a severe energy crisis during 2007 and 2014. The shortage of electricity largely emerged from three main reasons: the inability of generation and distribution companies to recover full economic cost from the consumers, existence of administrative and line losses, and high cost of maintaining subsidies (to finance energy sector deficit). Table 1 indicates that in 2014–15, the distribution companies had not received PKR 633 billion from the end-consumers and therefore were unable to cover their operational expenses. On top of this, transmission and distribution losses accounted for 2.0 and 2.6 per cent respectively. Such poor financial health of electricity distribution companies also had implications for service delivery.[6] Table 2 exhibits the high number of outages faced by the residential and commercial consumers of electricity. Despite planned outages, Pakistan Electric Power Company (private) limited (PEPCO) also resorted to forced outages.

Table 1: Power Sector Losses 2014–15

Receivables of Distribution Companies	PKR 633 billion
Transmission and Distribution Losses of Distribution Companies (DISCOs)	34.81%
Auxiliary Consumption and System Losses of PEPCO for 2014–15	
Auxiliary Consumption	2.7%
Transmission Losses	2.6%
Distribution Losses	19.9%

Source: State of Industry Report 2015 NEPRA.

Table 2: Transmission Lines Tripping in PEPCO 2014–15

Description	Planned Outages		Forced Outages	
	500 kV	220 kV	500 kV	220 kV
No. of Outages	469	777	76	250
Total duration in minutes	267,263	230,783	85,656	727,395

| Maximum duration of any single outage (minutes) | 3729 | 1990 | 12347 | 244,003 |

Source: State of Industry Report 2015 NEPRA.

The situation in the gas sector is not very different. Independent estimates suggest that Pakistan could run out of domestic natural gas supply within the next 15 years. Currently, a 2.5 billion cubic feet gap between demand and local supply of gas costs the exchequer 2 per cent of the country's national income. The energy mix remains heavily dependent on gas and this source accounts for 41 per cent of all energy consumed in the country. Almost 51 per cent of energy consumed by the industrial sector is derived from gas. There are no deeper reserves in sight and a move towards re-gasified liquid natural gas will lead to 30 per cent increase in energy spending by the industry. Key reasons for such a state of affairs in the gas sector include: shallow reserves found in newly drilled wells, security threats to new drilling enterprises, delays in divestment of OGDCL shares, high receivables of OGDCL and Pakistan Petroleum Limited, delays in utilization of Gas Infrastructure Development Cess (GIDC), provision of new gas connections by Sui Northern Gas Pipelines Limited (SNGPL) and Sui Southern Gas Company (SSGC) despite increased shortages, gas sector distribution losses (-15 per cent for SSGC and 12 per cent for SNGPL), and high unaccounted for gas (UFG) losses, e.g., 51 per cent in the case of Balochistan.

The overdraft provided to cover financial losses of energy companies (see Table 3) and the existence of untargeted subsidies in the textile and food sectors had severe fiscal repercussions. These subsidies were financed through heavy domestic borrowing (through the banking channels), which in turn led to reduction in loanable funds available for the private sector. As no strong brakes were applied to the ballooning circular debt in the energy sector, therefore this also resulted in pressures on fiscal deficit and inflation, particularly during the period 2010–13. Second, as most of these subsidies were untargeted, their impact on intended beneficiaries was weak. Such inefficient management of subsidies (and federal grants) is not just limited to the energy sector but also extends to other areas such as procurement of wheat and sugar and operations of Utility Stores Corporation. While the pressures of compliance with IMF's structural targets compelled the government to temporarily reduce these subsides, however in the recent past these were also extended to oil refineries, the fertilizer sector, and the Trading Corporation of Pakistan.

Table 3: Subsidies and Grants by the Federal Government

PKR Million

Description	Revised 2015–16	Budget 2016–17
PEPCO	117805	95400
K-Electric*	53400	22600
Support to the Textile Sector	33	-
PASSCO	10000	15300
USC	5000	7000

Others	10000	300
Sale of Wheat and Sugar	303	-
Total	196541	140600
Grants	409875	441616

Source: Budget in Brief 2016–17, Ministry of Finance.

*K-Electric: Karachi Electric, PASSCO: Pakistan Agricultural Storage & Services Corporation Limited (PASSCO), and USC: Utility Stores Corporation.

So why are PSEs in Pakistan providing limited and unreliable services at economically unviable returns? The overarching cause is that the operations of these entities are not managed as per professional standards. In the case of most of these enterprises, the information regarding the financial situation is not fully disclosed. The lack of competition is also not allowing the public sector's management to achieve minimum levels of efficiency. The commercial incentives in these enterprises also remain weak, and lack of incentives for improved performance limit the potential of HR. A failure to address these issues has led to significant fiscal costs borne by the taxpayers, anti-poor redistributive effects, and distortions leading to allocative inefficiencies (ADB 2014).

While the above-mentioned governance challenges require continuous reform, it is important that the regulatory framework and accountability institutions in the country should maintain a pressure for reform. Thus, a simultaneous reform of governance and regulation of markets is essential. Currently, there is a vacuum of regulatory policy. This is hindering collaboration between the various regulators in the country (e.g., the need for a strengthened working relationship between SECP, FBR, SBP, and the Ministry of Finance (MoF) for regulation of capital and money markets). A regulatory imbalance is seen in the case of several sectors, for example, in the insurance sector, SECP is unable to take remedial actions due to slow (legal) revisions to the available set of insurance laws which govern this sector. This gap is also seen for professional service providers. As there is weak or at times missing legal framework[7] to govern the operations of several services, therefore it is not easy to monitor the conduct of markets for these services.

A key challenge facing regulatory reform is the rising costs associated with the compliance of market laws, rules, regulations, and directions. A serious effort is required to harmonize the entire chain of legal framework and make it less complex for the private sector. There are also delays in the law-making process that can result in regulatory inefficiencies. For example, in the case of SECP, it can draft rules under the laws it will be administering. However, lengthy review and approval by MoF and vetting by the Ministry of Law and Justice often delays the notification of rules by SECP.

A lack of widely available information regarding economic and business rights and entitlements results in low levels of regulatory compliance. The power of the regulator is further eroded due to high rates of growth seen in the informal segment of the economy. This issue can be addressed in the medium term, and regulatory compliance can be improved through addressing the misperceptions related to the harassment of private sector participants in the markets.[8] Lack of compliance is not helped by the weak (implicit) regulatory enforcement framework in the country. The adjudication process is carried out by the courts and the commission can assist the court towards this pursuit. However, the high volumes of litigation in the country slow down the judicial process, adversely affecting effective enforcement in turn. This has continued to poorly reflect on Pakistan's global 'rule of law' rankings (Figure 2).

Figure 2: Rule of Law Index 2014

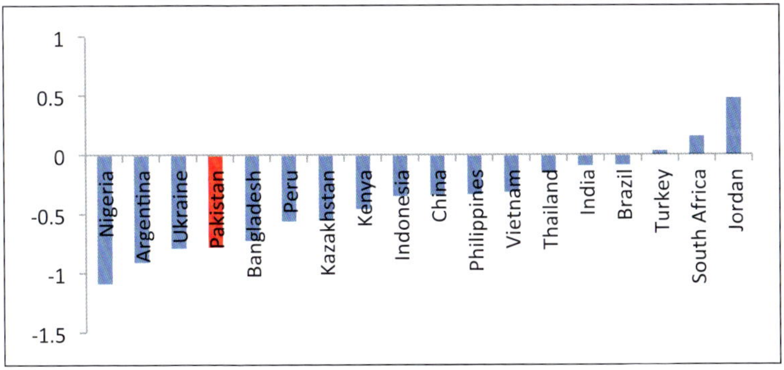

Source: Worldwide Governance Indicators, www.govindicators.org.

Note: The standard normal units range from -2.5 to 2.5 with higher values corresponding to an improvement.

Issues of conflict of interest across the governance structures of regulatory bodies require careful attention. Staying with the example of SECP, as MoF is also an active player in the financial markets, therefore the Federal Secretary should not head the Securities and Exchange Policy Board. This board has to provide strategic guidance to SECP and having MoF to head this board can result in conflict of interest. Several of these constitutional requirements are ignored due to the dominance and centralization of economic affairs at a single institution i.e., MoF.[9]

Finally, two related problems render the existing regulation of markets irrelevant. The first is the lack of periodic regulatory impact assessment (RIA), and secondly, the lack of capacity to conduct RIA. Such regular assessment is necessary so that the proposed regulation or changes to the existing regulation are targeted at the correct group of stakeholders, and do not lead to any excessive costs to the party involved.

4. Reform of Economic Management

Our methodology to attempt this section is three-pronged. We first rely on the author's past and on-going work on institutional reform of MoF, Ministry of Planning, Development and Reform (MoPDR), Ministry of Commerce (MoC), and FBR. We have also made use of existing literature available on the subject. Second, we aim to incorporate findings from in-depth interviews specifically aimed to inquire reforms for regulatory oversight. Third, on HR management for improved economic governance, we aim to update the recommendations from Husain (2012), GoP (2011), pay and pensions commission, etc. The updating exercise draws from the author's recent work with the World Bank and Sustainable Development Policy Institute.

The limitations of our policy recommendations include: a) lesser focus on provincial economic governance, and b) analysis related to the federal government is confined to HR challenges, internal reorganization for a leaner and more effective management, and select desired changes in laws which can enhance the service delivery capacity of the federal government's ministries and attached departments. A more comprehensive update of the work in Husain (2012) is still desired and may be pursued by taking a 'whole of the government' approach.

Let us start by outlining key objectives of economic governance. In order to keep the context familiar, we take lead from already defined principles of sound fiscal and debt management in FRDL Act. The future economic governance reform agenda should aim to:

- Build HR and technical capacities for improved revenue collection.
- Upgrade civil service and accounting systems to minimize wastages and leakages in government expenditures.
- Ensure through appropriate accountability and financial monitoring tools that the incidence of social and poverty alleviation related expenditures is pro-poor and leads to a reduction in various forms of inequalities.
- Ensure through strengthening of law and accountability systems that fiscal deficit and total public debt remain within prudent limits.
- Review and strengthen the mechanisms required for the follow-up of decisions taken at inter-ministerial and inter-

governmental forums such as CCI, Cabinet Committees, NEC, and NFC.

Human Resource Management in public sector

To achieve the above-mentioned objectives, the foremost concern is that no federal or provincial economic management institution can improve its service delivery without the basic reform of civil services. The quality of civil service determines the policymaking, service delivery, resource management, and regulatory outcomes. This matter has already been highlighted in detail in Husain (2012), GoP (2011), Ahmed (2015), Ahmed (2016), Cyan (2012), Laking (2007), and Haque (2006). The aim of this chapter is not to deep dive into the reform of civil service at economic management institutions. However, it is important to strongly suggest here that the key changes required to the recruitment, training, induction, evaluation and appraisal, compensation, and promotion should include:

a) Transparent and strictly merit-based recruitment through public service commissions at all levels of service i.e., federal, provincial, and district.
b) Minimization (through appropriate law) of political interventions in postings, transfers, and rewards (e.g., promotions, trainings, allowances, and increments).
c) Improvement of monetary incentive structure (including pay, entitlements, and pension) in line with the market

for similar services in the private sector, and not-for-profit organizations.
d) Removal of hidden and discretionary perks and entitlements which allow nepotism to flourish. Such benefits can be made part of the gross salary in order to promote transparency.
e) Regular skills upgradation and guaranteed up-take of lessons learnt through security of tenure.
f) Linking of promotions with performance review, diversity of experiences, qualification, and ability to demonstrate essential behaviour and skills required for the next level.
g) Ensuring accountability systems that do not increase complexity of public sector functioning yet ensure that the civil service remains responsive to the society. These can include both demand- and supply-side accountability mechanisms.
h) Reducing time and transactions costs involved in accessing civil service grievance redress mechanisms e.g., ombudsman.
i) Benchmarking civil service output and outcomes with norms in better performing peer economies.
j) Regular feedback from private sector and local communities on satisfaction from public service delivery and using this feedback to improve civil service structure, composition, and competencies.[10]

A recent powerful proposal shelved due to perceived opposition by incumbent civil service was to initiate the new National Executive Service and hire senior level talent at BS-20 to BS-22 positions. This would have also ensured inducting technical expertise into the current structures of the civil service. This proposal was accompanied by abolishing of rather redundant tiers such as BS-21 and BS-19. Once human resources are in place, the proposal recommends putting in place performance contracts for ministries, departments, and their officials. These contracts will be translated into the still missing, entity-wise key performance indicators.[11]

A Performance Management Fund was also proposed with the aim to award and incentivize the well performing ministries, departments, and their officials. For this a new system of annual performance review (unlike the currently practiced annual confidential review) will be put in place. An Excellence and Innovation Fund is also proposed to help entities in proposing and implementing new methods of improving governance under their jurisdiction. The Establishment Division's objectives and outputs are envisaged to be reformulated so that it can play its due role in improving the HR performance across the government. A Governance Expo will be organized every year to allow government entities a chance to present their output directly to the stakeholders. Finally, there was a proposal to have three new civil service groups namely, energy, legal affairs, and transport and communication.[12] A strong political will is required to implement these proposals as there will be pressure and resort to legal action by the incumbent civil servants.

Revisiting the working relationship between CCI and the federal government

It was discussed earlier that NEC has the mandate of formulating plans 'for advising' the government including the provinces; this advice requires a legal approval forum for operationalization. The economic planning which is on part-II of the federal list implies that this is the domain of CCI (see Figure 3). CCI perhaps cannot perform its duties unless it has supervisory control over NEC and all other economic planning institutions. If this process is allowed to happen, this will imply a shift from centralized planning of a development budget to a more federalized planning (Tahir and Tahir 2013). There is also a need to revisit the working relationship across various other cabinet and inter-ministerial committees and line departments.[13]

We also observe that several constitutional steps are often found missing in tactical economic governance. For example, CCI needs to meet as per the schedule under the 18th Amendment; advice of standing committees needs implementation and compliance; several cabinet committees which now stand defunct, should either be abolished or reinvigorated with a new set of objectives; inter-ministerial committees also need to be revisited for their post-18th Amendment utility; monetary and fiscal policy coordination board will require greater independence and a more effective follow-up for implementation of post-IMF economic agenda, along with strategic guidance to SBP. The central bank's own board needs expansion as several key segments of economic activity are not represented.

Figure 3: Federal economic governance—back to the basics

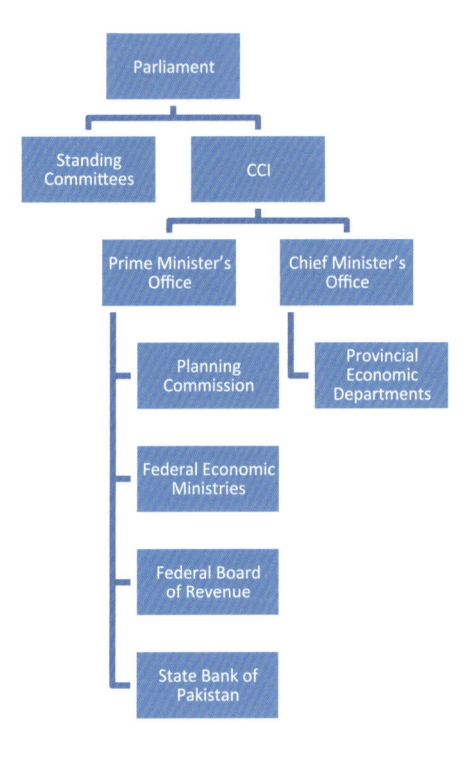

```
                    Parliament
                    /        \
        Standing Committees   CCI
                              |
                 Prime Minister's Office — Chief Minister's Office
                              |                    |
                    Planning Commission    Provincial Economic Departments
                    |
                    Federal Economic Ministries
                    |
                    Federal Board of Revenue
                    |
                    State Bank of Pakistan
```

The reform of various regulatory constraints on competitiveness now rests with the provinces. For example, the provinces will have to ease compliance with local taxes, enforcement of legal contracts, execution of real estate transactions, obtaining utilities connection (e.g., electricity) for commercial purposes, and dealing with permits (e.g., for construction and trade). For this the provincial governments will need to propose specific measures for approval by CCI.

The CCI urgently needs to suggest ways to improve federal-provincial coordination to harmonize the regulatory regime for production and exports. After the 18th constitutional amendment, provinces have come forward with their own tax regime, and growth and investment strategies. The export and industrial promotion incentives provided under these strategies requires harmonization to avoid wastage of potential fiscal resources. Several current incentives hurt product sophistication in non-traditional exports and geographical diversification of Pakistani exports. Furthermore, they have given rise to unfair business practices which have strengthened monopolies and allowed businesses to relocate and evade their tax and other liabilities.

A balance is also required between the various federal-level committees. Currently, there are a vast number of committees being chaired by the Finance Minister, which puts a single ministry (i.e., MoF) in a position where it can dominate economic governance. This issue can be resolved by giving Planning Commission (Chaired by the PM) its due role in driving the long-term economic reforms agenda. Today's Planning Commission (PC) has been reduced to a division dealing with Public Sector Development Programme (PSDP), therefore we do not see a strong ownership of Planning Commission's Vision 2025—the government's long-term development agenda. This has remained the case for the former governments as well, e.g., during the regime of Pakistan People's Party Parliamentarians, the Framework for Economic Growth, formulated by the Planning Commission, was not funded by the Finance Division and hence operationalization of this plan was halted. Back then the frictions between both Planning and Finance Divisions have resulted in different economic foci i.e., economic growth and macroeconomic stability respectively.

Another key area which needs to be insulated from the dominance of MoF and FBR is the administration of trade policy at MoC. Recently, the Commerce Minister had to write to the Finance Minister requesting him not to make protectionist instruments such as customs duties and tariffs a cornerstone of the government's revenue mobilization strategy (Ghumman 2016). It is important to revisit the role of MoF and FBR in export promotion. Given the arbitrary changes in the fiscal regime faced by exporters, a tax incidence analysis is required to understand which sectors are being hurt by: multiplicity of taxes and double taxation at federal and provincial levels; exemptions provided in the tax code for select sectors, business entities, and individuals; and the inability to rationalize tariffs, arbitrary imposition of regulatory duties, and cascading in the sales tax system. The tax incidence analysis should then guide the next Finance Act in June 2016 and directives related to export promotion by Economic Coordination Committee (ECC).

Our interviews with former senior-level officials suggest that CCI will need to ensure that institutions such as PC, FBR, and

SBP have complete autonomy. Unless these institutions are empowered the economic governance structure at the federal level (Figure 3) will remain centralized at MoF.

Reimagining the objectives of the Planning Commission

Under the Rules of Business 1973, the Planning Commission is the apex body for preparing and coordinating the national development plan and reviewing and evaluating its implementation. The weakest link at the Planning Commission is service delivery monitoring. This also applies to the provincial Planning and Development Departments. It is recommended that the Planning Commission should be positioned by the Prime Minister as the apex planning and budgeting body in the country and should be transitioned to act as a Secretariat of CCI. This will also strengthen the follow-up mechanism for decisions by CCI. For PC to perform its due role, it will need to act as the government's lead think tank and develop expertise in economic and sectoral policy planning. This, however, is not possible unless the brain drain at PC is curtailed. Historically this has been a result of two important issues. First, qualified and technical human resource was made to work under stringent rules of business (which govern the civil service). They were usually found working on processing of PSDP projects rather than actual research and development. Their performance evaluation was conducted often by non-technical superiors in the hierarchy. Second, PC's inability to design its own recruitment, induction, training, evaluation and appraisal, promotion, and compensation rules, has kept the good brains from providing their services to the Planning Commission. Both issues need to be resolved if PC has to envisage an innovative and long-term perspective plan and follow through with its implementation.

In order to provide assistance to CCI, PC will also require assistance of think tanks and academia for putting in place computational infrastructure which can formulate development scenarios on the basis of scientific simulations. PC has not updated its macroeconomic model, earlier used in simulations for GoP (2011), Ahmed and O' Donoghue (2010, 2010b), and Ahmed et al. (2010). The micro simulation setup developed for PC and used in Ahmed and O' Donoghue (2009) has also not been updated. A high quality of economic analysis at PC can also support the research and evaluation work desired at the provincial level. The Planning and Development Departments at the provinces can contribute to the improved development administration if they (along with PC) can develop an integrated national economic modelling framework.

PC's core task of management of Public Sector Development Programme (PSDP) is performed through a set of project proposals, feasibility designs, and monitoring and completion forms which are fairly obsolete.[14] A cursory look at the completed and approved PC-I (project proposal) forms reveals lack of regard for the environment and gender appraisal as part of the approval exercise, not due to intentional neglect, rather the lack of capacity to think about risks around these themes.

Other technical aspects of PSDP that require attention have been discussed in Chapter 4.

The already approved and pending reforms to improve the functioning of MoPDR need to be expedited. These include: rationalization and new configuration of sectoral units at the Ministry, reappropriation of human resource strength in each unit, redefining reporting lines to improve functioning and accountability, defining key performance indicators (KPIs) and job descriptions of each employee, and strengthening coordination with line ministries and provincial government departments. Finally, the Advisory Committee at the Planning Commission needs expansion to include a greater number of well reputed non-governmental organizations, think tanks, private sector associations, and social enterprises.

Shedding non-essential tasks of MoF

The sheer size of this ministry and the desire of past Finance Ministers to centralize the work of the federal government have resulted in diseconomies of scale. Several wings under this ministry are overburdened with slow case disposal rate. Therefore, a key recommendation here is to update the organizational workflow assessment using scientific tools. This should guide the Ministry on how to shed the non-essential roles and responsibilities and perhaps shift these tasks to a more relevant ministry. A key example is the Economic Reforms

Unit at the ministry. This unit is functioning despite the same mandate given to MoPDR.

Another important issue is to map those areas where short-term and ad hoc consultants are aiding the regular affairs of the ministry. A detailed mapping will then exhibit key areas where the ministry needs to build in-house capacity for delivery of efficient and effective fiscal policy. Like PC, current human resource at the ministry lacks the capacity to perform scientific policy analysis using standard modelling techniques to demonstrate the incidence of tax and expenditure policies. This also implies that the ministry cannot trace the outcome and impact of its own work performed over the medium to longer term. Perhaps, the Economic Advisor's Wing at the ministry should be the starting place for reform of this institution. A competent team of macroeconomists with the ability to conduct high frequency *expost* and *exante* economic analyses and make them available for the government in easy-to-understand and non-technical language can go a long way in improving the quality of policymaking.

There are several good initiatives started by the ministry which continue to be performed by ad hoc consultants. Such initiatives can easily be made full-time and regular functions within the ministry and charged to the recurrent expenditures. A key example is the Medium Term Budgetary Framework (MTBF) in the ministry. This effort requires the government to set three-year spending priorities for all ministries and the government as a whole. This system is now also under implementation at the provincial level. However, the key concern is that even at the federal level MTBF has not been fully integrated with the budget wing. In fact, the budget wing lacks the capacity and expertise to update the basic financial programming required to manage MTBF across the federal government. Perhaps a more important advice will be to raise a separate technical cadre within the Finance Division with its own service rules and regulations, and which would be responsible for institutionalizing and updating the MTBF process.

A careful review is also required to bring greater focus to the tasks performed by the regulation wing. A lot of key decisions processed under R-10 and R-14 Sections should rest with the Establishment Division. This includes, for example, allowances provided to civil servants, pay packages for serving in projects, and appointments of attendants at Pakistani missions abroad. MoF also has its own 12 senior level officers dedicated to human resource management, acting again as an (internal) Establishment Division. Most ministries do not have their own human resource management units as these matters, by law, have to be managed by the Establishment Division.

The Minister of Finance is also the Minister for Economic Affairs Division (EAD) and hence ends up playing the role of a central figure for economic diplomacy. Currently, there are over 60 Joint Economic Commissions (JECs) formed to follow up trade and investment cooperation decisions with various countries in the world. While the decisions of some JECs are being effectively followed up, others remain dormant. A careful review should rationalize the number of JECs and for those requiring a more robust follow up (e.g., with neighbouring countries such as Afghanistan and Iran) there should be a dedicated focal resource person at the Finance Minister's office to follow up the decisions with the rest of the government. This will effectively rationalize the scope and work of EAD.

During the 1980s and 1990s, EAD's core task was to procure and manage debt for running government operations. This task has also been formally taken over by the MoF with the establishment of Debt Policy Coordination Office (DPCO). This office is meant to work as a Secretariat for managing affairs necessary for implementation of FRDL Act. Specific tasks include preparing a debt reduction path, monitoring and evaluation of external and domestic borrowing strategies, analysing the foreign currency exposure of Pakistan's external debt, providing consistent information on public and external debt, and government guarantees including total guarantees outstanding (GoP 2014). A lot of these tasks are a duplication of work entrusted to EAD under the rules of business. More specifically, EAD is responsible for assessment of requirements, programming, and negotiations of external economic assistance.

Building ownership of line ministries in the work directly related to them should also be an important goal for MoF. There are several functions that concern other ministries however these entities are not on-board various important decisions. One such example is the work performed by the Provincial Finance Wing. This wing is responsible for federal transfer of provinces and rarely communicates matters related to such financial flows to the Inter Provincial Coordination Division in the Cabinet Secretariat.

The already approved and pending reforms to improve the functioning of MoF need to be expedited. This should also include an evaluation of the Quality Assurance (QA) programme initiated in 2006.[15] The evaluation should inform if the quality objectives of the various wings in the ministry have been met. MoF also receives assistance from external development partners to improve internal functioning and build capacity. For example, the ministry will receive USD 150 million from Asian Development Bank to execute Public Sector Enterprise Reform Programme. The six-monthly evaluations of such programmes should be presented to the parliament and uploaded on the website for public knowledge.

For strategic guidance to the MoF, it is important to expand the membership of both the Economic Advisory Council, and the Monetary and Fiscal Policy Coordination Board. The members should include economists who have past experience in varied sectors. Pakistani economists working outside of Pakistan and in international civil service may be invited for online participation in these meetings. Similarly, the Council and the Board may be allowed to bank on the capacities of policy think tanks and local research institutions wherever they require technical assessments.

Administrative reforms at FBR

FBR remains the apex entity for federal level tax administration. In 2015–16, federal revenues accounted for almost 93 per cent of total national revenues. Unfortunately, lack of effective governance reforms in this entity has resulted in difficulties for both tax officials and taxpayers. Currently, revenue targets are not forecasted using scientific tools in turn leading to increased pressure on officials, who then resort to forceful demand of advance tax and stopping refunds of genuine taxpayers in order to achieve a respectable revenue number. The failure to expand the tax net has also resulted in: burdening of existing taxpayers through distortionary withholding taxes (SDPI 2013), higher corporate tax rates (Ahmed & Talpur 2016), higher and protectionist custom duties (Ahmed et al. 2014), and a discriminatory tax regime for domestic versus foreign investors (Ahmed & Khan 2015). Due to the lack of research capacity at FBR, the welfare incidence of the above-mentioned distortions has not been recently estimated.

For improving the tax administration, a Tax Administrative Reform Project (TARP) was initiated in 2005. According to a World Bank evaluation the programme could not achieve its goals. A function-based organizational structure could not be fully put in place in the FBR (SDPI 2013). A meagre amount is collected through tax demands, which presents an opportunity for improvement in the tax administration system. Making use of policy suggestions provided in SDPI's research on this subject spanning over a period between 2010 and 2016, we can provide some updated recommendations for the administrative reforms at FBR.[16]

First, FBR should be made an autonomous organization on lines similar to SBP. A more autonomous entity will face lesser political pressure and control by federal government. Similarly, FBR will have greater freedom in revamping human resource management through improved recruitment, postings, transfers, career elevation, and reward mechanisms. The autonomous FBR should be headed by a governor, who has a tenure post under a proposed FBR autonomy law and his/her selection should be done through the board of governors. A performance review mechanism may be introduced and linked with FBR's commitments to revenue collection under MTBF.

Second, a stronger legal framework for tax administration is required so that FBR can effectively charge the tax evader and defaulters. Due to lack of balance between the rights of taxpayers and the powers of the tax agency, those not paying taxes have a fair certainty that they can get away with this crime.

Third, the Customs and Excise, and Inland Revenue civil service groups should remain a single cadre so that functional expertise can be developed. The entire organization should be reorganized around functional lines i.e., tax policy, enforcement, audit, human resources, and financial management with minimal management layers and appropriate spans of control, streamlined field operations, and organizational alignment to key taxpayer segments (e.g., a large taxpayer office), and sufficient numbers of staff assigned to each level of the organization and each function.

Fourth, in line with more efficient and effective revenue authorities across the world, a performance-based pay and reward structure should be introduced in FBR. This will result in the abolishment of basic pay scales which have already been termed obsolete (Husain 2013). FBR may be allowed through a legal provision the use of 0.5 per cent of the cost of collection for financing its capacity-building and skills upgradation activities. This should also lead to building expertise in risk-based audit and other tax validation measures. Such skills will help in detecting taxpayers who avoid taxation while also strengthening dispute resolution. The research and statistics wing at FBR should be revived with a full-time member heading this wing. The member should be selected on a competitive basis and must have technical knowledge and ability to design alternate tax policy scenarios.

Fifth, a clear audit plan should make way for separation of tax assessment auditor, tax recovery manager, and reduction of discretionary powers of income tax officials. The responsibility of appeals and their redress also needs to be done by a third party. In this regard FBR may carve future grievance redress reforms in collaboration with the Tax Ombudsman's office. In fact the Ombudsman's office can provide redress on its own for various disputes, if its powers are enhanced by law and the decisions are binding on the tax administrative machinery.

Sixth, the simplification of tax procedures and rules and publication of tax forms in Urdu language should be made a practice. A detailed study is required to estimate the transaction costs faced by various types of taxpayers and how these can be minimized. FBR's own spending on taxpayer facilitation units may not render optimal results unless the compliance process is simplified. These reforms can be supported by internally adopting e-governance to run FBR's official affairs. The already established IT systems in FBR may be integrated with other national databases to improve identification of tax evasion e.g., National Database and Registration Authority (NADRA) and SBP data warehouses. Similarly, there should be an 'Integrated Tax Management System' which should compile information from different tax systems at the federal and provincial level. This will also help in validation of tax bases and true estimation of taxpayers' incomes and wealth across the country. This can also help in the wider exercise of harmonizing the tax regime across provinces. There have been controversies on the selection of off-the-shelf application versus programming customized solution by the Pakistan Revenue Authority Limited. It is recommended to adopt an internationally accepted off-the-shelf application (which is being regularly updated and addressed for any bugs) for customs, sales tax registration, and enforcement management.

Finally, a high-level Advisory Board for providing strategic guidance to the FBR may be constituted. The board should be headed by an independent economist of international repute and vast experience of policy design and execution. The board should include economists having specialization in public finance and international trade, lawyers, chartered accountants, and senior politicians who can advise on legislative changes to strengthen the FBR.

Restructuring and enhancing the role of the MoC

The MoC will need to carefully analyze the binding constraints to export growth. For each constraint a desired policy response will be beyond the domain of the MoC and hence the need for an expanded role of the MoC (in economic decision making), with help from an inter-ministerial coordination group. The MoC can also be helped by the revival of the Cabinet Committee on Exports. Such a high powered coordination forum can then protect budget allocation for trade policy initiatives, credit guarantee support for exporting Small and Medium Enterprises (SMEs), and reducing anti-export taxes. Similarly, the MoC will also need to propose to the Cabinet a more robust and certain mechanism for inter-ministerial coordination which in turn could ensure utilization of the Export Development Fund (EDF). The future vision should be to use this fund for incentivizing services exports, promoting a 'make in Pakistan' agenda, help marketing endeavours of exporters, and expanding the support which the 'GSP Plus Support Mechanism Unit' at the MoC can provide to the provincial governments.

The MoC also needs to shed its non-core functions.[17] This

will allow the ministry to maintain its focus on the core objectives of STPF. The MoC should look into letting go of the administrative charge of Trade Development Authority of Pakistan, Trading Corporation of Pakistan, State Life Insurance Corporation of Pakistan, National Insurance Company Limited, Pakistan Reinsurance Company Limited, Pakistan Tobacco Board, and Pakistan Institute of Fashion and Design. In the case of the TDAP it may be reorganized on functional lines and made autonomous in its working. This will allow the TDAP to manage its own finances and hire human resource in line with the demands of global and regional marketing. Several other attached departments can also be reviewed for either making them autonomous or ensuring their reattachment with a more relevant ministry or department.

A permanent research and evaluation unit within the MoC is also required to provide timely analysis. Currently, this task is being performed by ad hoc consultants and the office of a permanent Economic Consultant. The latter's capacity has been on a decline for reasons similar to the Planning Commission's brain drain. Several forms of analyses are required at a high frequency, e.g., on revision of FTAs, analysis of possible impact of FTAs by competitor economies and blocs, such as, Trans-Pacific Partnership, Regional Comprehensive Economic Partnership, and India-ASEAN FTA. The same unit can be tasked to develop a communication strategy for key messages to the provincial governments. This is now essential as the MoC is responsible for ensuring and helping the provinces in their compliance with conventions to be ratified under GSP Plus and other market access agreements. This unit will require high quality professionals having a background in quantitative economics and law. The recruitment and regular training of such professionals should be given to Pakistan Institute of Trade and Development (PITAD), which should be detached from the MoC and transitioned to become an independent Pakistan University of Trade and Development with the status of an HEC-recognized federal university.

It is also recommended that civil servants having a background in commerce and trade (C&T) should be responsible for holding the highest positions in this ministry. The qualification requirements for those in the C&T cadre should be increased and they should be supported to complete advanced degrees in international trade and finance, commercial law, trade policy analysis, negotiating multilateral and regional trade agreements, technical barriers to trade, trade and environment, trade-related aspects of Intellectual Property Rights, Sanitary and Phytosanitary Measures, and trade in services.

In line with the practice in several other countries it is recommended that the Ministry of Industries and Production, the Ministry of National Food Security and Research (de facto Ministry for Agriculture), and the Ministry of Textile should be merged with the MoC. Besides improving the coordination across the government (much desired to achieve production and export targets), this measure will significantly reduce the government's recurrent expenditure.

As part of a related exercise, the author conducted a set of key informant interviews with government officials working in trade-promoting public sector organizations including the MoC. The respondents informed that in the past, top-level leadership at the MoC lacked the necessary experience to execute trade reforms. Higher level officials such as the Secretary or Additional Secretaries at the MoC should be from the specialized Commerce and Trade or Customs cadre. The ministry also has a shortage of staff which in turn has prompted ad hocism whereby existing officers have been granted additional charge. These officials also have a vested interest in keeping the additional charge of multiple positions due to monetary and in-kind returns such as the additional charge allowance, project allowance, and deputation allowances. As it stands today, the MoC remains understaffed, and a summary should be moved by the MoC and put up to the Prime Minister for filling up of vacant positions of Joint Secretaries, Deputy Secretaries, and Section Officers at the MoC.

Address fragmented governance and regulation of the energy sector

There are over two dozen government institutions and three regulatory bodies involved in the governance and regulation of the energy sector in Pakistan (Ahmed 2013). It has been widely recommended that both National Electric Power Regulatory Authority (NEPRA) and Oil and Gas Regulatory Authority (OGRA) should be merged. The latter is on record to have endorsed this recommendation. Similarly, the manifestos of all mainstream political parties recommend that the Ministry of Water and Power and the Ministry of Petroleum and Natural Resources should also be merged.

Second, the element of conflict of interest (a key contributor to Pakistan's poor governance ranking) needs to be reduced and the practice of retired government officials being posted as regulators need to be revisited. There is a need for professional management with relevant technical qualification in the energy sector regulatory bodies. Appropriate legislative changes will be required to further strengthen the autonomy of both regulators in this sector.

Third, the technical capacity at both ministries will also need to be upgraded. For example, the transmission of electricity in the country is being optimized manually (without the use of widely practised scientific techniques). It is widely understood that recruiting and retaining technical staff has been a challenge for both ministries. This matter can be resolved through formation of a working group involving the ministries, relevant regulators, and the Federal Public Service Commission. The working group's recommendations can then be made part of the civil service reforms being formulated at the Planning Commission. The latter has already proposed a separate cadre for energy management in the country.

Fourth, the arbitrary changes in the prices of oil, power, and gas (through various levies) should end. This has harmed the longer term investment decisions. Strong economic reasoning is required for all forms of sectoral pricing, however the variation between prices for the same fuel provided to different categories of consumers e.g., households versus industry should be minimized.

Fifth, the goal of cheaper energy supplies in the future cannot be achieved without curbing theft, and distribution and transmission losses. The installation of smart metering or other technologies should be explored. Furthermore, relevant changes in the law should demand from the provinces an effort to bring down the default payments (and distribution and transmission losses). The Ex/En should have a third party check outsourced to a private sector monitor to help in achieving this task (Ahmed 2013).

Sixth, given the size of the circular debt and the lack of a long-term solution in the public sector it is important that the government should reconsider its full ownership of electricity generation companies (GENCOs) and distribution companies (DISCOs). In the case of some of these entities, public sector mismanagement is resulting in continuous increase in recoveries. For privatization or even public-private partnerships (PPP) in GENCOs and DISCOs a key step will be to underwrite the entire stock of the circular debt and make it part of the overall government liability. Once this is done, these entities can then be offered for privatization or processed for PPP. Additional investment can be attracted even while these entities have a majority public sector ownership; however significant deregulation will be required beforehand (Ahmed 2015).

Finally, there is enough evidence to suggest that Pakistan will run out of domestic natural gas within the next 15 years. Some key administrative measures are required to expedite discovery of new reserves, to conserve current stock, and to improve the public sector's management of the gas sector. The specific administrative and regulatory reforms, as also highlighted in author's recent work (Ahmed 2016) include:

- Merging regulatory bodies i.e., petroleum concessions office, OGRA, and NEPRA.
- Implementing already available recommendations by CCP to improve the state of competition and incentives in the gas sector.
- Enforcing regulation that should prevent sub-standard and inefficient products in the gas sector.
- Expediting judicial reforms that can ease the stress faced by the gas sector. The growth in gas theft persists as those involved know that lengthy conviction processes and legal lacunas cannot bring about certainty of punishment.
- Unbundling the transmission and distribution of gas will allow a single transmission company with several distribution companies having specific and time-bound key performance indicators.
- Curtailing UFG losses through installation of smart meters network and prudent gas accounting.
- Finally, bringing ECC decisions on gas sector

allocation and pricing for approval to the Council of Common Interests.

A MIX OF DEMAND-SIDE AND SUPPLY-SIDE ACCOUNTABILITY

The initial part of this chapter provided a dismal picture regarding Pakistan's low ranking on global governance indicators. A key reason for this milieu is weak accountability and regulatory arrangements. On most occasions, accountability institutions such as National Accountability Bureau (NAB), Federal Investigation Agency (FIA), PM Inspection Commission, and anti-corruption cells at provincial level will come into action once a misdeed takes place and is reported and followed by the applicant. There are instances where these institutions fail and the Supreme Court ends up resorting to its *suo moto* powers.

A special working group should be constituted by NAB to look in to various impediments in effective implementation of existing laws and judicial decisions on combating corruption. Some major laws that provide the legal framework for accountability include (see also Qureshi 2016): Sections 161 and 171 of the Pakistan Penal Code, Prevention of Corruption Act 1947, Public and Representative Office (Disqualification) Act 1949, Elective Bodies Disqualification Order 1959, Holders of Representative Offices (Prevention of Misconduct) Act 1976, Disqualification for Membership

Act 1976, Holders of Representative Offices (Punishment for Misconduct) Order 1977, Parliament and Provincial Assemblies (Disqualification for Membership) Order 1977, Ehtisab Ordinance 1997, and NAB Ordinance 1999. The same working group may also advice on issues curtailing the effective functioning of public accountability bodies exhibited in Figure 4.

Figure 4: Public Accountability Institutions

```
                    Public
                Accountability
                    Bodies
    ┌───────────────┬───────────────┬───────────────┐
  Public         National        Federal         Provincial
  Accounts    Accountability     Bodies           Bodies
  Committee      Bureau
                              Prime Minister's   Chief Minister's
                                Inspection       Inspection Units
                                Commission

                              Parliamentary      Provincial
                               Committees       Parliamentary
                                                 Committees

                                Federal          Provincial
                               Ombudsman         Ombudsman

                                Federal
                              Investigation
                                 Agency
```

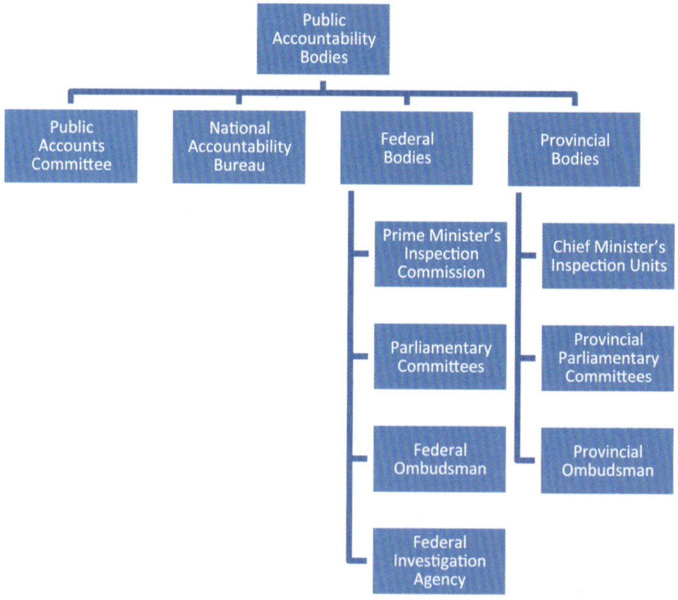

At a national level there is weak understanding of economic issues, in particular taxation and trade related matters, within most accountability institutions. On several occasions a weak working relationship between the accountability institutions (e.g., NAB or even the Supreme Court) and regulators (e.g., CCP) has resulted in the continued existence of consumer exploitation. The independence of various accountability bodies is also compromised on occasions. For example, most heads of NAB, in the past have complained of interventions by the Ministry of Interior. Similarly, the weak support provided to the accountability institutions by the various national intelligence agencies results in poor preparation of cases against perpetrators. This support is essential to access forensic services only available with a few agencies.

There is also a need to induct professionals in accountability institutions with corporate sector's knowledge. Currently, most institutions lack or do not have positions for macroeconomists or actuaries, having the ability to forecast fair prices in domestic and foreign markets. The inability to do so continues to result in sub-optimal pricing, excessive tax levies and surcharge, and consumer exploitation. Furthermore, lack of skills in tracking financial and merchandise flows allows growth in illegal and informal trade.

It will remain a challenge for the state to put in place a system of supply-side accountability that can fully deliver the desired outcomes. It is therefore necessary to also promote demand-side accountability mechanisms which can be accessed by the private sector and local communities to exert pressure for reforms. Such social accountability tools have been explained in Yaseen (2013). A responsive judiciary, vibrant media, democratization of political parties, strengthened civil society organizations, public access to information (e.g., through Right to Information Act), constitutional protection to whistle-blowers, and hotline communication channels for vulnerable communities can help strengthen social accountability mechanisms.

NEED FOR REGULATORY IMPACT ASSESSMENT—WHAT TO REGULATE AND HOW?

Pakistan's low rank in worldwide governance performance is also attributed to weak regulatory institutions responsible for the accountability of both outputs and outcomes of economic managers. We have two immediate questions. First, how can Pakistan improve the functioning of already existing regulatory institutions (mentioned in Figure 4), inter-governmental forums, and inter-ministerial arrangements responsible for the regulation of the economy and the corporate sector? Second, what new or more focused regulatory arrangements can be put in place which could lead to improved outcomes (and rankings)? There is also the issue of over regulation of markets at the micro level which provides select players to manipulate the rules at provincial and district levels and resort to anti-competitive practices.

Figure 5: De facto economic regulatory arrangement

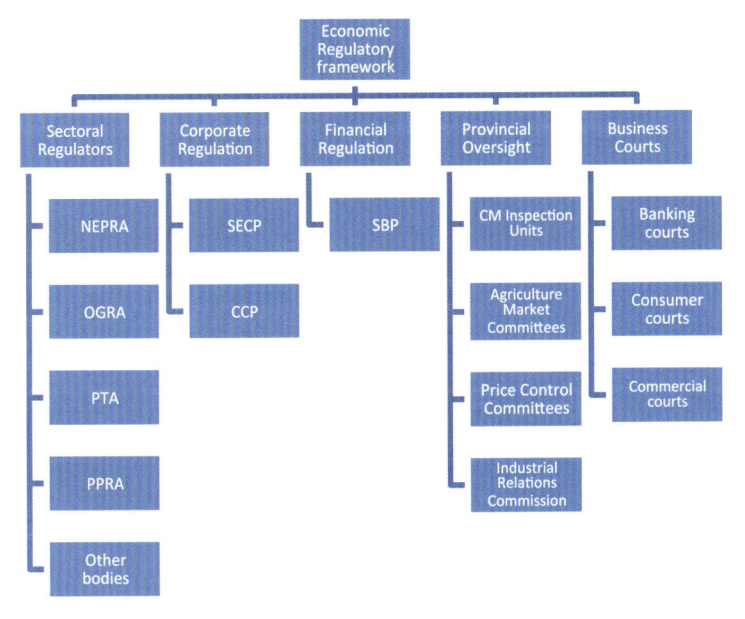

```
                    Economic Regulatory framework
    ┌───────────┬──────────┬──────────┬──────────┬──────────┐
 Sectoral   Corporate   Financial   Provincial   Business
 Regulators Regulation  Regulation  Oversight    Courts
    │           │           │           │           │
  NEPRA        SECP        SBP     CM Inspection  Banking
                                       Units      courts
  OGRA         CCP                  Agriculture   Consumer
                                      Market       courts
                                    Committees
  PTA                              Price Control  Commercial
                                    Committees     courts
  PPRA                               Industrial
                                     Relations
                                    Commission
  Other
  bodies
```

Note: NEPRA: National Electric Power Regulatory Authority, OGRA: Oil and Gas Regulatory Authority, PTA: Pakistan Telecommunication Authority, PPRA: Pakistan Procurement Regulatory Authority.

To answer the first question we first need to assess and remove the duplication of work across the entities involved in economic and corporate regulation. This can be addressed through: (a) revisiting their objectives and carrying out legislative changes removing such duplication of effort; and (b) putting in place an inter-agency coordination mechanism so that they are able to meet more frequently to address issues involving more than one regulatory body. The latter measure will also help in better understanding of viewpoints at each regulatory body.

Coordination among different institutions can be both vertical and horizontal. In the case of, for example, CCP, a vertical collaboration may be with the Supreme Court or its attached departments such as the Law and Justice Commission of Pakistan. This could allow a better understanding of each other's viewpoint leading to early disposal of cases initiated by CCP and currently stuck due to stay orders. In the case of, for example, SECP, a horizontal collaboration may be with other regulatory bodies such as SBP.

In order to make economic regulation holistic it is important to announce a schedule for coordination committee meetings. Such a committee (and a quarterly meeting schedule) already exists between SECP and SBP. It is further recommended that the minutes of these committee meetings should be uploaded on the websites of both institutions.

In order to avoid excessive and unnecessary regulation, which in turn can add to the transaction costs for producers and consumers in the economy, regular economy-wide regulatory impact assessment (RIA) is necessary. However, before a formal RIA it is important to ground the objectives of this exercise into the current challenges faced by the markets (SECP 2004). These may include:

- Promote effective corporatization: While there may be growth in the number of formally registered companies, however their survival and graduation into larger entities has not been proven through the recent data. A significant number of microfinance institutions and SMEs continue to operate in the informal economy. While targeted and time bound tax breaks and subsidies may be important for SMEs, however these entities can also be encouraged through ease of regulation and reducing financial costs of compliance with current regulations.

- Provide incentives for product diversification: Pakistan's manufacturing sector continues to operate in low value added production. Even in the case of services sector, there have not been major innovations in for example services provided by IT, telecom, banking and insurance, and transport sectors. Through ease of regulation one could for example encourage inclusive financial services which in turn could reach a vast population associated with agriculture and rural non-farm sectors. The agriculture sector is still not approached by formal insurance sector firms due to information asymmetry and lack of investor confidence.

- Allow regional and global market integration: There are significant regulatory steps required to further integrate Pakistan's services economy, particularly banking and insurance sectors with the regional and global markets. The uptake of e-commerce and online money transfer services remains weak due to several missing regulatory interventions at both legal and practice levels. This is also curtailing the growth of start-up companies in Pakistan e.g., in the IT sector, which have the ability to sell their services abroad.

- Provide a framework for professional service providers:

The missing (or on occasions incomplete) rules for professional services are leading to both informalization and exploitation in this sector. In several sectors even the basic code of ethics, formally announced by the regulator is also missing. This can be seen in the case of unregulated market for IT services, private education, accountants, tax solicitors, freelance consultants, personal grooming services, fitness centres etc. The lack of accreditation also does not let local firms bid for foreign opportunities.

Turning to RIA, an important aspect is to make the process of re-regulation as regular as possible. Currently, most regulatory bodies can only recommend changes or updates in rules and regulations to the government, and the relevant department can take time to update. This has in the past led to unnecessary delays in the issuance of new rules and regulations. A proposal may be to either bring a law which binds the government to update certain regulations after a fixed period of time, or this task may be delegated to the relevant regulatory bodies.

Finally, any RIA should first look into: the current necessity (if any) of a regulatory measure; and if the regulation is targeted towards the right entity, sector, or market. The proposed regulatory amendments should be cost-effective and implementable given the current capacities of the government. Like the issue of re-regulation RIA should be made a regular exercise at the federal and provincial planning departments. If they lack the capacity to undertake this then the same could be delegated to the relevant regulatory authorities.

Specific measures for the 'Rule of Law'

While this may not be the main subject of this chapter, however the rule of law certainly impacts the service delivery at institutions responsible for economic management. It has been advised in the past evaluations that the transactions cost of approaching and receiving justice from the courts need to be rationalized. For facilitating the business community, more efficient commercial courts need to be established in all cities with population above one million. Alternative Dispute Resolution forums, where present, need to be reinvigorated. These may be established, if absent, to help clear the backlog of cases. To facilitate the public Urdu translation of relevant legal documentation, rules and regulations need to be published under the auspices of provincial law departments. A more updated evaluation is required which may also highlight the resistance to the above-mentioned desired changes.

5. Conclusion

This chapter is a brief attempt to explain the structure of rather fragmented economic governance in the country, highlight political economy challenges in managing institutions responsible for economic governance, and suggest policy recommendations based on recent research derived from the author's own work, already available literature in the public domain, and in-depth interviews with parliamentarians, officials at the CCP, SECP, NAB, SBP, PC, MoF, MoC, and FBR.

We discuss how post-18th Amendment changes will impact national and sub-national economic policy and its coordination. There is a need to align the various legislative changes in economic governance initiated by the federal government, regulatory bodies such as CCP and SECP, and provincial governments. Greater clarity in the objectives of prudent economic governance will allow the federal and provincial governments to improve human resource management in the public sector and also reorganize the economic management institutions on modern lines.

If Pakistan aims to attract greater volumes of local and foreign investment, a concerted effort is required to improve the ranking in worldwide governance indicators (discussed in this chapter). In more specific terms this effort should require: a more efficient civil service at federal, provincial, and district levels; revisiting the working relationship between the CCI and federal government, reimagining a new set of objectives for PC and provincial planning and development departments, shedding non-essential tasks of the MoF, administrative reforms at FBR, restructuring and enhancing the role of the MoC, addressing fragmented governance and regulation of the energy sector, complementing the government's accountability efforts with the promotion of demand-side accountability, introducing judicial and police reforms to improve the rule of law, and conducting a regulatory impact assessment to avoid excessive and unnecessary regulation.

Our analysis on economic governance has several limitations. We have not focused here on the reform of economic governance at the provincial level which would have required a greater time given some variation across (economic) laws in the provinces. Even at the federal level we have confined ourselves to minimum changes in macroeconomic management institutions that could bring about efficiency in operations. Finally, we have not covered the management of the State Bank of Pakistan. We hope that future attempts will aim to bridge these gaps.

References

Abbas, M, H. and Ahmed, V., 'Challenges to Social Accountability and Service Delivery in Pakistan', *Sustainable Development Policy Institute, Working Paper No. 145*, 2014.

ADB, 'Sector Assessment—Public Sector Management', Public Sector Enterprise Reforms Project (RRP PAK 48031). Asian Development Bank, Islamabad, 2014.

Ahmad, Ejaz, R. Abida, E. and Hameedur, R, B., 'Political Institutions, Growth and Development in Pakistan (2008-2013)', *Journal of Political Studies*, Vol. 21, Issue-1, 2014, 257:269.

Ahmad, N., 'Governance, Globalization and Human Development in Pakistan', *The Pakistan Development Review*, 44:4, 2005, pp. 585–94.

Ahmed, V. and Donoghue, C. O., 'Redistributive Effect of Personal Income Taxation in Pakistan', *Pakistan Economic and Social Review*, Volume 47, No. 1, 2009, pp. 1–17.

Ahmed, V. and Donoghue, C. O., 'Tariff Reduction in a Small Open Economy', *Seoul Journal of Economics*, 2010.

Ahmed, V. and Khan, H. D., 'Fund-raising for Energy Projects in Pakistan', *Sustainable Development Policy Institute, Working Paper No. 149*, 2015.

Ahmed, V. and Khan, H. D., 'Fund Raising for Energy Projects in Pakistan', (ed) *Solutions for Energy Crisis in Pakistan,* Islamabad Policy Research Institute & Hanns Seidel Foundation, 2015.

Ahmed, V. (2016) 'Taxation Reforms in Sindh', Policy Brief (unpublished). Sustainable Development Policy Institute, Islamabad.

Ahmed, V. and Donoghue, C. O., 'External Shocks in a Small Open Economy: A CGE Micro-simulation Analysis', *The Lahore Journal of Economics,* 15: 1, 2010, pp. 45–90.

Ahmed, V. and Ahmed, S., 'Poverty and Social Impact Analysis of Expanded Programme on Immunization in Pakistan', *Sustainable Development Policy Institute, Working paper No. 143.* Islamabad, 2014.

Ahmed, V. and Talpur, M., 'Corporate Tax Reforms in Pakistan', *Sustainable Development Policy Institute, Working Paper No. 155*, 2016.

Ahmed, V. et al., 'Public Infrastructure and Economic Growth in Pakistan: A dynamic CGE Micro-simulation Analysis', *Springer*, 2013, 117–43.

Ahmed, V., Sugiyarto, G. and Jha, S., 'Remittances and Household Welfare: A Case Study of Pakistan', *ADB Economics Working Paper Series,* 2010.

Ahmed, V., 'Focusing on the Gas Sector' http://tns.thenews.com.pk/focusing-gas-sector/#.V4XvxKK3syt, *The News on Sunday,* January 24, 2016.

Ahmed, V., 'Improving Education & Skills Using Innovation & ICT', (ed) *Building Knowledge-Based-Economy in Pakistan: Learning from Best Practices,* Islamabad Policy Research Institute, 2016.

Ahmed, V., 'Overcoming Fragmented Governance—The Case of Energy Sector in Pakistan', *Social Science and Policy Bulletin*, 2014.

Ahmed, V., 'Sustainable Economic Development in Pakistan', (ed) *Pakistan's Security Problems & Challenges in the Next Decade*, National University of Sciences and Technology, 2015.

Akhtar, A., S. Amirali, A. & Raza, M. A., 'Reading between the Lines: The Mullah-Military Alliance in Pakistan', *Contemporary South Asia, 15:4*, 2006, 383–97, DOI: 10.1080/09584930701329982.

Akhtar, S., 'Regulatory and Supervisory Framework', International Bankers Annual Washington Conference, Washington DC, 5 March 2007.

Amin, M., Ahmed, A. and Zaman, K., 'The Relationship between Corruption and Economic Growth in Pakistan—Looking Beyond the Incumbent', *Economics of Knowledge*, Volume 5, Issue 3, 2013.

Andlib, Z. Khan, A. and Haq, I, U., 'The Coordination of Fiscal and Monetary Policies in Pakistan: An Empirical Analysis 1975–2011', Paper presented at the 28th Annual General Meeting of Pakistan Society of Development Economics, 2012.

Arby, M. F. and Hanif, M. N, 'Monetary and Fiscal Policies Coordination: Pakistan's Experience', *State Bank of Pakistan Research Bulletin*, Volume 6, No. 1, May, 2010.

Avinash, Dixit., 'Governance Institutions and Economic Activity', *The American Economic Review*. Vol. 99, No. 1 (Mar., 2009), pp. 3–24

Avinash, K., Dixit, 'Economic Governance', from *The New Palgrave Dictionary of Economics* 2008 edition.

Aziz, K. K., *Religion, Land and Politics in Pakistan: A Study of Piri-Muridi*, Vanguard Books, 2001.

Candland, C., Workers' Organizations in Pakistan: Why No Role in Formal Politics? Editors R. Agarwala and R. J. Herring: *Whatever Happened to Class? Reflections from South Asia*. Lexington Books, 2009.

Chaudry, A., *Political Administrators—The Story of Civil Service in Pakistan* Oxford University Press, 2011.

Cyan, M. R., 'Civil Service Management in Devolved Government: Reconciling Local Accountability and Career Incentives in Pakistan', *The Lahore Journal of Economics,* 17, 2012: pp. 425–45.

Farooq, A. et al., 'Does Corruption Impede Economic Growth in Pakistan?' *ELSEVIER*, Volume 35, 2013, pp. 622–33.

Ghumman, M., 'Commerce Minister Criticizes Import Tariff Regime', http://www.brecorder.com/top-stories/0/59084/*Business Recorder*, 10 July 2016.

Haider, A., Din, M. U. and Ghani, E., 'Consequences of Political Instability, Governance and Bureaucratic Corruption on Inflation and Economic Growth: The Case of Pakistan' *Pakistan Institute of Development Economics*, 2011.

Haq, N. and Khawaja, I., 'Public Service: Through the Eyes of Civil Servants. (Governance Series) *PIDE Series on Governance and Institutions*, 2007.

Haq, R. and Zia, U., 'Does Governance Contribute to Pro-poor Growth? Evidence from Pakistan', *PIDE Working Papers*: 2009, 52.

Haq, R. and Zia, U., 'Governance and Pro-poor Growth: Evidence from Pakistan' *The Pakistan Development Review*, 45:4, Part II, 2006, pp. 761–76.

Haque, N. U., 'Why Civil Service Reforms Do Not Work', *PIDE Working Papers* 24, 2006.

Husain, I., 'Institutions of Restraint: The Missing Element in Pakistan's Governance', *The Pakistan Development Review*, 38:4, 1999, pp. 511–36.

Husain, I., *Reforming the Government in Pakistan*, Vanguard Books, 2012.

Hussain, A., 'Institutions, Economic Growth and Participatory Development' *Lahore School of Economics*, 2013.

Hussain, A., 'Power Dynamics, Institutional Instability and Economic Growth: The Case of Pakistan', Manuscript, *The Asian Foundation*, 2008.

ICG 'Reforming Pakistan's Civil Service' International Crisis Group.' *Crisis Group Asia Report no. 185*, 16 February, 2010.

Javaid, U., 'Corruption and its Deep Impact on Good Governance in Pakistan', *Pakistan Economic and Social Review*, Volume 48, No. 1, 2010, pp. 123–34.

Kemal, A. R., 'Regulatory Framework in Pakistan', *The Pakistan Development Review*, 41:4, Part I, 2002, pp. 319–32.

Khawaja, M. I., and Khan, S., 'Reforming Institutions: Where to Begin', *PIDE Working Papers*, 2009:50.

Khan, S., Yasin, F., Kakakhel, S., Sohaib, M., (2013), 'The Dynamics of Access: Implications of 'Voice', 'Exit' and Accountability in the Provision of Public Goods.' *Working Paper 135*, Sustainable Development Policy Institute, Islamabad.

Kirk, T., 'Citizen-Led Accountability and Inclusivity in Pakistan', *London School of Economics and Political Science*, 2014.

Laking, R., 'International Civil Service Reform: Lessons for the Punjab', Asian Development Bank, 2007.

Nabi, I., 'Public Policy Fundamentals for Sustainable and Inclusive Growth', *The Lahore Journal of Economics*, September 2008, pp. 95–116.

PIDAT, 'Accountability Structures: A Comparative Analysis', *Pakistan Institute of Legislative Department and Transparency*, 2015.

Qasim, A. W., Kemal, M. A., and Siddique, O., 'Fiscal Consolidation and Economic Growth: A Case Study of Pakistan', *PIDE Working Papers No. 124*, 2015.

Qayyum, A. and Khawaja, I., 'Growth Diagnostics in Pakistan' *PIDE Working Papers*, 2008:47.

Qureshi S. A., 'Governance Deficit: A case study of Pakistan', Sang-e-Meel Publications.

Samad S., 'Combating Corruption: The Case of the National Accountability Bureau, Pakistan', *JOAAG*, Vol. 3, No. 1, 2008.

Sanchez-Pages and Straub., 'The Emergence of Institutions', *The B.E. Journal of Economic Analysis & Policy*. Volume 10, Issue 1, September 2010.

SDPI, 'Reforming Tax System in Pakistan' Sustainable Development Policy Institute, Draft Study, 2013.

SECP Annual Report, Securities and Exchange Commission of Pakistan, Islamabad, 2004.

Shah, S. K., 'National Level Accountability Framework: Key Issues With Respect to Corruption', Presentation at Sustainable Development Policy Institute. Islamabad, 2012.

Shahbaz, M., Hye, Q. M, A. and Shabbir, M. U., 'Does Corruption Increase Financial Development? A Time Series Analysis in Pakistan', *MRPA*, Paper No. 29640, 2011.

Tahir, P. and Tahir, N., 'Implications of the 18th Constitutional Amendment for National Planning and Economic Coordination', Presentation at International Conference on Federalism & Decentralization. UNDP Pakistan, 2013.

Yaseen, F., 'Social Accountability in Pakistan: Challenges, Gaps, Opportunities and the Way Forward', *Sustainable Development Policy Institute, Working Paper No. 133*, 2013.

Yaseen, F., 'Social Accountability in Pakistan: Challenges, Gaps, Opportunities and the Way Forward', *Sustainable Development Policy Institute, Working Paper No. 133*, 2013.

Zakaria, M. and Fida, B. A., 'Democratic Institutions and Variability of Economic Growth in Pakistan. Some Evidence from the Time-Series Analysis', *The Pakistan Development Review*, 2009, pp. 269–89.

Zubair, S. S. and Khan, M. A., 'Good Governance: Pakistan's Economic Growth and Worldwide Governance Indicators', *Pakistan Journal of Commerce and Social Sciences*, Vol. 8 (1), 2014, 258–71.

Annex-I: Linking Governance and Economic Growth[18]

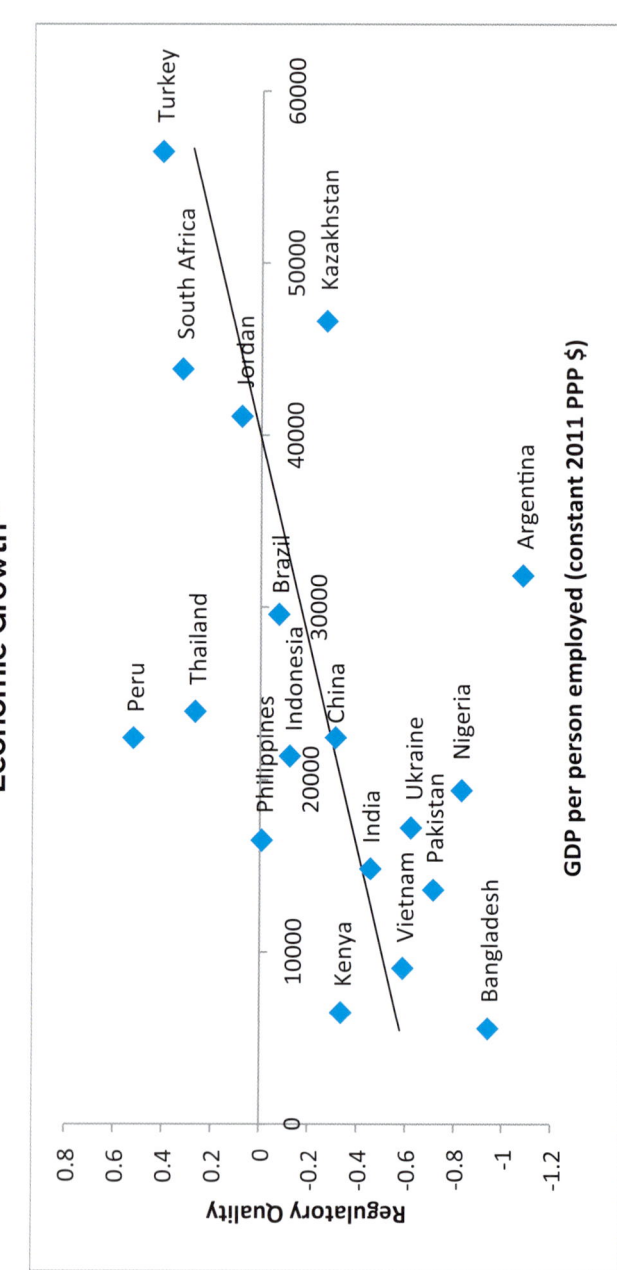

Source: Author has derived data from World Development Indicators (http://data.worldbank.org).

Note: As per the World Bank Group's definition 'regulatory quality captures perceptions of the ability of the government to formulate and implement sound policies and regulations that permit and promote private sector development'. The standard normal units range from −2.5 to 2.5 with higher values corresponding to an improvement.

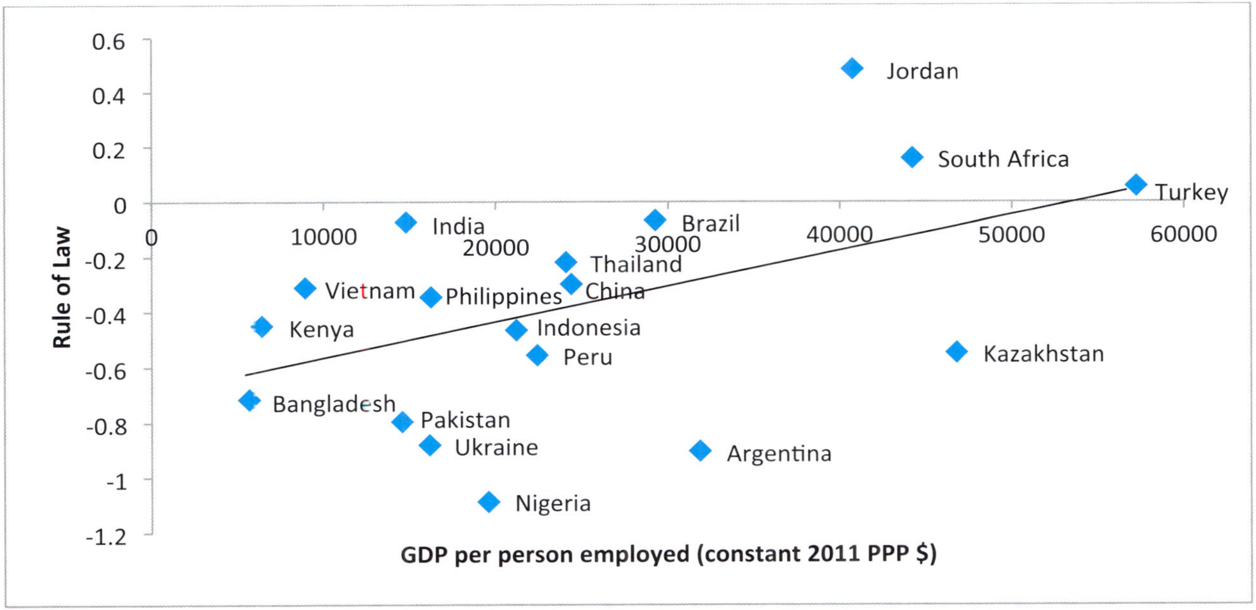

MACROECONOMIC POLICY GOVERNANCE   99

Source: Author has derived data from World Development Indicators (http://data.worldbank.org).

Note: As per the World Bank Group's definition 'rule of law captures perceptions of the extent to which agents have confidence in and abide by the rules of society, and in particular the quality of contract enforcement, property rights, the police, and the courts, as well as the likelihood of crime and violence'. The standard normal units range from −2.5 to 2.5 with higher values corresponding to an improvement.

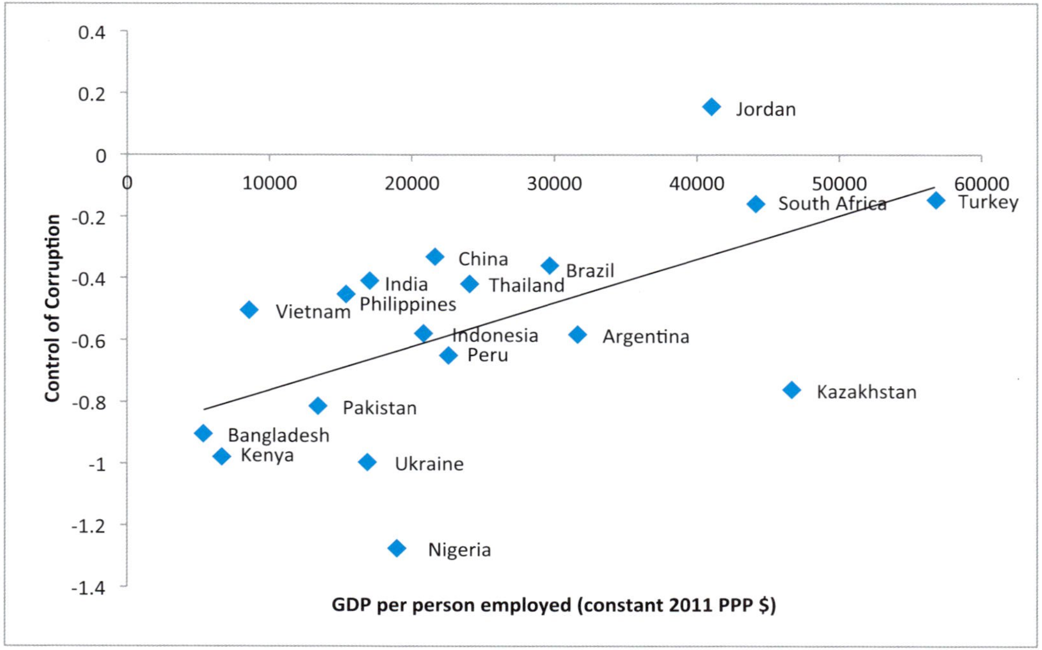

Source: Author has derived data from World Development Indicators (http://data.worldbank.org).

Note: As per the World Bank Group's definition 'control of corruption captures perceptions of the extent to which public power is exercised for private gain, including both petty and grand forms of corruption, as well as capture of the state by elites and private interests'. The standard normal units range from -2.5 to 2.5 with higher values corresponding to an improvement.

MACROECONOMIC POLICY GOVERNANCE 101

Source: Author has derived data from World Development Indicators (http://data.worldbank.org).
Note: As per the World Bank Group's definition 'government effectiveness captures perceptions of the quality of public services, the quality of the civil service, and the degree of its independence from political pressures, the quality of policy formulation and implementation, and the credibility of the government's commitment to such policies'. The standard normal units range from -2.5 to 2.5 with higher values corresponding to an improvement.

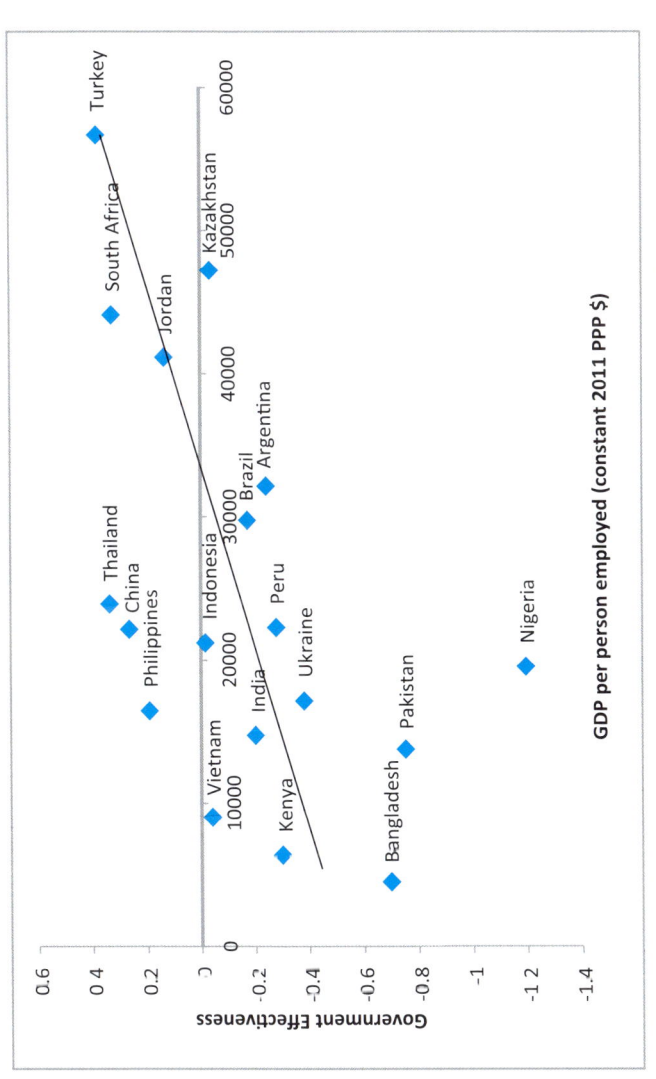

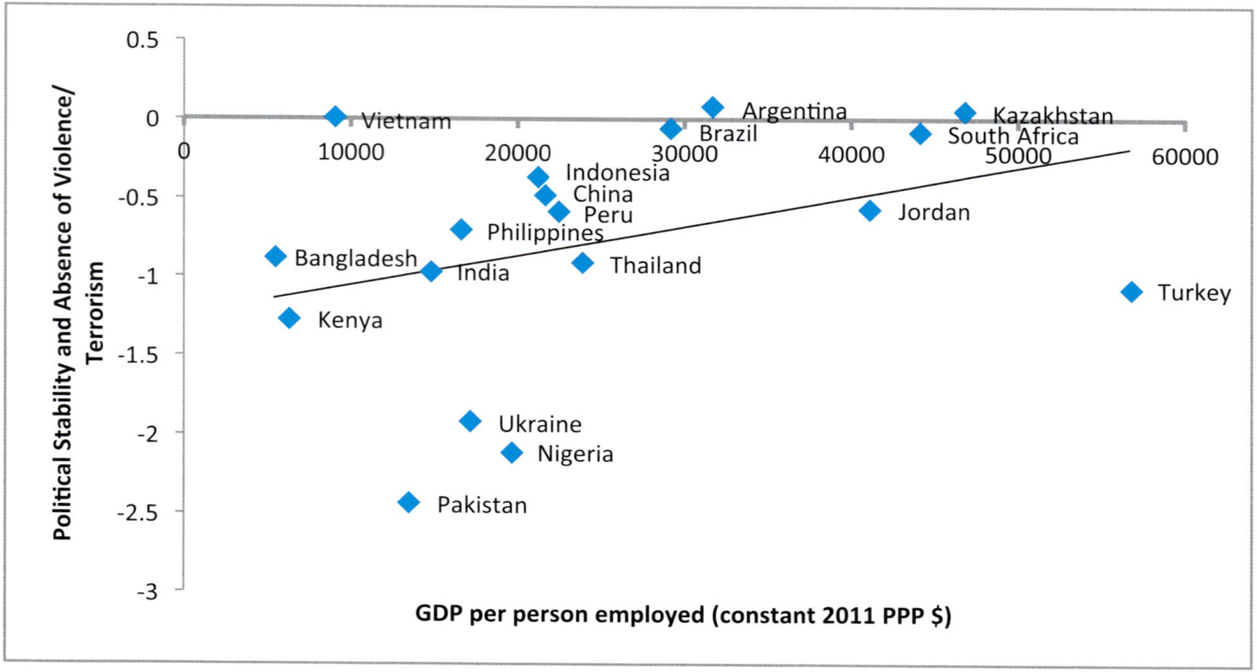

Source: Author has derived data from World Development Indicators (http://data.worldbank.org).

Note: As per the World Bank Group's definition 'political stability and absence of violence/terrorism measures perceptions of the likelihood of political instability and/or politically-motivated violence, including terrorism'. The standard normal units range from -2.5 to 2.5 with higher values corresponding to an improvement.

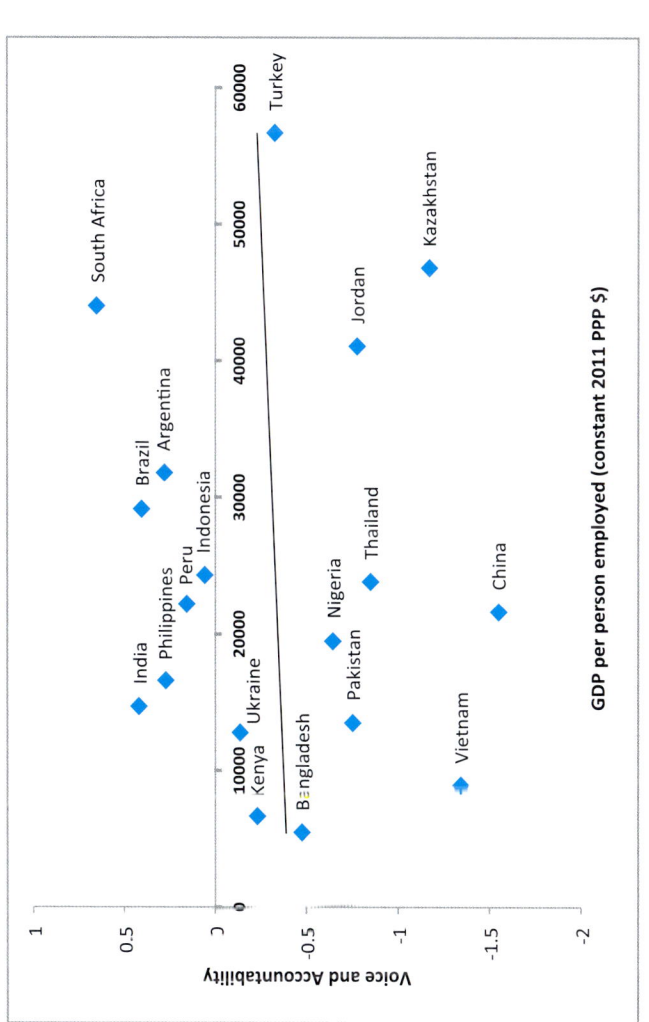

Source: Author has derived data from World Development Indicators (http://data.worldbank.org).

Note: As per the World Bank Group's definition 'voice and accountability captures perceptions of the extent to which a country's citizens are able to participate in selecting their government, as well as freedom of expression, freedom of association, and a free media'. The standard normal units range from -2.5 to 2.5 with higher values corresponding to an improvement.

Annex-II: Financial Position of Select Public Sector Enterprises

Pakistan International Airline (PIA)

Rs. Million

	2010	2014
Operating revenues	107,532	118,049
Operating expenses	4,065	14,939
Operating Loss	**(20785.12)**	**(32,222)**

Source: Annual Report 2014 PIA.

Pakistan Railway

Rs. Million

	2010–11	2014–15
Gross Earning	18,612.07	31,924.76
Operating expenditure	31,464.91	42,000.13
Interest expenditure	4,956.74	-
Loss	**(29,947.02)**	**(27,246.78)**

Source: Pakistan Railway Yearbook 2014–15.

Oil & Gas Development Corporation Limited (OGDCL)

Rs. Million

	2010	2015
Net sales	142572	210625
Other revenues	3360	20230
Profit before taxation	88550	127030
Profit for the year	**59177**	**87249**

Source: Annual Report OGDCL 2015.

Pakistan State Oil (PSO)

Rs. Million

	2010	2015
Sales Revenue (net of discounts)	877,173	1,114,409
Net Revenue	742,758	913,094
Gross Profit	29,166	23,579
Other Income (including share of associates' profits)	8,090	14,403
Marketing & Administrative Expenses	6,996	11,419
Other Operating Expense	2,417	3,513
Operating Profit	27,328	22,671
Finance Cost	9,882	11,017
Profit before Tax	17,963	12,033
Profit after Tax	**9,050**	**6,936**

Source: Annual Report 2015 PSO.

Lahore Electric Supply Company Limited (LESCO)

Rs. Million

	2010	2014
Total revenue	128,529	225,175
Operating cost	217,669	124,597
Operating profit	7506	3932
Profit before interests & tax	12118	7071
Less: Financial charges	1098	581
Profit for the year	**11020**	**6490**

Source: LESCO Financial Statements.

Multan Electric Power Company Limited (MEPCO)

Rs. Million

	2013	2015
Electricity sales—net	140,240	156,759
Cost of electricity	118,277	130,804
Gross profit	21,964	25,955
Operating cost	13,757	19,356
Other income	2,492	2,109
Financial charges	390	791
Profit for the year	**11,885**	**9,797**

Source: MEPCO Financial Statements.

Sukkur Electric Power Company (SEPCO)

Rs. Million

	2013	2014
Revenue	46,759	41,400
Operating cost	62,887	54,729
Loss from operations	(16,128)	13,329
Other income	568	389
Finance cost	3,865	8,419
Loss after taxation	**(19,430)**	**(14,810)**

Source: SEPCO Financial Statements.

Quetta Electric Supply Company Limited (QESCO)

Rs. Million

	2013	2014
Electricity sales	46,957	47,699
Cost of electricity	49,624	53,933
Gross loss	2,667	6,234
Distribution cost	4,665	4,969
Other income	2,690	3,119
Finance cost	2,486	2,580
Profit/(Loss) after tax	**(13,773)**	**8,313**

Source: QESCO Financial Statements.

Faisalabad Electric Supply Company Limited FESCO

Rs. Million

	2012	2015
Sale of electricity (net)	72,645.1	99,993
Cost of electricity	95,292	105,627
Gross profit	7,934	16789.0
Operating expenses	10096.4	14,454
Operating profit	17,170	3,432
Other income	2,035	2,312
Finance costs	14.7	208
Profit before taxation	15,149	5,536
Taxation	-	306
Profit/(Loss) after taxation	**(15,149)**	**5,230**

Source: FESCO Financial Statements.

Notes

1. Including Pakistan International Airlines and Pakistan Railways.
2. A Bill or Amendment shall be deemed to be a Money Bill if it contains provisions dealing with the: imposition, abolition, remission, alteration, or regulation of any tax; the borrowing of money or the giving of any guarantee by the Federal Government, or the amendment of the law relating to the financial obligations of that Government; the custody of the Federal Consolidated Fund, the payment of moneys into, or the issue of moneys from, that Fund; imposition of a charge upon the Federal Consolidated Fund, or the abolition or alteration of any such charge; receipt of moneys on account of the Public Account of the Federation, the custody or issue of such moneys; audit of the accounts of the Federal Government or a Provincial Government; and any matter incidental to any of the matters specified in the preceding paragraphs.
3. See World Governance Indicators for detailed definitions: http://info.worldbank.org/governance/wgi/index.aspx#doc.

4. These include Access to Justice Programme, Tax Administration Reform Programme, and Civil Service Capacity-Building Programme led by the Establishment Division.
5. See web link: http://ow.ly/NfOS302KH7M. Accessed on 30 July 2016.
6. A summary of the financial position of select electricity distribution companies (and some other PSEs) is given in Annex-II.
7. Depending on the specific sub-sector under professional services.
8. Harassment by, for example, FBR, SECP, provincial labour, and environment departments.
9. The ministry has been found to breach the autonomy of the central bank. For example, it was widely reported in the news when the Finance Minister revealed changes in the monetary policy before the announcement by the central bank, in turn confirming the perception that at some level the central bank was being dictated to by the exchequer. See *Express Tribune* report, 24 January 2015, weblink: http://tribune.com.pk/story/826936/discount-rate-cut-by-1-ishaq-dar-reveals-ahead-of-sbp-announcement/. Weblink accessed on 12 July 2016.
10. While the structure will focus on issues such as hierarchy versus flat organizational systems (depending upon the need of the task), the composition could include a mix of management and technical professionals working at the same level of seniority however collaborating to deliver a better mix of services.
11. Past exercises on key performance indicators are available with Medium Term Budgetary Framework office at the Ministry of Finance. At the provincial level, there are examples from Punjab Resource Management Programme.
12. Some news coverage on these issues may be seen here: http://tribune.com.pk/story/1020530/upgrading-bureaucracy-govt-finalises-civil-service-reforms-package/.
13. For example, the Cabinet Committees on economic matters include Committees on Exports, Privatization, and Energy.
14. Manual of Development Projects is available on Planning Commission's website: http://www.pc.gov.pk/wp-content/uploads/2014/05/Manual-for-development-projects.pdf.
15. For details: http://www.finance.gov.pk/qa_performance.html, accessed on 17 July 2017.
16. This research benefited from views and contributions by Hafiz A. Pasha's team under the project entitled 'Research and Advocacy for the Advancement of Allied Reforms'. The author also benefited from discussions with Ahmed Qadir and Nohman Ishtiaq.

17. In formulating these recommendations, the author received technical advice from Mr Shahid Kardar and Mr Abdul Wajid Rana.
18. Definition of governance indicators used here may be seen at Worldwide Governance Indicators: http://info.worldbank.org/governance/WGI/#doc.

Chapter 3

Tax Policy and Administration

1. Introduction

The government's tax policy can impact poverty and inequality levels in several ways. Depending on the demographic structure, level of economic growth, and existence of economically backward regions and communities, a progressive tax policy with efficient administration can lead to income and wealth redistribution. However, this also depends upon the government's willingness to improve the efficiency of public spending. Historically, countries have also relied on tax cuts to stimulate growth during recessionary periods but reduced taxes may not always be sufficient to attract investors' interest if not accompanied by other regulatory measures that reduce the cost of doing business in the country.

In order to increase tax collection, authorities often compromise on two important principles of taxation. The first is the efficiency principle which demands that the imposition of a tax should result in a minimum possible economic cost to the society and should not stifle production activity. Second, the principle of fairness requires that the tax should be designed in a manner that the rich pay a larger share of their incomes relative to the poor.

A key question for any government is to see who bears the tax burden? In the case of Pakistan, Wahid and Wallace (2008) explained that despite several tax concessions allowed to the rich, the overall burden of taxes in Pakistan could be termed progressive i.e., the rate of the tax increases as the taxable income increases. The authors however suggest that further improvement may be required to improve distribution of taxes. While progressivity may be seen in the case of the top income bracket, however, this may not be the case for the rest of the income distribution including the middle income group. This indicates room for increasing tax efforts for various income groups above the threshold.

Ahmed and Donoghue (2009) also suggest that the structure of personal income taxation since the Income Tax Ordinance 2001 has resulted in greater redistribution. The deductions allowed to those in wage-employment contributed the most towards progressivity. However, authors had argued that given the increasing pre-tax income gap, tax-related changes may not be the only remedy for reducing inequality.

Pasha (2014), while discussing the above-mentioned findings, argues that there are reasons to believe that the burden of taxes may be less progressive since 2008. Key reasons include: an increase in indirect taxes faced by the lower income groups, sharp increase in taxes from petroleum products, particularly the fuel type used in public transportation and farming, and regressive impact of the rising number and rate of withholding taxes (WHTs)[1] on electricity, communications, imports, and contracts.

The period between 2007 and 2015 saw Pakistan experiencing one of the lowest economic growth rates in comparison to peer economies. This affected revenue collection which was already below potential due to administrative gaps and concessions allowed on political economy grounds (Ahmed 2015). The government expenditure during this period could not be decreased due to the escalated war on terror, inability of the government to reduce losses of state-owned enterprises, and untargeted subsidies. Lower revenues and higher expenditures in turn resulted in increased government borrowing and fiscal deficit.

During the same period, the export sector's competitiveness was under pressure due to electricity and gas shortages, prevalence of distortionary taxes, regulatory requirements introduced through Finance Acts between 2013–15, overvalued exchange rate, and the inability of revenue authorities to clear the refund of exporting entities. This situation was further exacerbated by a slowdown in growth and dampening of demand in the advanced economies. The private sector's response was to refrain from locking themselves into longer term export commitments. This was also reflected in reduced credit off-take by the private sector from the banking system in 2014–15.[2]

Pakistan also committed to an ambitious set of goals agreed during the Sustainable Development Summit in

September 2015, known as the 2030 Agenda for Sustainable Development. This includes 17 goals aimed at combating poverty, inequality, social injustice, and climate change. A key lesson from the experience of Millennium Development Goals (MDGs) was that these goals are harder to achieve if governments are cash starved, unable to improve governance of social sectors (e.g., health, nutrition, education, and skills) and cannot effectively spend on human development and well-being of the citizens (Hulme 2013, Ahmed et al. 2014). The economies with low levels of tax revenue found it harder to create fiscal space for sustained expenditures in social sectors over the medium and longer run. The inability of the state in raising revenues or bringing efficiency in public spending can also lead to higher deficit and debt burden. This also contributes to inflationary and exchange rate pressures. Tax policy alone will not be sufficient to meet the Sustainable Development Goals (SDGs). An alignment of current public expenditure portfolio with SDGs will also be essential, particularly at the provincial level.

Our next section will provide a brief situation analysis of tax collection in recent years and challenges faced by revenue authorities and taxpayers. We also look at how changes in the tax regime may be contributing to the rising cost of doing business and hurting the objectives of trade policy in Pakistan. In section three we will provide policy recommendations based on existing literature, the author's own research and key informant interviews with experts, representatives of the private sector, and government officials. Many of these interviews were conducted as part of the pre-budget consultations organized by the Sustainable Development Policy Institute (SDPI) in 2016 and 2017.

2. Taxes in Pakistan: Situation Analysis

The revenue authorities have found it challenging to raise the collection at a scale desired for maintaining the government's current and development expenditures. The inability to make people pay their due taxes has forced the state to expand the scope of withholding taxes and indirect taxes. These taxes sometimes take distortionary and regressive forms. Such taxes were routinely imposed between 2010 and 2015 on items more intensively consumed by the poor, for example, food and fuel. According to some estimates this move may have contributed to an increase in poverty (Pasha 2014b) and food insecurity (Jamal and Javed 2013).

The direct taxes by definition are levied on the proceeds from wage- and self-employment, profits, and capital gains. Wealth taxes have also been used in the past to boost revenues. The indirect taxes are imposed on consumption (general sales tax), imports (customs duty), and expenditure on items which are thought to carry negative externalities (excise duty). Besides these, the state can also collect non-tax revenues in the form of levies, surcharges, fees, royalties, dividends, and profits.

Between 1998 and 2014, the share of direct taxes increased from

35 to 39 per cent (Table 1). One reason for this increase was the heavy reliance on presumptive taxes, also regarded as a kind of indirect tax. An important example of this is the increased share of withholding taxes in the overall direct tax collection. Such taxes withhold a certain payment at the time of transaction and can be adjusted in the final year-end tax liability. There are several issues with this system e.g., a person performing the transaction and paying the withholding tax (e.g., on electricity or gas consumption) is assumed to be a tax filer and an income earner—this may not always be true, particularly for the poorest income quintile. Secondly, the year-end adjustment in the tax liability does not account for any within the year changes in inflation. Thirdly, the month-end filing of withholding tax returns impose an additional compliance cost. This is particularly hurting the small businesses that do not have the resources to outsource such obligations.

Table 1: Federal Tax Collection (PKR Billion)

Year	Total (FBR)*	Tax % of GDP	Direct Taxes	Indirect Taxes			
				Cus-toms	Sales	Excise	Total
2013–14	2,255	9.0	877	243	996	138	1377
			{39.0}	[17.6]	[72.3]	[10.0]	[61.1]
2014–15 B.E	2,810	9.7	1,180	281	1,171	178	1,630
			{42.0}	[17.2]	[71.8]	[10.9]	[58.0]

*Source: Federal Board of Revenue.

[ ] as % of indirect taxes. { } as % of direct taxes. B.E = budget estimate.

Lower revenues also hurt the ability of the state to invest in an enabling environment for businesses. This, in turn, affects competitiveness of local businesses and exporters vis-à-vis other economies. Box 1 exhibits that tax collection in Pakistan as percentage of GDP is lower than Bangladesh, China, India, and Indonesia. Second, tax-to-GDP ratio has not significantly increased since the levels seen during the past decade. Third, share of indirect taxes in the overall tax collection has remained high overtime—indicating a weak effort to broaden direct tax base, which in turn could lend greater share of revenues from progressive corporate and personal income taxes. Fourth, while sales tax remains the highest contributor to overall indirect tax collection, it may be observed that there is no deliberate effort to: bring down taxes on international trade, and phase-out distortionary excise duties. A key element that adds to the overall regressivity of the indirect taxes is the rising share of revenues from imposition of various surcharges.

Pakistan is also witnessing low tax buoyancy, calculated as growth in tax collection due to growth in national income (Rasheed 2006, Bilquees 2004). The annual average tax buoyancy between 1976 and 2013 was 1.0. This dropped to 0.9 during 2004 and 2013. A key reason for realizing lower than potential tax revenues has been the vast number of exemptions, concessions, and preferential treatment (Table 2) allowed to select sub-sectors under agriculture, industry, and services.

Box 1: Tax Collection in Pakistan

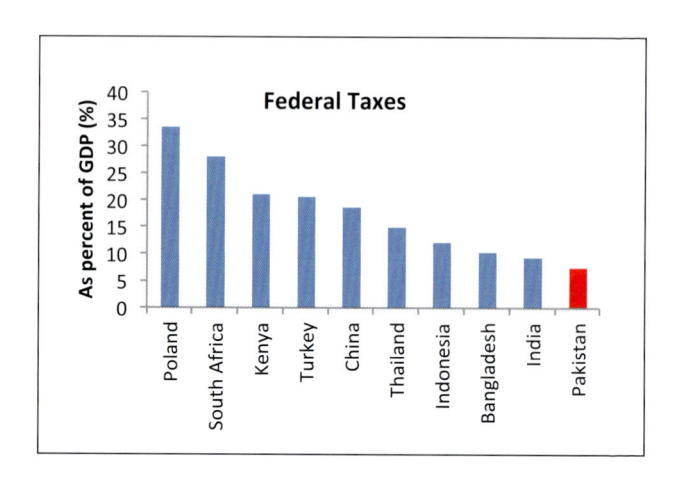

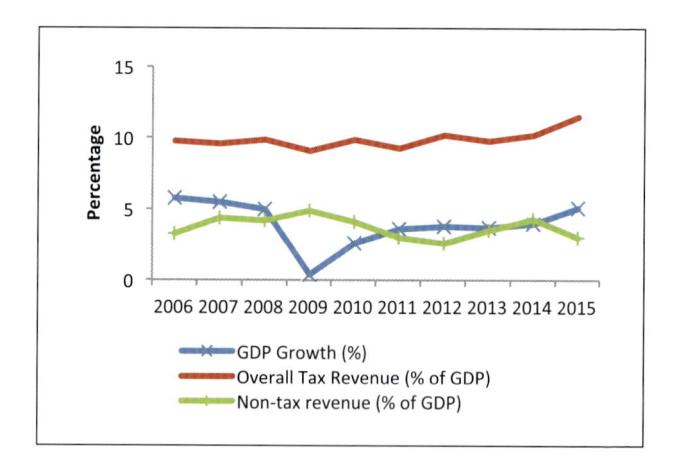

Federal Taxes (As percent of GDP (%))

Country	%
Poland	~33.5
South Africa	~28
Kenya	~21
Turkey	~20.5
China	~18.5
Thailand	~14.5
Indonesia	~12
Bangladesh	~10
India	~9
Pakistan	~7

Legend (second chart, 2006–2015):
- GDP Growth (%)
- Overall Tax Revenue (% of GDP)
- Non-tax revenue (% of GDP)

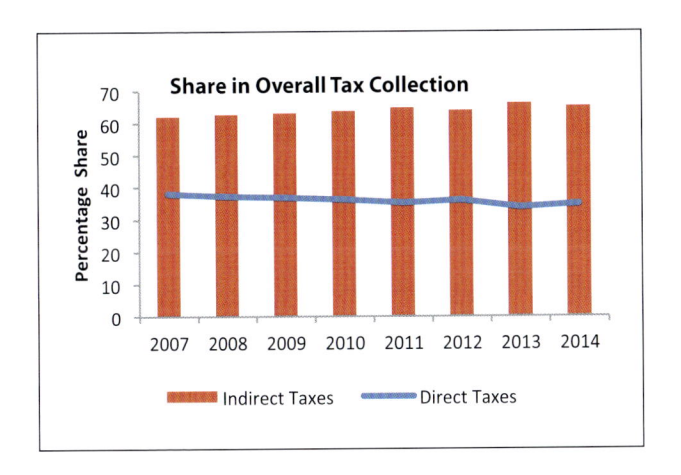

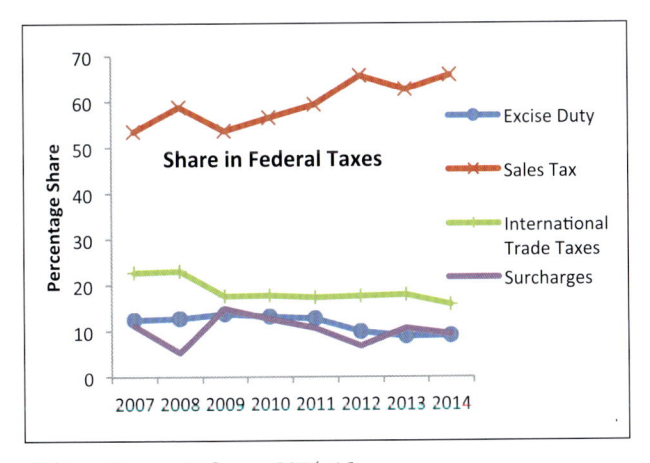

Source: Pakistan Economic Survey 2014–15.

Table 2: Tax Expenditure (PKR Billion)

Taxes	2014–15	2016–17
Income Tax	84	14
Sales Tax	478	250
Customs Duty	103	152
Total	665	416

Source: Federal Board of Revenue.

Secondly, after the 18th Constitutional Amendment, GST on services (GSTS) is now a provincial subject. The necessary measures required to collect the due GSTS will now depend on the political will and administrative capacity of each of the provinces. Some have argued that the incentives for provinces to tax their own constituency have declined as the 7th National Finance Commission Award 2010 has already allowed them the necessary fiscal space to accommodate an increase in their provincial spending (SDPI 2013).[3]

Thirdly, weak audit and enforcement capacity has resulted in reduced capacity of the federal and provincial revenue authorities to effectively make an example of the tax evaders. The ability of large economic sectors, e.g., transport, and the wholesale trade and retail sector to remain and expand in the informal sector, has resulted in an expansion of undocumented economy.[4]

In May 2013, the government agreed as part of the support from IMF to impose several new tax measures including a gas levy. The commitment on the part of the government aimed at rationalization of concessions in the tax schedule, sending tax notices to over 100,000 persons considered to be involved in evasion, and improving tax administration.

While significant changes in tax policy have been made since 2013, however, tax administration reforms have still not been fully implemented. The World Bank's assessment of the Tax Administration Reform Project (TARP) informs that the project could not achieve the desired outcome due to slow integration of FBR along functional lines, under-utilization of IT-enabled systems, and weak audit capacity. The report attributes the less than anticipated success of the programme to lack of reform ownership by FBR officials, frequent changes in FBR leadership and management, indefinite postponement of broad-based GST legislation, divisions among staff from various service groups, and weak internal monitoring and evaluation (World Bank 2012).

The federal government also made a commitment with the IMF to help provinces build capacity for mobilizing revenues. Despite a large provincial tax base, the current contribution by the provinces is only 7 per cent in overall revenues. Going forward as the cities expand, and there is larger non-farm activity in rural areas, provincial governments will need to increase revenue mobilization in untapped sectors, e.g., agriculture, services, transport, and property, and also improve tax administration (Nabi and Sheikh 2013, Nasim 2014, Ahmed 2015b).

Traditionally, the provinces have continued to rely on old tax rates charged under property taxes, stamp duties, motor vehicle levies, agriculture income tax, electricity duties, professional tax, capital value tax, infrastructure cess, and entertainment duty. Apart from these, the non-tax revenues of provinces come from irrigation, community services, law and order, and general administration.

The province-level legislation on services sector taxation (e.g., Punjab Sales Tax on Services Act 2012, and Sindh Sales Tax on Services Act 2011) now allows provinces to increase the scope of GSTS. Some of the large sub-sectors under services include wholesale and retail trade, electricity and gas operations, agriculture and extension services, transport, storage, communications, ownership of dwellings, and banking and finance. The provinces have also identified that hotels, clubs, caterers, advertisements, telecom, insurance, banking companies, non-bank financial institutions, stock brokers, shipping agents, and courier services can offer significant revenues. However, under several of these areas, provinces have differences with the federal government on three accounts: (a) incidence of double taxation in some cases, (b) issues of definition of a taxable activity or income, and (c) the federal government may have allowed a certain exemption to a sub-sector or activity. Weak audit capacity also limits the understanding of books maintained by such businesses.

Even for the optimal collection of GSTS, none of the provinces have conducted a census of services establishments. The already undocumented economy in services allows a large off-the-radar activity in: private education, medical centres, transportation, accountancy services, retail outfits, and beauty parlours.

The provincial revenue reforms are harder to implement as currently these collections are being done in a fragmented manner. In Sindh, for example, collections are being undertaken by: (a) Excise, Taxation, and Narcotics Departments, (b) Board of Revenue, (c) Sindh Revenue Board, and (d) government of Sindh directly collecting levies (e.g., electricity duty).

The efficiency of tax collection at provincial levels is also hurt by the large number of taxes imposed in the past for specific purposes and then never repealed. The Sindh Tax Revenue Mobilization Plan 2014–19 correctly points out that 9 out of the total 15 provincial taxes in Sindh render 99 per cent of collected revenues. The remaining 6 taxes only contribute 1 per cent (GoS 2014).

Agriculture taxation is another area where both federal and provincial governments are losing tax revenues (PILDAT 2011). The federal government in 2014 had constituted a Tax Reforms Commission (TRC) which pointed out that land utilization data across the country has not been updated. This is also preventing a correct estimation of property and real estate holdings and proceeds from such assets. Even in the case of agriculture, the land-based taxes charged through land revenue rates between PKR 100–300 per acre need to be updated on scientific lines. Currently, the land tax is not calculated in a manner that reflects potential income from land. The penalties by the government for non-compliance are not effective either.

Finally, most of the changes in the tax system are being

introduced without a thorough incidence analysis by the tax authorities. This has welfare implications for the entire society. Taking the case of GST, the complexities of input invoicing in the current system allows a 'cascading' of the indirect tax to take place. Ahmed et al. (2015) explain that even a small change in the GST rate, keeping the GST slabs the same, will lead to an inter-sectoral burden which is bound to be higher than the original rate. In their example for the fertilizer sector, a ten per cent point increase in GST for fertilizer and petroleum products leads to a distortive impact on the cotton sector and therefore also impacts value addition in textiles.

3. Towards an Equitable Tax System

Improving tax policy

Taxes should not merely be seen as a means to run the government machinery. As a key instrument of fiscal policy, taxes can incentivize: private sector expansion, inflow of foreign investment, enhancement in producer and consumer surpluses, and redistribution of incomes and wealth. We present below some possible measures that can help in the achievement of a holistic tax reform.

Update estimates of tax gap: Ahmed and Rider (2008) had estimated tax gap for 2004 at 69 per cent of tax receipts. A gross tax gap is usually defined as the variance between taxes paid during the fiscal period and overall taxes owed. FBR's own study updated these estimates in 2012, which informed that the tax gap had risen to 79 per cent of the actual tax receipts.[5] Independent economists have also calculated the tax expenditures using a different methodology.[6] With new data being published on the federal and provincial tax bases, it is important to update the gap under each tax heading. FBR should make this a regular feature to estimate and report consolidated tax gap in Pakistan as part of the annually published budget documents and Economic Survey of Pakistan. Existing studies also indicate that taxing the shadow economy at a sales tax rate of 17 per cent could be enough to increase the public expenditure on, for example, the health sector by up to five times. This could also imply that the tax-to-GDP ratio would almost double (SDPI 2013).

Rationalize the number and size of concessions: It is recommended that all incomes, beyond a minimum threshold, decided by the parliament, should be treated equally for the purpose of taxation. This argument is undermined when several forms of agricultural incomes and holdings are exempt from any form of taxes. This then implies a more than proportional tax burden on sectors already under the tax net e.g., the manufacturing sector.

Second, according to Article 77 of the Constitution, taxes by the federal government can be levied by an act of the parliament. However, lacunas in the existing tax laws allow the government to give exemptions without any parliamentary approval. This allows the parliament to be over-ruled by tax administrators and the government. There is also no requirement in the law to report the value of these exemptions to the parliament on a regular basis. Only recently the Finance Standing Committees in both houses of parliament have started to demand estimates of tax expenditures. However, the irregular frequency of meetings by the committees reduces the pressure on tax administrators to update their estimates.

While the government had committed in 2013 to the IMF to gradually phasing out these exemptions and concessions through a reduction in Statutory Regulatory Order (SROs), however due to political pressure, we witnessed in 2015 a revival of fiscal concessions to the agriculture and textile sectors. This will continue to happen unless the Finance Standing Committees of the Senate and National Assembly keep a more regular and effective check on FBR.

An amendment in the Finance Act can introduce a provision whereby FBR will report the value of tax expenditures (by tax type) as part of the FBR Quarterly Review and annual budget documents. This should be accompanied by a brief annex that covers specific SROs through which these expenditures will be implemented. Equally important is to report the methodology of calculating the tax expenditures as part of the annually published Economic Survey of Pakistan. The section on analysis of tax expenditures can also provide the incidence of such expenditures. A presentation of SRO-wise incidence will also prompt the authorities in case there is some misuse of any concession or exemption allowed by the government.

Broaden the tax base: Out of a total employed workforce of 56 million, less than 2 million are registered taxpayers, and in 2016 only 1.2 million were tax filers. This is 2 persons in every 100 employed. Even the lawmakers in the country have been reluctant tax filers (Cheema 2012).Of the total income tax collected, around one-third is collected through 'withholding tax' which is not a best practice. Several argue that such a tax is against the fairness principle usually regarded necessary for any tax imposition.

People also seem afraid to register with the tax department (Figure 1). SDPI's 2013 survey of informal enterprises found that 22 per cent of the respondents did not register with the tax authorities due to fear of unnecessary intrusion by tax officials. The tax department has a perception of rent-seeking which has unfortunately grown with the passage of time. There are also technical difficulties in tax compliance. Pakistan ranks 162nd in the World Bank's 'paying taxes' index. It takes an average of 560 hours (highest across South Asia) to comply with annual tax obligations. A key recommendation from several business associations, as part of 2016–17 pre-budget proposals, was to reduce the frequency of tax payments at federal and provincial levels (Ahmed and Wahab 2015).

A broadening of the direct tax base will also allow a gradual shift away from the WHT. The excessive reliance on presumptive taxation is distorting incentives to save and invest. The compliance of small businesses with WHT monthly reporting has increased costs. Furthermore, the government should stick

Figure 1: Why we do not register with FBR?

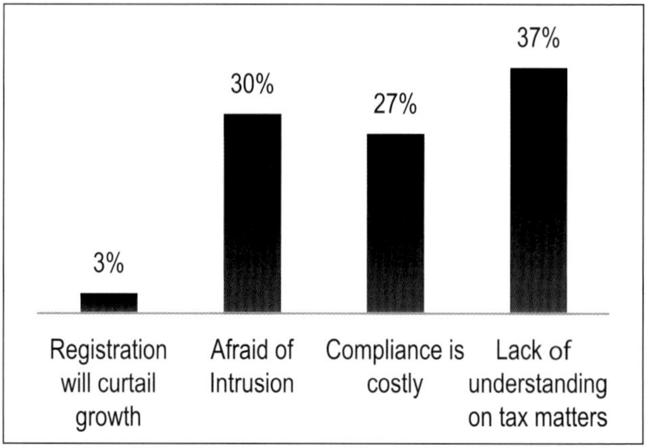

Reason	Percentage
Registration will curtail growth	3%
Afraid of Intrusion	30%
Compliance is costly	27%
Lack of understanding on tax matters	37%

Source: Ahmed and Adnan (2014).

to a long-term policy of adjusting WHT against final liability of the taxpayer. On occasions, for example, Budget 2013–14 had demanded that WHT be claimed as refunds. The refunds from revenue authorities take much longer to materialize. From the private sector's viewpoint, a delay in receipt of refunds translates into a decline in liquidity and working capital.

Reform of the corporate tax regime: There are three different rates for corporate tax. This variation allows companies to report incomes and profits in a manner that can keep tax liability to a minimum. For example, a public company will be charged a rate of 33 per cent.[7] A banking company is charged 35 per cent and a small company is charged a reduced rate of 25 per cent. Similarly, a lower rate of 20 per cent is applied in case the company is in the industrial sector and was set up between

July 2014 and June 2017 for at least a period of five years, provided their 50 per cent equity is through foreign direct investment. Remittance of profits to the head office is treated by FBR as a dividend income and therefore subject to 10 per cent withholding taxes. The corporate entities also register their subsidiaries for a different scope of work, however, with the intention of seeking lower tax liability.

Further complexity in the corporate tax regime has been introduced through concepts such as minimum and alternate taxes. For example, if tax liability is less than 1 per cent of the turnover, and the company is in profit, a minimum tax equivalent to 0.5 per cent of the turnover will be paid. Similarly, an Alternate Corporate Tax (ACT), introduced in 2014, defines that minimum tax liability will be the higher of 17 per cent of accounting income or the tax liability.[8]

There is a case for simplification of the corporate tax regime in Pakistan (Ahmed and Talpur 2016) as the current regime is a disincentive to corporatize. The corporate taxes still generate a significant share of government revenues however, 2015 data shows that 62 per cent of enterprises are not paying taxes. A four-pronged strategy to increase corporate taxes through: (a) simplification of corporate tax laws, (b) eliminating unfair exemptions from corporate taxes, (c) broadening of the corporate tax base, and (d) building capacity of the tax administration to evaluate and audit new forms of corporate incomes, can help raise greater revenues. The appeals management and grievance redressal mechanisms will also need to be sharpened in order to build trust.

A gradual move towards a modified value added tax (VAT): The existing GST on goods regime is not realizing its potential due to over invoicing of inputs and the inability of FBR to process the refunds in a timely manner. At the federal level, a reform towards a modified VAT will include setting of input-output norms across major industries, and pre-fixing the export rebate across major exported commodities. The proposed norms by industry are given in Table 3. This table only provides norms for those industries that are contributing more than PKR 500 million in revenue. Once the modified VAT takes ground, a more broad-based VAT system should be introduced through the VAT bill after review of the CCI. A draft VAT bill 2010 is already available with the Ministry of Finance for reference. It was estimated for 2014–15 that the above-mentioned move towards modified VAT can bring an additional PKR 55 million (Pasha et al. 2016).

Table 3: Input-Output Norms

90%	80%	70%	60%	50%	40%
Iron & Steel (138)*	Natural Gas (80)	Food Products (75)	Cement (60)	Fertilizers (59)	Cigarettes (48)
Motorcycles (92)	Oil Marketing Companies (89)	Motor Cars (79)	Storage Batteries (64)	Liquid Glucose (56)	LPG (49)
IPPs (104)	Beverages (80)	Fruit & Vegetable Juices (74)	Biscuits (67)		Fertilizer** (48)
Electrical Goods (138)	Tea (81)	Toilet Soap (74)	Detergents (69)		Pickles in Oil (42)

Machinery, Mechanical (101)	Auto Parts (87)	Paper & Paper Board (78)	Ceramic Tiles (64)		
Plastic Prod (95)	Paints & Varnish (82)	Nylon Chips (72)	GI Pipes (62)		
Electrical Energy (98)	Tyres & Tubes (86)	Pesticides (76)	Glass Bottles (62)		
Confectionery (90)	Paper Prod (87)		Syrups & Squash (61)		
Iron & Steel (145)	Deep Freezers (80)		Acid (68%)		
Iron & Steel Ingots (829)	Resin Material (83)		**30 %**	**20%**	**Below 20 %**
Buses, Tractors (97)	Glass & Glassware (81)		Concentrates (39)	Explosives (24)	Oil Exploration
Printing (93)			Sugar (37)		
Perfumery & Cosmetics (101)			Alcohol (38)		
Footwear (98)					
Refrigerators (118)					
Power Looms (217)					
Insecticides (90)					
Milk & Cream (119)					
Chemicals Org (94)					
Elec. Generators (96)					
Medicines (125)					
*Current I/O Ratio in GST Payments *Fertilizer other than Urea					

Source: Pasha et al. (2016).

A large part of evasion in GST on goods takes place due to high rates imposed on sectors which are not performing well due to the ongoing energy crisis and depressed demand. A sectoral growth analysis can guide which sectors should face a temporary lower rate of GST. This will enhance the capacity of SMEs to face economic shocks.

An incidence analysis of GST regime should be a routine feature at FBR, especially before any significant changes in the rates and slabs. In this regard, it is important to mention the example of GST on petroleum products. In 2015–16 the incidence on high-speed diesel had increased to 64 per cent (Ahmed et al. 2015). This had implications for rising costs in the transport sector besides affecting the transportation of essential goods. One recommendation is a return to the pre-2007 parity between HSD and motor spirit. Before the start of the fiscal year 2007–08, the rate for HSD was lower than for motor spirit.

Correcting customs duties: The effective rate of customs duty falls as the number and value of concessions (from customs duties) increase. Such concessions need to be reconsidered, unless they are part of a preferential or free trade agreement, or based on humanitarian grounds. Imports are also hurt by multiple slabs and differentiated rates across sectors. The tariffs have also been termed high in comparison to peer economies. This, in turn, affects the competitiveness of exporting sectors which intensively use imported raw material and machinery. The multiple slabs are also prone to misuse and under-invoicing.

This view is endorsed, through formal explanation in Ahmed and O' Donoghue (2010). The authors explain that economy-wide impact of a reduction in tariffs benefits exports in the form of reduced prices of imported raw material, machinery, and related inputs. In overall terms, trade liberalization promoted through a reduction or simplification in the tariff regime will benefit the economy if the exporting sectors expand and compensate for the increase in imports.

In order to promote regional trade in line with the vision in the Strategic Trade Policy Framework, there is a need to harmonize Pakistan's customs duty codes with the Economic Cooperation Organization (ECO) and Central Asian countries. This can also be helped by moving to a three-tier structure where the slab of 15 per cent will be removed. The three slabs of 5 per cent, 10 per cent, and 20 per cent will ensure that items currently facing a 15 per cent tariff will either go under the 10 per cent head (if these are intermediary inputs) or under the 20 per cent (if these are end products).[9]

The country also loses revenue due to under-declarations (e.g., in case of China-Pakistan FTA). There are discrepancies between trade data at the origin and the destination country (Ahmed et al. 2016). For example, Table 4 exhibits under-invoicing in Pakistan's trade with China. One short-term solution to this issue could be to adopt a minimum import price regime for key import items. The already established minimum import price regime in India can serve as an example. It is also important to revise the minimum import prices annually to take account of inflation and exchange rate changes. In the longer term, however, the reform to strengthen the border-related trade information systems and monitoring should be emphasized.

Table 4: Pakistan's Trade with China 2014—Import of Top 20 Items

(in million USD)

Sr. #	Product Code	Product Label	Imports from China (A)	Exports by China (B)	Under/Over Invoicing (C)
1	8517	Electric app for line telephony, incl. curr. line system	1,054	806	248
2	3105	Mixtures of nitrogen, phosphorous, or potassium fertilizers	294	358	(64)
3	5402	Synthetic filam. yarn, not put up	255	256	(1)
4	3102	Mineral or chemical fertilizers, nitrogenous	255	150	105
5	8502	Electric generating sets and rotary converters	205	89	115
6	8541	Diodes/transistors and sim. semiconductor devices, etc.	184	204	(20)
7	7225	Flat-rolled products of other alloy steel, of a width of 600mm or more	184	317	(134)
8	4011	New pneumatic tires, of rubber	159	189	(30)
9	5403	Artificial filam. yarn, not put up	143	138	5

10	5503	Synthetic staple fibres, not carded	143	148	(5)
11	8471	Automatic data processing machines, optical reader, etc.	140	121	19
12	7208	Flat-rolled products of iron/non-al/s width>/=600mm, hr, not clad	124	2	122
13	7210	Flat-rolled prod. of iron or non-al/s width>/=600mm, clad, plated, or coated	124	143	(19)
14	3907	Polyacetal, polyether, epoxide resin, polycarbonate, etc., in primary form	112	85	28
15	8501	Electric motors and generators (excluding generating sets)	109	67	42
16	8504	Electric transformer, static converter (for example, rectifiers)	101	162	(61)
17	7304	Tubes, pipes, and hollow profiles, seamless, or iron or steel	100	81	19
18	8539	Electric filament or discharge lamps	98	116	(19)
19	8414	Air, vacuum pumps; hoods incorporating a fan	94	82	12
20	8419	Machinery, plant/lab, involving a change of temp ex heating, cooking, etc.	88	118	(30)
	TOTAL	All products	9,588	13,246	(3,658)

Source: Ahmed et al. (2015).

Revisiting the case for excise duty: The government has yet to deliver on its promise of phasing out excise duties. There remains a need to see on a case-by-case basis where GSTS and federal excise duties are contributing to double taxation. The federal government will need to resolve the definition issues that create instances of multiple taxation. However, as the federal government reduces its levy on activities now under GSTS, the federal government can still expand the tax base for excise duty. This can be done by revisiting the production activities with negative externalities, and import of luxury goods and services. On welfare grounds it is suggested that excise duties on edible oil, vegetable ghee, and sugar may be gradually phased out particularly in the case of rural and backward areas.

Reform of provincial taxes: The GSTS now allows provinces to secure a large revenue stream if appropriate measures are taken. First, the issue of double taxation, where FBR is found to be charging excise on activities already paying GSTS at the provincial level, may be resolved. The identification and assessment of services sector incomes and assets can be improved through a provincial census of services establishments.

The definition issues have also led to a rise in the cost of doing business at the provincial level. For example the federal government in 2013–14 had introduced a WHT on retailers, builders, and schools. The rates of WHT and advance tax were also enhanced in case of professional services. All of these activities are also facing GSTS, in turn increasing their cost of doing business, reducing consumer surplus, and also increasing the cost of compliance for taxpayers. Such measures also incentivize expansion of the undocumented sector under a weak audit regime.

There remains a need to conduct a detailed study on the incidence of provincial taxes. The 18th Constitutional Amendment allows management of progressive taxes including wealth tax, capital gain tax on immovable property, gift tax, and estate duty. Such taxes have vast potential to promote redistribution and social justice. The provincial assemblies may introduce and strengthen the levy of these taxes. For this the federal government may be asked through CCI to remove any federal exemptions or concessions allowed to provincial tax bases (Ahmed and Naqvi 2016).

In the case of agriculture, the existing mechanism of collecting taxes through output and land-based estimation of liability needs to be revisited. The current land (revenue) rates range between PKR 100–300 per acre and have not been updated. This tax should reflect (potential) income from the land holding. For 2010, the potential revenue from agriculture was estimated between PKR 55–75 billion per year.[10] The penalties for non-compliance with agriculture taxes are not effective either. Legislative changes that enhance the enforcement powers for the revenue authorities will be required, along with appropriate check on the misuse of enhanced powers.

As agriculture taxation is a politically sensitive subject for both elected representatives and voters, therefore a win-win suggestion could be to introduce a revenue-neutral change[11] in burden of tax, where: (a) proceeds from agriculture, beyond a certain threshold may be subject to direct tax, and (b) indirect taxes, levies, and surcharges on agriculture inputs may be reduced. This will help broaden the tax net and document incomes falling under agriculture sector. The provincial governments should also consider decentralizing agriculture tax collections. For example, through appropriate revision in the Local Government Acts, land revenues and its administration, up to a certain percentage may be transferred to the union councils.

To realize the potential of Urban Immovable Property Tax (UIPT) a periodic survey of urban properties is recommended so that the regularly revised rates accurately represent any changes in property and rental value. The concessions allowed under UIPT may be revisited. The rating areas also need to be regularly notified in order to help an expansion in tax coverage. Currently the high rates of UIPT are also a reason for tax evasion. There is also a differential between owner- and lessee-occupied properties. Differences also exist between rates for similar size and type of properties in various cities. Such anomalies may be corrected through appropriate changes recommended to CCI for approval. The gains in revenue from updating UIPT valuation tables have been simulated in Aziz et al. (2014).

IMPROVING TAX ADMINISTRATION

Tax policy changes may not be of much use unless supported by reform of tax administration. For example, the administrative structures at FBR follow the national civil service norms, governed by the Rules of Business 1973. These sets of rules have lost their relevance given the current challenges facing revenue mobilization in the country. Past efforts to introduce results-based management with clear key performance indicators remained a mere rhetoric (GoP 2011). We provide the following entry points to gradually move towards raising the administrative standards which can help in fair and equitable tax reforms.

Revisit lessons from TARP Evaluation: The project which started in 2005 and lasted until 2009 with assistance from DFID and the World Bank could not render the anticipated results and failed to improve the efficiency of the tax administration and to broaden the tax base (Haq and Bukhari 2014). The less than anticipated success of TARP calls for an updated independent evaluation to help the tax authorities understand why the current organizational structure in FBR is not delivering the desired results. Similarly, the automation reforms at FBR were not accompanied by continued capacity-building and updating of business processes. The lessons from TARP will provide important insights for designing a new administration reform with inputs from all stakeholders including representatives of the business community. Some of these lessons are documented in the World Bank (2012). A consultative process of administration reform will also help create a buy-in from the taxpayers. SDPI's Survey of eligible taxpayers conducted in May 2013 reveals the lack of trust and perceptions of corruption in tax administration (Box 2).

Box 2: Rent-seeking and a Lack of Social Capital[12]

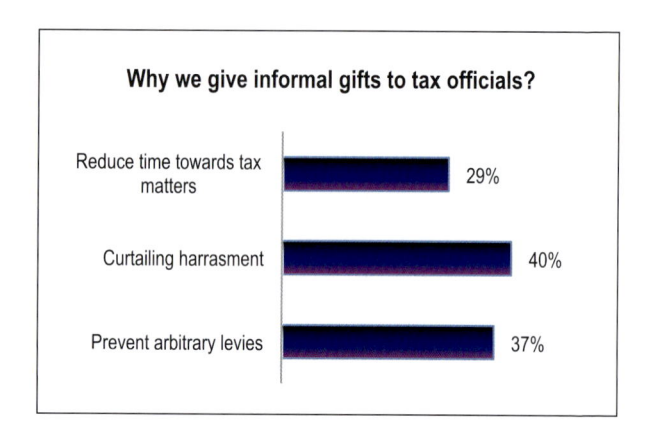

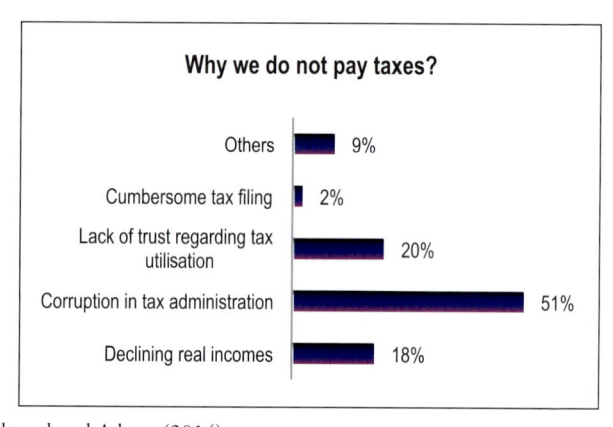

Why we give informal gifts to tax officials?

- Reduce time towards tax matters: 29%
- Curtailing harrasment: 40%
- Prevent arbitrary levies: 37%

Why we do not pay taxes?

- Others: 9%
- Cumbersome tax filing: 2%
- Lack of trust regarding tax utilisation: 20%
- Corruption in tax administration: 51%
- Declining real incomes: 18%

Source: Ahmed and Adnan (2014).

Management reforms at FBR: The new vision for FBR should not only be to focus on optimizing revenue for the government, but also to help the private sector in the reduction of tax compliance costs, and take trade facilitation measures that boost competitiveness of Pakistani enterprises. FBR will need to look into how much of its efforts actually lead to redistribution of incomes and wealth in Pakistan. The organization has come under criticism for its large expense towards managing its affairs. Rana (2015) argued that 95 per cent of the total income tax can be collected even after closing down the FBR. In specific cases of 15 FBR stations the cost to collect tax was found higher than the actual amount collected through FBR's own assessment.

A full autonomy of FBR, similar to what was seen in the case of the State Bank of Pakistan, between 2000 and 2006 may be considered. FBR's own human resource should be insulated from any political influence of the government, may it be in tactical functioning or related to recruitment, promotions, accountability, and reward. FBR will also require restructuring for creating functional expertise including a separation of tax policy and administrative functions.[13] This however can only happen if FBR formulates and adheres to a medium-term strategic plan with clear key performance indicators. The progress on these indicators should be demanded by the parliament's standing committees on a bi-annual basis. Like the SBP, FBR should be headed by a governor having a tenured posting.

Following the example of SBP and Securities and Exchange Commission of Pakistan (SECP), FBR's recruitment should be delinked from the cadre-based admissions through the Federal Public Service Commission. FBR should be autonomous to select candidates on the basis of their education, experience, and relevance to the demands of the vacancy.

A complete overhaul of the reward structure will be required. It is therefore appropriate to suggest that basic pay scales for FBR officials may be abolished and all forms of compensation should be linked with performance. Furthermore, in order to promote career growth, FBR may be allowed to use a specific percentage of the excess of annual revenue target towards capacity-building purposes. The capacity-building expense can be ascertained after a third-party needs-assessment exercise, commissioned by the Establishment Division, Government of Pakistan.

The private sector has long demanded that the process of appeals should be made more transparent. Frequent changes in discretionary powers vested with the FBR, without approval of the parliament, compromise the transparency of taxpayer obligations. The information on tax liabilities and administrative procedures is not available in easily understandable and less technical language for the understanding of laypersons. The hearing of appeals should be conducted strictly by an independent party held in regard by both the revenue authority and the taxpayer. As FBR struggles with the piling court cases it is important to make the Alternative Dispute Resolution Committee more active. An urgent study is also required to inquire as to why taxpayers are reluctant to approach Tax Ombudsman's office even for their genuine issues.

A risk-based audit along with forensic capabilities can help in the validation of tax returns. A medium-term audit reform plan can help in clearly defining the roles of tax assessment auditor and recovery managers. This will also reduce the role of discretion by tax officials. The audit will also be helped by a simplification of rules, procedures, laws, and relevant forms. This will reduce the transactions cost of both revenue officials and taxpayers.

Strengthen Grievance Redressal Mechanism (GRM): A key issue faced by the business community is the lack of an effective mechanism to address their complaints. None of the tax authorities in the country have a documented and publicly communicated GRM. The private sector's recommendations on increasing the efficiency of taxes should not just be evaluated as part of the annual pre-budget consultations exercise, however a permanent Tax Reforms Committee which meets on a quarterly basis may be constituted to act as a bridge between the government and the private sector. After the 18th Amendment, the number of complaints by taxpayers has significantly increased. However, at the time of writing this chapter, no province has yet appointed a provincial tax ombudsman to help in the disposal of the past and new cases.

GRM is again one area of improvement which can quickly help in establishing trust between the state and the taxpayers. Ahmed and Adnan (2014) explain that in a national sample of 300 enterprises, 77 per cent said that they had not registered any grievance to a tax department whereas 23 per cent respondents had done so. Those who had approached the authorities with their complaint were asked to rate their level of satisfaction with the remedial measures put in place to address the complaint. 13 per cent were not satisfied, however 67 per cent expressed satisfaction. Many acknowledged that FBR's efforts such as one-window and taxpayers' facilitation unit should be further expanded, particularly in new towns and cities. Taxpayers can access GRM more confidently if transparency and accountability mechanism are respected. During the survey there were responses which revealed a sense of fear if FBR was approached for guidance and documentation was exposed to them.

Merge revenue departments at the provincial level: The newly formed bodies to collect GSTS may be structured as independent bodies, having legal cover through appropriate provincial legislation. The board of revenue, excise departments, and other tax revenue collection bodies may be gradually merged into the newly formed entities e.g., Khyber Pakhtunkhwa Revenue Authority, Punjab Revenue Authority, Sindh Revenue Board, and Balochistan Revenue Authority (Ahmed and Jamali 2016). The automation reforms at these entities should include access to and integration with Pakistan Revenue Automation (pvt) Ltd. (PRAL's) database for validation of income and wealth statements. The automation exercise can also allow greater revenues through e-stamping and e-token taxes.[14]

Like the recommendation for FBR, these provincial revenue collection bodies should also be autonomous entities with their own recruitment, and reward and accountability mechanisms.

They should not be reporting to the provincial civil service or politically elected ministers. Unless this is done, politically sensitive taxes, such as the system of agricultural taxation cannot be reformed.

4. Conclusion

This chapter focused on key reforms necessary to make the taxes fair and efficient. It is important to realize that taxes can be used to support economic growth and wealth redistribution objectives. The tax policy also has implications for labour and capital markets. The lowering of tax wedge i.e., difference between gross and after-tax incomes helps strengthen incentives for work and retention of skilled labour force in the economy. Similarly, taxing profits efficiently can reduce distortions and promote greater inflow of investment. Productivity enhancements can be promoted through targeted and time-bound tax incentives.

The efficiency of direct taxes in Pakistan can be enhanced through elimination of obsolete and untargeted concessions in the tax schedule, and broadening of the base (in particular tapping the untaxed agricultural and services sector incomes). These reforms will also need to be complemented with innovative tax administration measures. It is proposed that results-based management with clear key performance indicators should be introduced in FBR and provincial revenue authorities. The audit and enforcement should be helped by improved IT systems, and plugging the gaps in laws that allow tax evasion and avoidance to remain high. FBR will also need to increase outreach efforts and effectively demonstrate a facilitation role for the private sector. The political leadership will also require moral authority to demand taxes.

The provincial revenue authorities can now establish a baseline of tax bases for each of the taxes under their jurisdiction. They should be able to introduce IT-based business processes for tax compliance to reduce human contact between taxpayers and payee. All provincial revenue authorities should have access to PRAL and NADRA databases for validation of tax returns and audit purposes. The GIS-based validation of land holdings, commercial wholesale, and retail activity may be pursued. A serious effort may be made to improve taxpayers' information regarding provincial taxes, ideally through effective one-window operations. The low yielding taxes such as cotton fee, entertainment tax, and tax on property transfers may be abolished.

The above-mentioned will also require a reform of the provincial tax administration. For example, in Punjab province the already announced merger of Excise and Taxation Department, Board of Revenue, and Punjab Revenue Authority may be expedited to ensure low administrative costs and better rapport with the taxpayers. Other provinces may also like to follow this example. The provincial tax ombudsmen may be appointed and strengthened with judicial powers. Finally, in order to ensure some level of social accountability, a tax directory of agricultural income tax and UIPT payments should be annually published and disseminated as part of the provincial budget.

References

Ahmed, V., 'Fiscal Challenges and Response', Chapter 2 in *Roadmap for Economic Growth of Pakistan*, Islamabad Policy Research Institute, 2015.

Ahmed, V., 'Time for provincial tax reforms' *The News*, 5 April 2015.

Ahmed, V., and Naqvi, A., 'Tax Reforms in Punjab', Policy Brief 53, Sustainable Development Policy Institute, Islamabad, 2016.

Ahmed, V., and Jamali, S., 'Tax Reforms in Sindh', Policy Brief 54, Sustainable Development Policy Institute Islamabad, 2016.

Ahmed, V., and Adnan, M., 'Energy and Tax Reforms: Firm-level analysis from Pakistan' *Working Paper 146*, Sustainable Development Policy Institute, Islamabad, 2014.

Ahmed, V. and Donoghue, C. O.,'Redistributive Effect of Personal Income Taxation in Pakistan', *Pakistan Economic and Social Review*, Vol. 47, No. 1, Summer 2009, p.1–17.

Ahmed, V., and Donoghue, C. O., 'Tariff Reduction in a Small Open Economy' *Seoul Journal of Economics*, Vol. 23, No. 4, 2010, p. 461–89.

Ahmed, V. and Talpur, M., 'Corporate Tax Reforms in Pakistan, *Working Paper 155*, Sustainable Development Policy Institute, Islamabad, 2016.

Ahmed, V. et al., 'Post MDGs: Issues for the Future', *Southern Voice Occasional Paper 5*, Centre for Policy Dialogue, Dhaka, 2014.

Ahmed, S., Ahmed, V., Donoghue, C.O., (2011) 'Reforming Indirect Taxation in Pakistan: A macro-micro analysis,' *eJournal of Tax Research*, Volume 9, Number 2.

Ahmed, V., and Wahab, M. A., 'Declining Investment Flows' *The News*. 13 December 2015.

Ahmed, V., Pasha, H. A., Sherani, S., Saleem, W., 'Agenda for Tax Reforms' *RAFTAAR*, 2015.

Aziz, D., Haider, S. and Raja, M. N. K. (2014), 'How much do you love Pakistan: A property tax revenue simulation for a municipal revolution in Punjab.' *Pakistan Strategy Support Programme, working paper* no. 18, April 2014.

Bilquees, Faiz (2004) Elasticity and Buoyancy of the Tax System in Pakistan. The Pakistan Development Review, 43: 1 (Spring 2004) pp. 73–93.

Cheema, U., 'Taxation by Misrepresentation: A comparative study of public representatives' income and tax declarations for 2012,' Sustainable Development Policy Institute Islamabad, 2012.

GoP, *Framework for Economic Growth*, Planning Commission, Government of Pakistan, Islamabad, 2011.

GoS, *Sindh Tax Revenue Mobilization Plan 2014–19*, Finance Department, Government of Sindh, Karachi, 2014.

Haq, I. and Bukhari, H. (2014), 'Making FBR Effective', *The News*, 9 November 2014.

Husain, I., 'Stubborn taxation regime'. *Dawn*, Published 11 March 2014, http://www.dawn.com/news/1092349.

Hulme, D., 'The Post-2015 Development Agenda: Learning from the MDGs' *Southern Voices Occasional Paper 2*, Centre for Policy Dialogue, Dhaka, 2013.

Jamal, H. and Javed, S., 'Incidence of General Sales Tax in Pakistan'. *Pakistan Journal of Applied Economics,* Vol. 23, No. 2, (73–95), Winter 2013.

Kemal, M. A. and Qasim, A. W., 2012, 'Precise Estimates of the Unrecorded Economy,' *The Pakistan Development Review,* Pakistan Institute of Development Economics, vol. 51(4), pages 505–16.

Nabi, I., and Sheikh, H., 'Reforming Urban Property Tax in Punjab, *Consortium for Development Policy Research,* 2013.

Nasim, A., 'Agriculture Income Tax in Punjab', *Consortium for Development Policy Research*, 2014.

Pasha, H. A., 'Progressive Fiscal Policy for Inclusive Growth', Economy of Tomorrow: n. pag. <http://library.fes.de/pdf-files/bueros/pakistan/11045.pdf>, 2014.

Pasha, H. A., 'Economy of Tomorrow: Case Study of Pakistan' Friedrich Ebert Stiftung, Pakistan, 2014b.

Pasha, H. A., and Pasha A. G., (2013), Pakistan Moving the Economy Forward. 'The Future Path of Tax Reforms in Pakistan', Lahore School of Economics.

Pasha, H. A., Sherani, S., Ahmed, V., Saleem, W., 'The Package of Budgetary Proposals' *RAFTAAR*, 2016.

PILDAT, 'Taxing the Agriculture Income in Pakistan,' *Briefing Paper No. 42*. Pakistan Institute of Legislative Development and Transparency, 2011.

Rana, S. (2015), 'The irony: Cost to collect tax higher than tax collection'. *The Express Tribune*, 6 May 2015.

Rasheed, F. (2006) An Analysis of the Tax Buoyancy Rates in Pakistan. Market Forces: Journal of Management, Business and Economics, Vol 2, No 3 (2006).

SDPI, 'Reforming Tax System in Pakistan', Sustainable Development Policy Institute Islamabad, 2013.

Wahid, U., and Wallace, S., 'Incidence of Taxes in Pakistan: Primer and Estimates' *Andrew Young School of Policy Studies, Working Paper* 08–13, December 2008.

World Bank (2012), Pakistan—Tax Administration Reform Project: Implementation Completion and Results Report. Washington, DC: World Bank. http://documents.worldbank.org/curated/en/2012/06/16489300/pakistan-tax-administration-reform-project.

Notes

1. A system in which advance tax is collected at the time of a transaction—e.g., when paying a mobile phone bill—and it is assumed that the person paying has an income (during 2015–16) of more than Rs.400,000 per annum—the minimum amount above which income tax is applicable.
2. Credit supply to the private sector had also declined due to rather large borrowing requirements of the government.
3. As a result of this award, federal and provincial governments agreed that transfers through national revenue divisible pool will increase from around 47 per cent in the previous award to 57.5 per cent.
4. Kemal and Qasim (2012) estimated that the size of the informal economy was between 74 and 91 per cent in 2008. Also see Husain (2014).
5. http://beta.dawn.com/news/634686/tax-evasion-hit-79pc-fbr-admits.
6. Hafiz A. Pasha and Aisha Ghaus Pasha (2013).
7. A public company is listed on stock exchange. A public company is also an entity

in which not less than 50% of the shares are held by the government or a public trust (source: http://taxsummaries.pwc.com).

8. ACT will apply to all companies except small companies, or companies dealing in the business of insurance, exploration, petroleum, and banking.
9. See Pasha et al. (2016) for a formal justification.
10. See also Nasim (2014). Economy-wide impact of a uniform tax on agriculture was also estimated in Ahmed et al. (2011).
11. Any decrease in a specific type of tax revenue is achieved with an equivalent increase in any other type of tax revenue.
12. Respondents were allowed to choose more than one option as answer to the question 'why we give informal gifts to tax officials?'
13. It is recommended that tax policy should be responsibility of Planning Commission.
14. See also SDPI 2013.

Chapter 4

Public Expenditure Management

1. Background

Public expenditure remains an important tool for stimulating economic growth, redistributing wealth, and in turn creating a dent in poverty and inequality. The key principles of public spending focus on: maximum social benefit i.e., the government will plan expenditures in a manner that promotes benefit for the largest number of people; the government will spend only the amount necessary for a particular objective which in turn develops productive capacity of the largest number of persons possible; the government should have approval of the legislature to incur any expenditure; the government should not resort to large deficit financing over longer periods of time, however to accommodate short-term changes in the economy or in the face of economic shocks, the government should have the flexibility to reduce or increase expenditures depending upon the economic cycle.

While the political economy of public expenditure makes it difficult to comply with several of the above-mentioned principles, however it is essential that policymakers involved in the process of managing budgets evaluate their work and its outcomes in the light of these principles. Such an evaluation is usually absent in the case of most developing countries, including Pakistan. The three main issues preventing effectiveness and efficiency of public expenditure in Pakistan are:

- Large recurrent expenditures, national security threats, and natural disasters leave little room for public investment in infrastructure and human resource development. Due to lack of proper planning and appraisal, at various tiers of the government, even these low levels of public investment are not optimally utilized and exhibit low value-for-money.
- A weak monitoring, evaluation, and learning mechanism at the Planning & Development departments results in reduced prospects for future improvements in service delivery.
- A large duplication of development programmes and projects across inter-province, intra-province, and federal-provincial domains results in waste of scarce public resources and prevents economies of scale.

Let us also turn to the existing literature on how effective public investment is in rendering favourable socio-economic outcomes in Pakistan. We see five main strands in recent literature. The first looks at how a persistently large defence spending impacts growth and poverty. The second at how spending on human resource development helps socio-economic goals. The third points towards the need for Pakistan to learn from peer economies in better targeting of public spending on welfare. The fourth highlights the need for expanding public infrastructure for future growth and expansion of private sector investment. Finally, post-18th Amendment literature highlights the need for greater alignment of public spending with provincial development strategies and Sustainable Development Goals (SDGs).

Increased defense spending leads to poor economic growth and poverty outcomes. Kalim R and Hassan M S (2014) indicate that public expenditure on defence consumes fiscal space that would otherwise have been used for poverty reduction goals. The study for the period 1976–2012 recommends reducing the share of defence spending and diverting the savings to human and social development. Shahbaz M et al (2013) also analyzed the link between defense expenditure and economic growth in Pakistan. Results pointed out that higher levels of defence expenditure strain economic growth.[1] Earlier, the study by Hussain F et al. (2008) had also pointed towards similar results. Furthermore, this study had shown that contrary to defence spending, government expenditure on education helps to reduce the poverty in both the short and long run.

Spending on human resource development contributes to growth and poverty reduction. Asghar Z and Zahra M (2012) demonstrated through a household survey in 2007–08 that the major advantage of public spending on primary and secondary education is for the lower income group both at the national as well as the provincial level. However, current levels of public spending on education are certainly not enough to fulfil the country's commitments towards 'education for all'. The bulk allocation of funds to education are still being spent on recurring expenditures while very little is contributed to improving capacity and quality outcomes in education sector (see Asghar N et al. 2011).[2]

For the health sector, Aurangzeb (2003) verifies a positive relation between economic growth and public health expenditure in Pakistan during both the short and long run (see also Asghar N et al. 2012). However, a deeper look into the incidence of public spending is necessary for future reform. For example, Hakro A N and Akram M (2007) use the benefit incidence method to observe that health spending is progressive at the national level while it seems regressive at the sub-national level. This implies that the lower income group is not a major beneficiary of health spending. We also see that health spending on mother and childcare is regressive at the provincial level (see also Mehmood, Y et al. 2015). Akram M and Khan F J (2007) also find existence of inequalities in resource allocation and service provision in public health spending. Rural areas are facing neglect in budget allocation and disbursement. Health spending is weakly targeted towards the marginalized segments of the society.

Pakistan can learn from the experiences of targeted and efficient public spending for growth and poverty reduction. South Asia as a whole needs to focus more on the reform of infrastructure and social sector spending. SDPI (2013) explained that large budget deficits in the Maldives, India, Pakistan, and Sri Lanka increased inflation and poverty (see also Zeeshan M and Ahmed V 2014). However in most South Asian countries social sector and poverty outcomes were at least better in comparison with Pakistan. Pakistan, in particular, seems to be lagging behind in some key social outcomes e.g. infant mortality. Wahab M A et al. (2013) observed that public spending on human resource development in Pakistan is proportionately less in comparison to most South Asian economies and this in turn could have implications for labour productivity. There is also literature on how Pakistan can improve targeting of social protection spending, possibly also learning from example of Mahatma Gandhi National Rural Employment Guarantee Act (Khan et al. 2016).

Public investment infrastructure can enhance the potential for long run economic growth. Ahmed V et al. (2013) show that infrastructure investment in Pakistan leads to gains in real GDP and reduction in poverty headcount. However, the impact of public investment also depends upon the efficiency with which this invested sum is utilized and absorbed. It also depends on which infrastructure sectors are targeted for government intervention (e.g., road versus energy infrastructure). RAFTAAR (2015) explains that infrastructure in Pakistan is insufficient according to its needs and if compared with peer economies. GoP (2011) had explained that even the governance of existing public infrastructure leads to resource wastage which if plugged can provide savings for future public investment (see also Pasha H et al. 2011).

Provincial expenditures need alignment with province-specific development strategies and SDGs. Almost all provinces have come up with their own medium-term development agenda. The Government of Sindh (2015) prepared Vision 2025 aimed at promoting education and health, besides also focusing on investment in energy, irrigation, communication, and mass transit. A focus on social sectors is also observed in the Government of Khyber Pakhtunkhwa (2010) and the Government of Balochistan (2013). The Government of Punjab (2015) prepared Punjab Growth Strategy 2018 with a large focus on employment generation and skills development. One observes that to reach a certain provincial growth target almost all provinces have a consensus to invest in human resource development. However, these initiatives suffer from duplicity, in turn leading to waste of resources. For example, having a common national-level programme (or even syllabus) for teachers' training, civil service capacity-building, management training for medical professionals, and advanced skills development for women can lend greater economies of scale. Currently one observes all provinces opening their own windows for such initiatives.

The next section provides a brief description of patterns of Pakistan's public expenditures. This is followed by a discussion on how service delivery outcomes are expected to improve under a devolution and fiscal decentralization milieu. Section 4 goes deeper into key reforms required to improve efficiency and effectiveness of public spending, including recurrent expenditure and development related public investment. The last section concludes with a brief discussion on the need to strengthen legislation on fiscal discipline.

2. Public Expenditure: Situation Analysis

There are three main issues keeping public spending from achieving the desired outcomes. The first is the inability to scale down those kinds of public expenditure which is either politically motivated or justified in the name of law and order. For example, over half of the federal government's expenditure is on debt servicing, defence, and salaries of public sector employees. Even if interest payments are not considered for a moment, there has not been a concerted effort to cut down the spending on defence and public administration. A large government size with weak ability to finance through own taxes, in turn adds to public borrowing and budget deficit.

Second, service delivery is hampered as the money available for public goods and services is inadequate. This applies to both inadequate spending on infrastructure and human resource development. In the case of the latter, the 7th NFC Award did lead to increased education and health spending by the provinces, however, most of this was consumed in the increased salaries and overheads component of both education and health sectors.

Third, existing ways of managing public resources are inefficient and lead to time and cost overruns. It is taking the government twice the originally projected time and almost twice the originally estimated cost to complete a publicly funded project (RAFTAAR 2015). The recurrent expenditure towards maintenance of existing public assets is not protected.

As a result of the above-mentioned, state spending has continued to outstrip government revenues since the 1970s (Box 1). The deficit was at its peak during the 1980s. Many have found Wagner's law of increasing state activities to hold true in case of Pakistan i.e., a situation where growth of public expenditure is a result of rising economic growth (e.g., see Afzal and Abbas 2010, Rehman et al. 2007). However, there have also been cases where the deficit continued to persist despite low economic growth. Pakistan, during recent years, continues to post high deficits compared with economies with similar levels of revenue mobilization. This is partly due to high debt servicing, rising share of civil administration costs, inability to significantly bring down the share of defence spending, and untargeted subsidies allowed to electricity, oil, wheat, fertilizer, and textile sectors (Ahmed et al. 2011). This has had implications for development expenditure, representing spending on social sectors, and infrastructure development. We can observe that development expenditure to GDP ratio could not go beyond 5 per cent between the period 2006–15.

The subsidy to the power sector has jumped in recent years. These subsidies continue to fund the losses of generation, transmission, and distribution in the power sector. As of end-June 2015, the circular debt in the power sector was 6 per cent of GDP (PRIME 2016). Both governance and efficiency factors are responsible for these losses (Ahmed 2015). In the case of the former, provincial governments have not reconciled

Box 1: Government Revenue and Expenditure Priorities

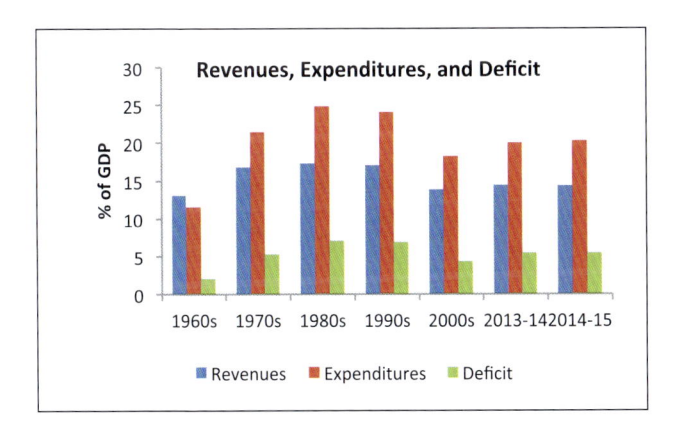

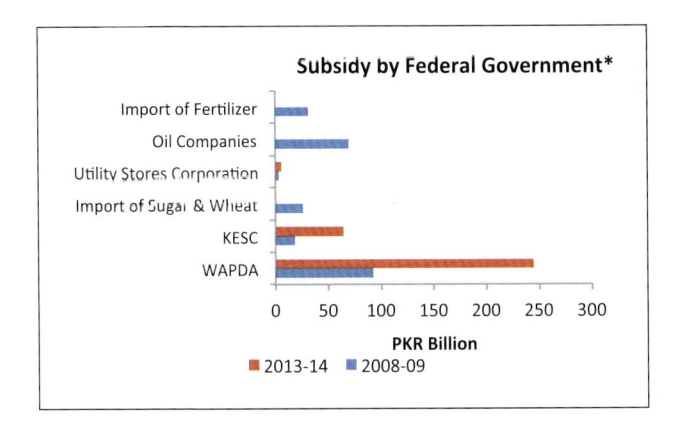

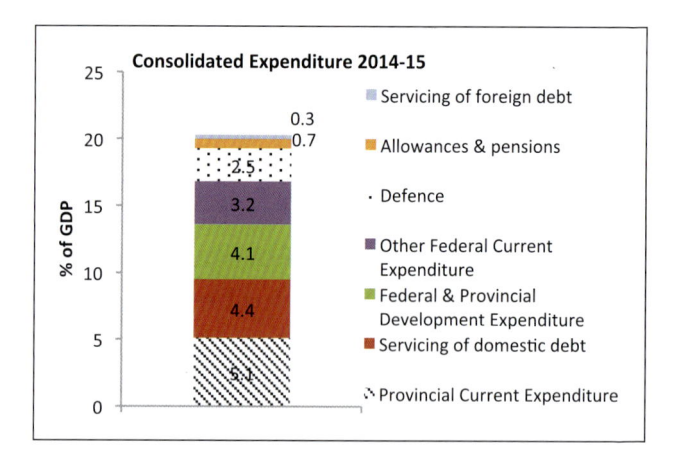

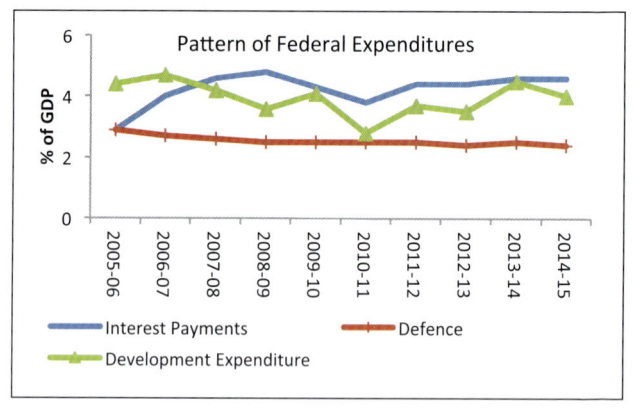

Consolidated Expenditure 2014-15

- Servicing of foreign debt: 0.3
- Allowances & pensions: 0.7
- Defence: 2.5
- Other Federal Current Expenditure: 3.2
- Federal & Provincial Development Expenditure: 4.1
- Servicing of domestic debt: 4.4
- Provincial Current Expenditure: 5.1

Pattern of Federal Expenditures (% of GDP, 2005-06 to 2014-15): Interest Payments, Defence, Development Expenditure

Source: Economic Survey of Pakistan 2014–15.

*WAPDA: Water and Power Development Authority, KESC is now called Karachi Electric (K-electric).

their payments; there has been a delay in the legal framework for curbing electricity theft; the federal government has been unable to make timely payments to the distribution companies, which in turn face a liquidity crunch; and there are delays in tariff determination and notification. The efficiency factors that contribute to the power sector's circular debt include: high transmission and distribution losses, and tariffs of independent power plants, which are not scientifically determined.

The federal and provincial national security expenditure increased from PKR 965 billion (4.8 per cent of GDP) in 2012–13 to PKR 1187 billion (4.1 per cent of GDP) in 2014–15. This was a growth of 11.6 per cent in comparison to the previous year i.e., 2013–14. This expenditure almost amounts to 150 per cent of the total public development expenditure incurred on education and health. In addition to these costs (Box 2) there were costs associated with one million internally displaced persons (Pasha 2014).

The government is also supporting loss making public utilities and special interventions in provinces through federal grants. These have substantial transparency issues. For example, the largest burden is contingent liabilities. The government claims that these are disbursements to bridge losses of public sector enterprises (PSEs) and supporting financing of essential commodities. However, there is no justification of why such large losses have continued to persist over time.

The cost of civil administration of the federal government also remains high. As a share of total current expenditure, this was 9.8 per cent in 2011 and increased to 11.6 per cent in 2014–15. This is despite the promises in the manifestos of all political parties that they will reduce the size of civil administration expenses.

Box 2: Financing National Security and Losses of Public Enterprises

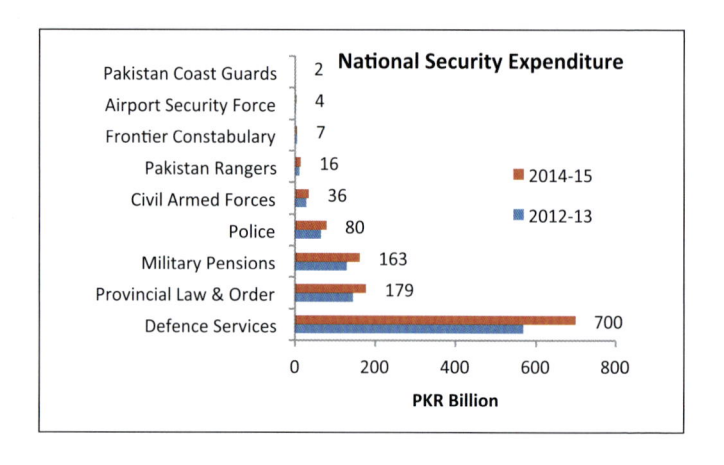

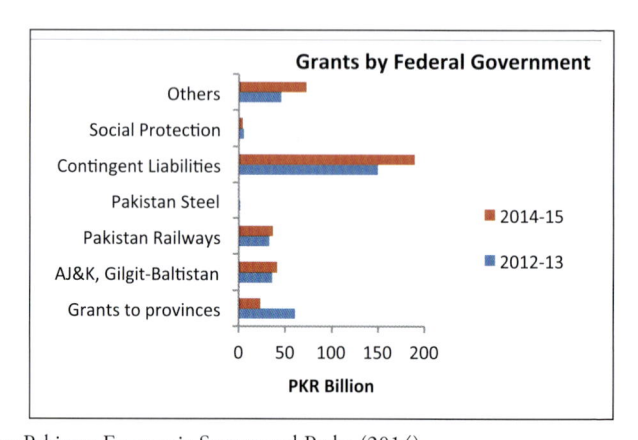

National Security Expenditure (PKR Billion), 2014-15 and 2012-13:

Pakistan Coast Guards	2
Airport Security Force	4
Frontier Constabulary	7
Pakistan Rangers	16
Civil Armed Forces	36
Police	80
Military Pensions	163
Provincial Law & Order	179
Defence Services	700

Grants by Federal Government (PKR Billion), 2014-15 and 2012-13:

- Others
- Social Protection
- Contingent Liabilities
- Pakistan Steel
- Pakistan Railways
- AJ&K, Gilgit-Baltistan
- Grants to provinces

Source: Pakistan Economic Survey and Pasha (2014).

The current structure of consolidated federal and provincial expenditures indicates little room for incremental expenditure on human development. In 2008–09, total federal and provincial expenditure on education was 1.8 per cent which touched 2.2 per cent in 2014–15. The expenditure on health was 0.6 per cent in 2008–09 and barely increased to 0.8 per cent in 2014–15. Similarly, the expenditure on clean water supply and sanitation was 0.2 per cent in 2008–09. This disbursement as a percentage of GDP remained at the same level in 2014–15.[3]

The share of the provincial government's spending on social sectors has been on the increase (Box 3). In 2008–09 this share stood at 82 per cent which increased to 87.4 per cent in 2012–13.[4] It is important to also see expenditure priorities in major sub-sectors. For example, in education there is an imbalance with almost 60 per cent allocation for primary and secondary education. Less than 3 per cent goes into technical and vocational training. For a labour force which faces major occupational and geographical mobility constraints, such a low allocation further decreases the likelihood of securing better opportunities. In the case of the health sector, 82 per cent is spent on running and maintenance of general public hospitals. The preventive facilities and measures receive less than 10 per cent. The mother and child hospitals and clinics receive less than 0.5 per cent of total expenditure on health. This is inadequate for a country where over 10 per cent of children between 1 to 2 years have not been through a full course of immunization (Ahmed and Ahmed 2014, Pasha 2014).

Box 3: Provincial Public Expenditure

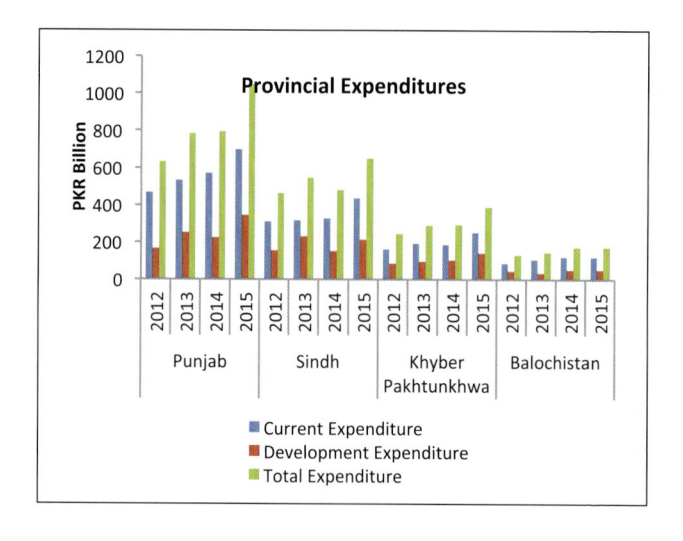

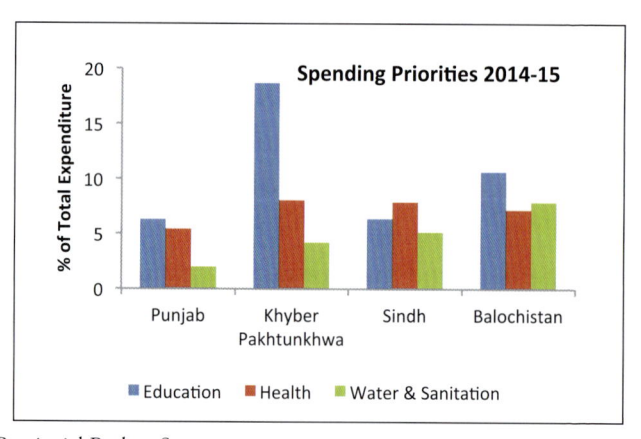

Source: Provincial Budget Statements.

3. Devolution and Fiscal Decentralization Outcomes

The 18th Amendment and the 7th NFC Award were significant steps towards empowering provinces and providing them with administrative and financial autonomy to manage their affairs and make efforts to bring about favourable outcomes in social sectors. Many believe that the process of devolution and fiscal decentralization is still not complete. Provincial governments need to act more proactively to devolve powers to the sub-national administrative tiers (Ghaus-Pasha 2012, UNDP 2015). The Council of Common Interests will need to be convened more regularly to look into issues related to inter-provincial and federal-provincial coordination gaps.

These coordination lapses have resulted in aggravating the asymmetric growth and human development patterns in the provinces. The World Bank (2014) had noted growing provincial financial mismanagement, as out of 32 provincial Public Expenditure and Financial Accountability (PEFA) indicators, one-third had deteriorated and only one-fifth had improved in Punjab and Sindh. The growing concern is that the expected improved provincial social sector outcomes that can be attributed to devolution have yet to be realized. Box 4 exhibits that infant and under-five mortality increased in at least two provinces between 2007 and 2013 i.e., Balochistan and Punjab. Similarly, the net primary enrolment ratio declined during the same period in Balochistan and Sindh. The literacy rate saw a decline in the case of Sindh province.

Box 4: Health and Education Indicators

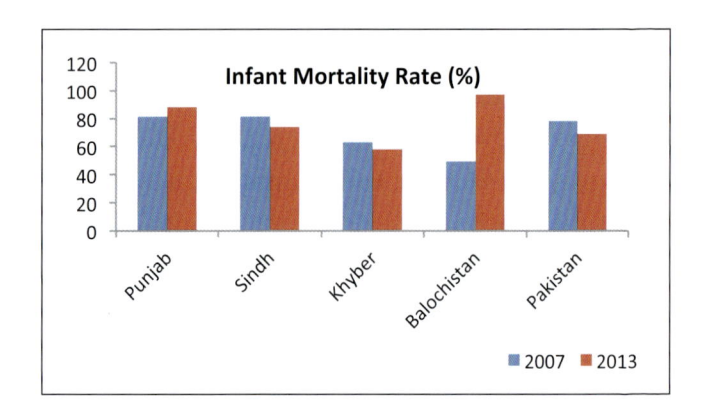

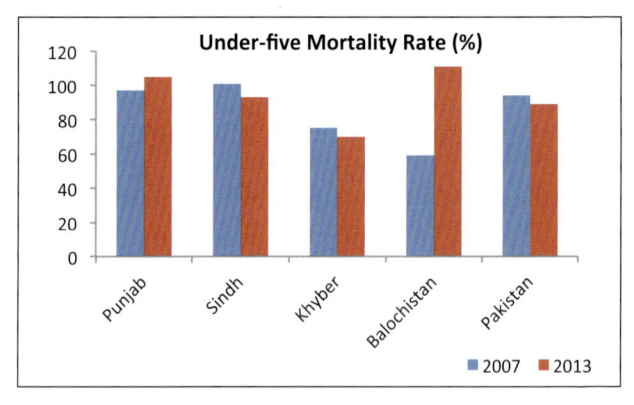

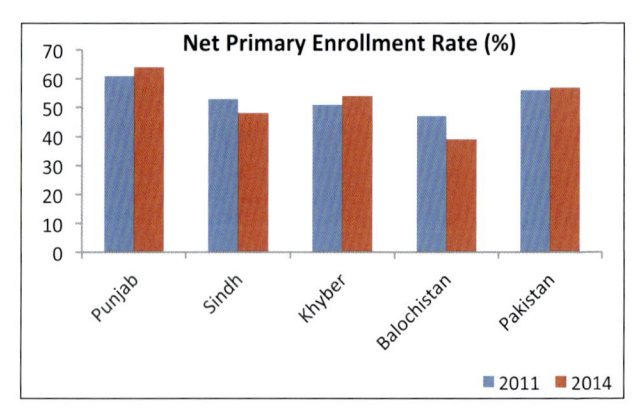

Literacy Rate 10 Years & Above (%)

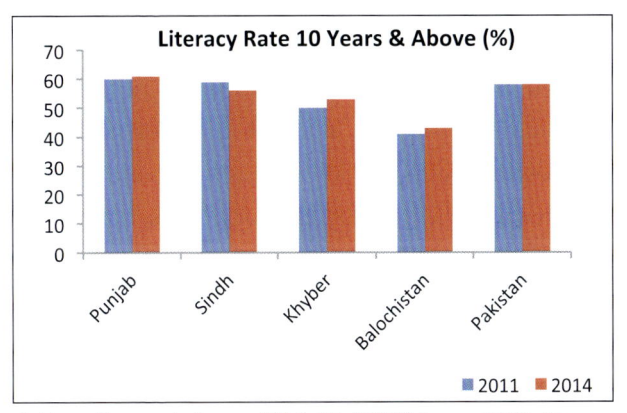

Source: Pakistan Economic Survey 2014–15, PDHS Survey 2012–13.

The failure to achieve improved social outcomes in the post-devolution period is attributed to reasons which are usually also put forward for weak attainment of Millennium Development Goals (MDGs) and scepticism that surrounds the implementation of SDGs. Ahmed (2014) had noted the lack of accountability and capacity-building reforms as a key reason for weak achievement of MDGs. In the context of localization of SDGs, it is now important that sectoral public investments should be carried out through community-based arrangements and public private models. The civil service which remains the only instrument for managing public expenditure should be encouraged and made comfortable with results-based management and clear key performance indicators (Ahmed 2015b). The reform of the civil service will need to accompany the transition towards outcomes-based budgeting.

The provincial governments now have the opportunity to create additional fiscal space that can complement the resources available under the 7th NFC Award. One way to do this is to enhance own fiscal effort to raise additional revenues through provincial progressive taxes. On top of this, local administrations can be empowered to collect local taxes which are progressive in nature. Revenue collection by the local government will have greater autonomy once provinces allow the process of Provincial Finance Commission (PFC) to move forward. At the time of writing this chapter three provinces have constituted PFCs however regular provincial award monitoring meetings are not taking place.

The existing framework of NFC awards also requires continuous reform. This is necessary if the state is to respond to fast evolving needs of the citizens. The delay in negotiating the next NFC award irks the smaller provinces which stand to gain relative to the larger provinces. The distribution formula should also be open to debate at the time of renegotiation of these awards. Here again the smaller provinces have long demanded that the formula should give greater weight to the low infrastructure endowment and weak revenue generation capacity, and vulnerability to climate change and food security. A more powerful and well capacitated Ministry of Inter-Provincial Coordination can play a proactive role in regularly exploring various distribution arrangements.

4. How to Reform Public Spending?

This section draws from in-depth literature review (cited above), research conducted by the author on linkages between public expenditure and economic growth during 2010–16, and key informant interviews and focus group meetings to discuss future reform of public expenditure in Pakistan.

A discussion regarding greater efficiency and effectiveness of public spending is important in order to achieve three important socio-economic objectives i.e., economic growth, poverty reduction, and decline in various forms of inequalities. We are interested in achieving the same or more output and increase value for money by having better outcomes at lower levels of spending. The efficiency and effectiveness framework forces us to think how we make the most out of scarce public sector monetary and non-monetary resources.

It is important to also understand the difference between efficiency and effectiveness. As indicated in Figure 1, the production of public goods and services will be considered efficient if for a given input the output is greater.[5] Efficiency in the production process can be termed as technical efficiency gains i.e., a movement towards best practices or allocative efficiency gains i.e., maximization of output through an optimal combination of inputs. Allocative efficiency takes into account costs and benefits of optimally combining several inputs (Mandl et al. 2008, Afonso et al. 2006).

Figure 1: Linking Development Programme Inputs with Outcomes

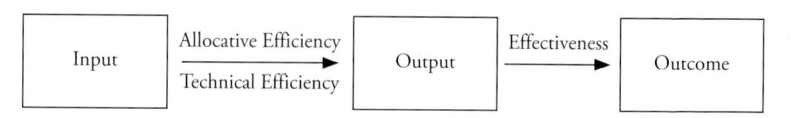

Input → [Allocative Efficiency / Technical Efficiency] → Output → [Effectiveness] → Outcome

Source: Adapted from Mandl et al. (2008).

This simple framework allows for a more standardized comparison across different economies. For example, two economies, A and B, have the same levels of public spending (input) but the former achieves higher output and is thus more efficient. This implies that country A has achieved maximum output achievable with the given set of inputs. Country B can move towards efficiency by raising output (output efficiency under given inputs) or reducing its inputs (input efficiency for a given output). This discussion has implications for national competitiveness and it is therefore important to look deeper into efficiency enhancing reforms (discussed below).

Reforms for greater efficiency of public spending

Efficiency gains can be achieved through reforming public administration, improving planning and appraisal processes, reducing losses of PSEs, and changing public expenditure mix in favour of human resource development, and targeted social safety nets. If administration is regarded as one of the inputs in public sector goods and service provision then an improvement towards cost and quality aspects of administration will be efficiency-enhancing. Let us turn to some of the measures that can render such gains.

The planning processes at the national and sub-national level require improvement: The current planning process is undermined due to politically motivated programmes and projects. The two democratically elected governments have been insecure about their tenure, leading to increased reliance on public expenditures which can lend quick and politically visible gains. This has hampered the implementation of longer term perspective plans formulated as part of Poverty Reduction Strategy Paper, Framework for Economic Growth, and Vision 2025.

There is a related concern of 'coordination in planning processes'. As the provinces come up with their own growth and development strategies, it is important to see which of the development initiatives can be implemented in synergy with other provinces. For this to happen, the Council of Common Interests (CCI) and the National Economic Council (NEC) will need to play a more proactive role in coordinating development schemes having inter-provincial domain. CCI however lacks a full-time secretariat which can steer the national planning process and also oversee implementation.

It is therefore recommended that the Planning Commission may be transitioned into a role where it can provide research, monitoring, and secretarial services to the CCI.[6] The Planning Commission already has mandate to either provide or arrange advice on almost all socio-economic issues. As the provinces complete the next round of local government reform and empower the sub-provincial administrations, the same role can be envisioned for provincial Planning and Development Departments.

Subsidies and grants should only be allowed after a scientifically conducted incidence analysis of benefits. The current levels of untargeted, hidden, and cross subsidies are not pro-poor and act as an additional burden on the fiscal deficit. Box 5 shows for the period between 2011 and 2013 that the benefit from electricity subsidies accrued the least for the poor segment of the population. In fact, the subsidies are being managed in such an arbitrary manner that the benefit for the poorest 20 per cent decreased between the fiscal year 2011 and May 2013, however the benefit for the richest 20 per cent increased during the same period.

Subsidies are also being managed at various different tiers of the government. This produces contradictory socio-economic outcomes. Dorosh 2005, Cororaton and Orden 2009 explain that Pakistan's trade and wheat pricing policies are taxing the wheat farmers. However, there are subsidies allowed through the commodity operations to wheat millers. This happens as the government sells wheat at below market price. Future subsidies should only be allowed after a benefit incidence analysis by the Finance Division with the aim to understand how subsidies can be better targeted towards the intended beneficiaries and if there is any leakage from intended beneficiaries to the other segments of the population (Trimble et al. 2011).

Box 5: Untargeted Subsidies

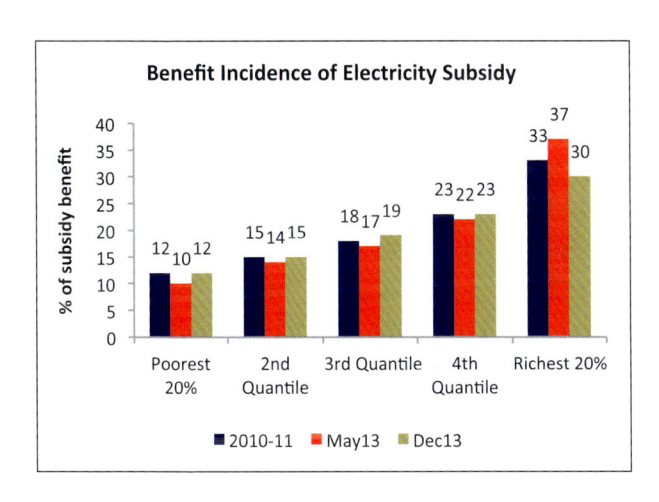

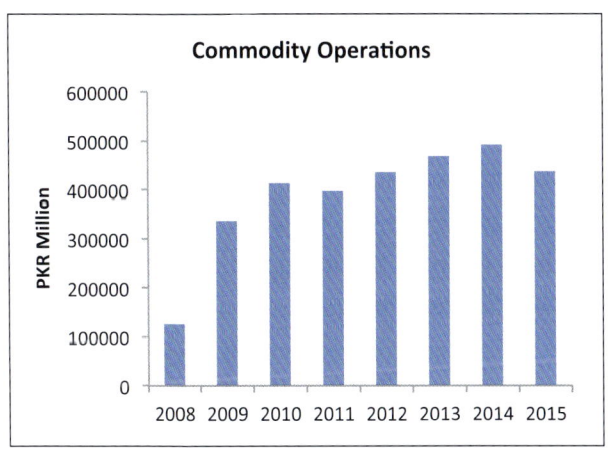

Benefit Incidence of Electricity Subsidy

Quantile	2010-11	May13	Dec13
Poorest 20%	12	10	12
2nd Quantile	15	14	15
3rd Quantile	18	17	19
4th Quantile	23	22	23
Richest 20%	33	37	30

Commodity Operations (PKR Million)

2008	~125000
2009	~335000
2010	~415000
2011	~400000
2012	~435000
2013	~470000
2014	~495000
2015	~440000

Source: Benefit Incidence: RAFTAAR 2015 (updated from World Bank estimates, 2014). Estimates for 2015 are provisional.

There is an urgent need to bring down the losses of PSEs and to restructure their liabilities. This however is not possible without the reform of management in these enterprises and legal provisions that insulate management from political pressures. Each of these entities is working under their own sectoral policy framework. The lack of scientific basis in setting policy rules also affects the losses of these enterprises. As an example, let us see the power and gas utilities, currently running high losses. While there are operational gaps that allow such losses, we also understand that the tariff structure is also a hindrance in cost recovery. Trimble et al. (2011) demonstrated that less than 10 per cent residential electricity consumers paid more than the cost-recovery level implying that 90 per cent of the consumers were net recipients of the subsidy.

The gas sector is also running higher than conventionally accepted losses. These losses in January 2016 stood at 15 per cent for Sui Southern Gas Company (SSGC) and 12 per cent for Sui Northern Gas Pipelines Limited (SNGPL). The globally recognized commercial and technical losses or theft is 2 per cent. For Balochistan province, the unaccounted for gas (UFG) losses were 51 per cent. While two-thirds of such losses are attributed to theft, the remaining is due to the dilapidated condition of pipelines and related infrastructure. This situation is further exacerbated due to the low recovery by these utilities from large consumers such as Pakistan Steel Mills and K-Electric. The pending recoveries add to the circular debt in the energy sector.

We have already discussed that the weak financial strength of

PSEs is contributing to rising contingent liabilities of the federal government, which include guarantees issued by the Finance Division of GoP to PSEs. Such liabilities have to be funded through grants by the federal government. Upon maturing, these liabilities act in the same manner as a contractual loan agreement. In 2015, this stock of guarantees by the federal government was at a record high of PKR 600 billion. This included a foreign currency component of USD 1.2 billion. Box 6 indicates the currently rising level of credit to PSEs and borrowing by autonomous bodies including WAPDA (including Pakistan Electric Power Company (Private) Limited), Oil and Gas Development Company Limited (OGDCL), Sui Northern Gas Pipelines Limited (SNGPL) and Sui Southern Gas Company (SSGC), Pakistan International Airlines (PIA), Pakistan Steel, and Pakistan Railways. These losses of PSEs reflect in the public sector borrowing and have economy-wide implications through prices, wages, interest rate, and exchange rate channels.

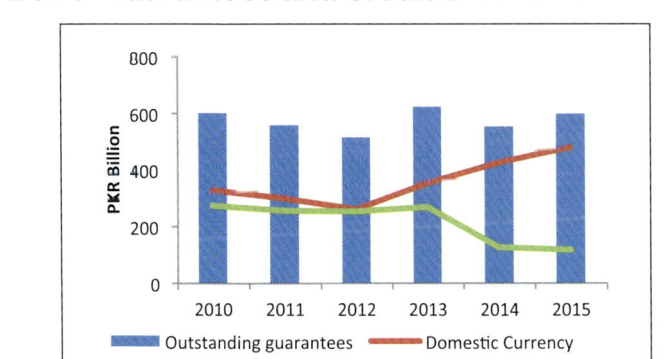

Box 6: Guarantees and Credit Extended to PSEs

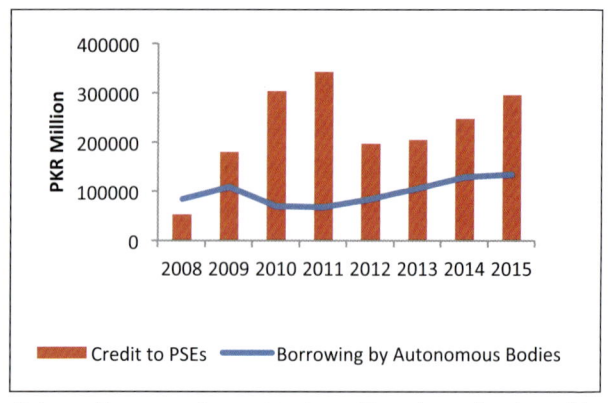

*Source: Pakistan Economic Survey 2014–15. The values of credit and borrowing by autonomous bodies are end-June stock.

There is also this broader question of how the government may like to exit from several production activities which now can be more efficiently conducted through public-private or solely private initiatives. Table 1 provides examples of some sectors and enterprises where the government is a provider of goods and services. In the case of some sectors, the government enters into active competition with the private sector, in turn distorting the latter's incentive to invest or remain in the market. The government as a service provider has also been found to be less responsive to consumer demands and preferences (GoP 2011).

Table 1: The Government in Business

Sector	Examples of Significant Enterprises[7]
Power	Power Generation Companies, Distribution Companies, National Power Construction, National Transmission and Dispatch Company, Sui South, Sui North etc.
Transport	Pakistan International Airlines, Pakistan Railways, National Highway Authority, Civil Aviation Authority, Port Qasim Authority etc.
Mining and Hydrocarbons	Pakistan State Oil Company, Oil and Gas Development Corporation, Pakistan Petroleum, Lakhra Coal Mines etc.
Manufacturing	Pakistan Steel Mills, Heavy Electrical Complex, Pakistan Machine Tool Factory etc.
Financial Services	SME Bank, National Bank of Pakistan, Industrial Development Bank of Pakistan, First Women Bank, National Insurance Company, National Investment Trust, State Life Insurance Company, Pakistan Reinsurance Company, Bank of Punjab, House Building Finance Corporation etc.
Other	Trading Corporation of Pakistan, Utility Stores Corporation of Pakistan, Pakistan Agricultural Storage and Services Corporation, Cotton Export Corporation, Rice Export Corporation of Pakistan, National Fertilizer Corporation, Pakistan Post, Pakistan Tourism Development Corporation, National Engineering Services of Pakistan etc.

Source: Speakman 2012.

It has been politically difficult for the government to undertake privatization of some of the units mentioned above. In this scenario it seems that the government will continue to manage the affairs of these entities for the foreseeable future. It is therefore important to put in place an overall policy framework for enterprises fully owned and operated by the state. Such a framework will provide autonomy, clear rules regarding scope of operations, and financial and operational reporting requirements (Speakman 2012). Providing a legal cover to this framework will be important in order to minimize the intrusion in management affairs of these enterprises. Second, it is equally important to revisit the ownership modalities e.g., the administrative control should be independent of any federal ministry or provincial department. This step will further allow commercialization of these enterprises. Furthermore, the monitoring and accountability functions should not be in the hands of government functionaries. An independent committee which includes the consumers and other important stakeholders in the case of fully corporate entities should have the oversight role.

In order to change the spending-mix in favour of greater infrastructure and social sector investments it is important to rationalize the size of the government. There remains plenty of room to reduce the operational size of federal and provincial governments. An audit at both levels to rationalize the government staff and consolidate operations was last done in 2003–04. A similar exercise may be undertaken again to guide the financial managers as to where the cuts may be undertaken. For example, in the case of the federal government several ministries with overlapping or related responsibilities may be merged. Already there is a single minister for the Ministry of Commerce and the Ministry of Textile. In a similar fashion the civil service working under the Ministry of Commerce can take care of the textile profile. Until late 1990s there was a single ministry taking care of both portfolios. Similarly, the Ministry of Industries can also be merged with the Ministry of Commerce. The former's role in economic decision-making has declined after privatization of PSEs in 1990s and 2000s. On the energy side, there are two different ministries and three different regulators. There is evidence from other countries which suggests that ministries may be merged into a single Ministry of Energy Affairs and regulatory bodies should also be merged in to a single entity. The manifestos of most political parties endorse this view.

The sheer size of several ministries can also be rationalized based on their performance or national priorities. For example, the number of foreign missions and embassies of Pakistan and staff working for these offices may be rationalized. A performance appraisal of staff working in the embassies from an outcomes lens (e.g., increase in trade due to the efforts of commercial attachés) is long due. The Ministry of Foreign Affairs can move towards a region-specific approach where a single embassy will be responsible for Pakistan's diplomatic relations with a group of countries.

It is important to also have a forward looking approach towards expenditure management and rationalization. A key aspect in this regard is the structure of pays and pensions. The employee-related expenditure has in fact increased after the 18th Amendment which provides another reason to believe that there may be some duplication of activities across the federal and provincial domains. The reform of future pay and pensions structure will require a joint working body comprising the Finance Division, Establishment Division, Finance Departments, and Services and General Administration Departments in the provinces. The starting point should be to find out if the administration of several attached departments within the ministries may be merged. Such a merging of operations will require an operations audit on functional lines. The facilities such as official staff, vehicles, and housing allowed to the civil servants, judiciary, and military officials should be monetized and indexed with inflation. Where such expenditures have already been monetized, there remain lacunas which require a regular evaluation. Any supplementary grant required by the ministries or departments, which exceed a certain limit of the approved budget should have endorsement of parliament's standing committees on finance and revenue. Pakistan has also made ambitious commitments towards SDGs. It is therefore important that the federal and provincial budgets should have alignment with national SDGs and sub-national targets.

Some fiscal space for social and infrastructure spending can also be created by rationalizing the tax expenditures. All SROs that provide tax concessions should be first discussed in parliament, relevant standing committees, and then approved by the National Economic Council. In a time of volatile commodity prices, infrastructure financing remains a challenge. It is therefore necessary to diversify the sources through which future infrastructure needs can be financed. The past practice of reliance on foreign assistance for financing such projects leads to *Dutch disease effect*. In line with the practice in some Asian economies, we recommend issuing long term tax-free bonds for infrastructure projects. It is expected that such bonds, backed by a government guarantee, will attract both local and foreign investors.

While greater public investment infrastructure is desired, however it is equally important to address governance of existing infrastructure. This is important as currently scarce resources are used to fund governance related losses. One such loss is in the form of circular debt in energy. Ahmed (2014) had noted that only the power sector losses amount to 2 per cent of GDP annually. Key reasons for such losses include: institutional fragmentation (leading to procedural delays), lack of scientific basis for tariff determination (full economic-cost pricing), fuel price adjustments and untargeted subsidies (with weak benefits to the poor), inability to reduce administrative and line losses (including theft), and weak capacity of distribution companies to recover dues (see also Ahmed 2015 and PRIME 2016). As discussed earlier such losses originating due to mismanagement are common in several PSEs.

REFORMS FOR INCREASED EFFECTIVENESS IN PUBLIC SPENDING

For government operations to remain lean and yet effective it is important to evaluate how they can remain focused on the core business of public service delivery and exit from areas which can be managed by other economic agents including the private sector. Ideally the policy and regulation functions should be retained and the management and production of goods and services should be left to competitive and transparent markets. Even in this framework there will be areas where markets will fail and for reasons of national security and human welfare, government intervention will be desired.

In order to keep government intervention to a minimum it is important to reimagine the objectives and coverage of Fiscal Responsibility and Debt Limitation (FRDL) Act. The act had a key focus on: (a) bringing revenue deficit to zero by the fiscal year 2008 and thereafter achieve a revenue surplus, (b) keeping total public debt to GDP ratio below or equal to 60 per cent, and (c) reducing public debt to GDP ratio by at least 2.5 per cent until the fiscal year 2013. These targets proved to be ambitious as Pakistan's revenue deficit continued to remain negative for the most part of the past decade. It may now be appropriate that the relevant committees in the parliament should demand a revision of this act. Such an overarching framework for fiscal discipline can create space for greater public investment and targeted welfare-related spending. A revision to FRDL Act is also important from the point of view of protecting budget allocation towards environmental protection, food security, and human development priorities under SDGs.

Planning Commission and Planning and Development Departments need strengthening for facilitating better implementation and outcomes. We discussed above how existing planning entities, given their resources, can be made more efficient. Here we now try to focus on how these planning entities, given their limited resources, may be able to derive more effective outcomes. We recommend that the focus of these entities should be more on design and monitoring of reform rather than management of public sector projects. They should be able to provide timely and state-of-the-art guidance to the line ministries and departments within the overarching development and growth framework. The ministries and departments should be encouraged to make their own service delivery plans and set achievable targets. While a system of monitoring quantifiable targets should be designed by the planning entities, focus on accountability of results is equally important. This also implies that while the line ministries and departments may be concerned more with the achievement of quarterly or annual output, planning entities should continuously focus on linking outputs with outcomes through effective coordination with provincial planning and development departments. The Planning Commission will be more empowered to play such a role if it is transitioned to become the secretariat for CCI.

On the Planning Commission's existing function of approval and oversight of public sector projects it is important to take stock of the missing link between resources invested and outcomes. The projects are being approved without scientific appraisal. The debate on cost benefit analysis of each project is not taking place in DDWP, CDWP, and ECNEC meetings. The fiscal consequences of approved projects are not carefully studied by the approving authorities. There are also multiple approving authorities for public sector projects which makes the process of accountability more difficult.

Special Delivery Units can strengthen results-based management (RBM). The government has established a Prime Minister's Delivery Unit and some provinces have also followed suit by creating such units at the Chief Minister's office. Instead of just overseeing the project implementation (which can be left to the Planning Commission), we recommend that these units should drive systematic implementation of RBM across the government. This process can start by having a medium term budget framework (MTBF) at both federal and provincial levels. The framework should be grounded in the overall growth and development strategy and provide short and medium term indicative budget ceilings (GoP 2011). MTBF process has been introduced at the federal level as well as in the case of at least two provinces. However, the ownership of this exercise remains limited to the Finance Division at the national level and Finance Departments at the provincial level. There is weak understanding of this process across the line ministries and departments.

Second, line ministries and departments will then prepare their sectoral plans in congruence with the overall growth and development strategy and budget ceilings provided under MTBF. These sectoral plans should have a clear mention of goals, inputs, outputs, outcomes, and impacts. In the third step it is expected that all entities will prepare output-based budgets which include costing of outputs and outcomes along with key performance indicators that measure these outputs and outcomes.

Fourth, the delivery unit will work with the finance ministry or department to develop an integrated accounting system that reports expenditure based on outputs and outcomes. This will allow this unit to furnish output and outcomes monitoring reports on a regular basis and present them to the parliament and CCI. Such reports may be accompanied by bi-annual submission of reports on results achieved by the Principal Accounting Officer in each department. Planning entities, which should ideally have the capacity of physical monitoring of these projects, will validate these results reports submitted by the Principal Accounting Officers.

Civil Service reforms can strengthen linkages between public sector operations and intended outcomes. The key objectives of such a reform should have a focus on efficient and effective public service delivery. This will involve attracting and retaining high quality professionals who have the autonomy to improve the government functioning at the national and sub-national level. The guiding principles for civil service reform may include: merit-based recruitment, transparent reward structure, job and tenure-specific capacity-building, output and outcomes based performance evaluation, security of tenure, and a revision of Estacode, Rules of Business, and Financial and Audit Rules to provide both autonomy and appropriate checks and balances (Husain 2012).

Taking a whole of the government approach and reforming civil service can complement the ongoing devolution process. The provincial governments now need to keep their promise and deliver administrative and financial autonomy to the sub-provincial administrations. This will have significant impact on the incentives and accountability of grass roots level service delivery. The local government acts promulgated by all provinces demand formation of Provincial Finance Commissions (PFCs) chaired by the provincial Finance Ministers. PFC award will provide local councils specific allocations. These acts also have some limitations. For example, there are only limited powers available for local councils to raise their own revenues.

It is important to also strengthen project design and management capacity in the public sector. This can have favourable outcomes from limited resources under Public Sector Development Programme of the Federal Government and the Annual Development Programme in the provinces. As stressed earlier this is only possible if planning and development entities move from traditional monitoring and evaluation (involving inputs, activities, and outputs) towards, results-based monitoring and evaluation (which also incorporates the evaluation of outcomes and long-term impact). Three levels of management capacity i.e., portfolio, programme, and project-level capacity will be required to improve the current supply chain of public sector service delivery. Both federal and provincial parliaments can help in reducing the throw-forward by: shutting down projects that do not provide socio-economic justification, and projects representing duplication across the federation. In future projects, throw-forward[8] can be reduced through alternate financing modes such as increased reliance on: public-private partnerships, built to operate and transfer, and built to operate and own. The element of rent-seeking can be reduced through: minimizing budget lines allocated to project management staff, appointing dedicated and accountable project directors, keeping consultancy charges to a minimum, keeping brick and mortar content in construction projects to a minimum, and disapproving allocation for contingencies at the approval stage.

Within the current approval process of public sector projects there is a need to strengthen feasibility, appraisal, and approval processes. Both federal and provincial governments may consider stronger financial and technical appraisal. Such a process can only be autonomous if outsourced and performed by a competitively selected entity. The appraisal should have a key focus on: social analysis (reflecting beneficiary population, dislocation, resettlement, and livelihoods), economic analysis (including domestic resource cost), and risk analysis (including an ex-ante assessment of time and cost overruns and expected content modification).

The federal government will need to strengthen coordination among public sector capacity-building initiatives. In 2012–13 federal PSDP had 17 different training facilities under different divisions leading to a fragmented capacity-building effort by the government. Such initiatives can be consolidated. An ideal solution will be to merge such initiatives under National School of Public Policy.

The provincial expenditure on education and health will

require alignment with demographic trends, national priorities under Vision 2025, and provincial development plans. In the case of education this will involve rationalizing current spending across primary, secondary, and tertiary education levels. In the case of primary schooling the spending per student is significantly lower than secondary and tertiary levels. Rationalization is also required in the budget allocation and disbursement between physical infrastructure (in schools) and investment in education quality. For example, there is a greater focus on building schools and procurement of fixtures and fittings. However, allocation for teacher's capacity-building is low on priority. Like the FRDL Act at the federal level, the provincial parliaments can pass a law that protects allocations for education. This equally applies to the health sector and allocations towards clean drinking water and sanitation.

Additionally, in the health sector, scarce financial resources can be saved if greater attention is diverted towards primary preventive healthcare. This can be done through an increase in the allocation for primary care (at the basic health unit level), mother and child health care, and immunization. The effectiveness of health sector programmes can be further increased through decentralized planning and budgeting of health activities (e.g., at the district level).

5. Conclusion

The efficiency and effectiveness of public spending in Pakistan is undermined due to weak portfolio management, lack of monitoring mechanisms, and duplication across programmes and projects managed by federal and provincial governments. A large expenditure on debt servicing, public administration, and defence leaves little room for spending on human resource development. The country has the lowest social sector spending to GDP ratio across the region. Even these low levels of expenditure lack alignment with provincial development plans and priorities under SDGs.

The ongoing process of devolution and fiscal decentralization has provided an opportunity to the provinces for exercising fiscal autonomy. However, the devolution process has yet to result in an overall improvement in outcome indicators for most provinces. This is partially because the increased share of social sector allocation available with the provinces has been invested in procurement and wage bill and less on improving quality aspects of the service delivery in education, health, water, and sanitation.

For a more equitable impact of public resources it is now imperative that the economic managers at the federal and provincial level refrain from politically motivated expenditures. To increase allocative and technical efficiency in spending we propose that the planning processes at the national and sub-national levels require substantial improvement. The untargeted, cross, and hidden subsidies (and grants) should be phased out and these should only be allowed after conducting a robust benefit incidence analysis. Parliamentary approval for such subsidies, grants, and even tax expenditures should be mandatory. The losses and liabilities of PSEs need to be restructured. Given the weak capacity of the public sector to manage PSEs, we recommend a move towards greater corporatization of these entities (even if the dominant ownership remains with the public sector). This is also important in the context of rationalizing the size of government operations and staff expenses overtime.

For strengthening the linkages between inputs and outcomes i.e., effectiveness of public spending, we recommend a revision of the FRDL Act. The proposed legal revision will keep public debt under check and protect the spending on human resource development. Second, the implementation of development schemes across the government can be improved through improved functioning of CCI, NEC, and NFC. Furthermore, greater coordination between planning and development departments and special delivery units at the Prime Minister and Chief Minister's offices will also help this goal.

Finally, for sustained improvement in the quality of portfolio, programme, and project implementation, it is important to undertake the long pending civil service reforms. Specific measures which improve recruitment, reward, tenure-structure, and accountability will go a long way in improving the service delivery at the grass roots level.

References

Afonso, A., Schuknecht, L. and Tanzi, V., (2006), 'Public sector efficiency: Evidence for new EU member states and emerging markets'. *European Central Bank Working Paper,* No. 581.

Ahmed, V., 'Towards Sustainable Economic Development in Pakistan' in *Pakistan's Security Problems & Challenges in the Next Decade*, pp. 141–68, National University of Sciences and Technology, 2016.

Ahmed, V., 'Economy and Energy Security for Pakistan—What Lies Ahead?', *COMSATS Institute of Information Technology,* 2014.

Ahmed, S., Vaqar Ahmed and Cathal O'Donoghue (2011) 'Reforming indirect taxation in Pakistan: A macro-micro analysis'. *eJournal of Tax Research,* Volume 9, Number 2, December 2011.

Ahmed, V, Abbas, A. and Ahmed, S., 2013, *Public Infrastructure and Economic Growth in Pakistan: A Dynamic CGE-Micro Simulation Analysis*, Springer, 117–43.

Ahmed, V. et al., 'Post MDGs: Issues for the Future', *Southern Voice Occasional Paper 5*, Centre for Policy Dialogue, Dhaka, 2014.

Akram, M. and Khan, F. J., 2007, *Health Care Services and Government Spending in Pakistan,* PIDE Working Papers, 32.

Ahmed, V. 2015, 'Contours of Pakistan's Power Crisis'. Editor Cheema, Z. I., Energy Crisis and Nuclear Safety and Security of Pakistan. Strategic Vision Institute.

Khan, A., Javed, A., Batool, S., Hussain, F., Mahmood, H., and Ahmed, V. (2016) The role of youth in sustainable development. Overseas Development Institute. Weblink: http://southernvoice.org/wp-content/uploads/2017/01/sdpi_paper_The-role-of-youth-in-sustainable-development.pdf, accessed on 9 June 2017.

Ali, S. 2010, *Does the Choice of Government Expenditures Affect Poverty? Time Series Evidence from Pakistan,* International Conference on Applied Economics, Coventry University, UK.

Afzal, M., and Abbas, Q., 'Wagner's Law in Pakistan: Another Look', *Journal of Economics and International Finance*, Vol 2 (1), pp. 12–19, 2010.

Asghar, N., Awan, A. and Rehman, H., 2012, 'Government Spending,

Economic Growth and Rural Poverty in Pakistan', *Pakistan Journal of Social Sciences*, vol. 32, No. 2, pp. 469–83.

Asghar, N. Azim, P. and Rehman, H., 2011, 'Impact of Government Spending in Social Sectors on Economic Growth: A Case Study of Pakistan', *Journal of Business & Economics,* vol. 3, No.2, pp. 214–34.

Asghar, Z. and Zahra, M., 2012, 'A Benefit Incidence Analysis of Public Spending on Education in Pakistan Using PSLM Data', *The Lahore Journal of Economics*, 17:2, pp. 111–36.

Aurangzeb 2003, 'Relation between Health Expenditure and GDP in an Augmented Slow Growth Model for Pakistan: An Application of Co-integration and Error-Correction Modelling', *The Lahore Journal of Economics,* vol. 8, No. 2.

Cororaton, C. B., and Orden, D., (2009), *Agricultural Price Distortions, Inequality and Poverty,* edited by K. Anderson, J. Cockburn and W. Martin, World Bank.

Dorosh, P. (2005), 'Wheat Markets and Pricing in Pakistan: Political Economy and Policy Options', Wheat Policy Note, South Asia Rural Development Unit, World Bank, Washington DC.

Ghaus-Pasha, A., (2012), 'Making Devolution Work in Pakistan'. *The Lahore Journal of Economics.* 17: SE (September 2012): pp. 339–57.

GoP (2011), 'Framework for Economic Growth'. Planning Commission, Government of Pakistan.

Government of Balochistan 2013, *Balochistan Education Sector Plan 2013–18,* Policy Planning and Implementation Unit, Education Department, Government of Balochistan.

Government of Khyber Pakhtunkhwa 2015, *Budget Strategy Paper 2015–16,* Government of Khyber Pakhtunkhwa.

Government of KPK 2010, *Khyber Pakhtunkhwa Health Sector Strategy 2010–17,* Government of Khyber Pakhtunkhwa.

Government of Sindh 2012, *Sindh Health Sector Strategy 2012–2020,* Government of Sindh.

Government of Sindh 2015, *Budget Strategy Paper 2015–16 to 2017–18,* Economic Reform Unit, Finance Department, Government of Sindh.

Government of the Punjab 2015, *Punjab Growth Strategy 2018: Accelerating*

Economic Growth and Improving Social Outcomes, Government of the Punjab.

Hakro, A. N. and Akram, M., 2007, 'The Incidence of Government Expenditures on Education and Health: Microeconomic Evidence from Pakistan', *The Lahore Journal of Economics,* 12:2, pp. 27–48.

Husain, I., (2012), *Reforming the Government in Pakistan.* Vanguard Books, Lahore.

Hussain, F., Hussain, S. and Erum, N., 2008, 'Is Defense Expenditure Pro Poor or Anti Poor in Pakistan?' *An Empirical Investigation,* Paper Presented at 30th Annual General Meeting, Pakistan Institute of Development Economics.

Hussain, F., Qasim, M. A. and Sheikh, K. M., 2003, 'An Analysis of Public Expenditure on Education in Pakistan, *The Pakistan Development Review,* 42:4, pp. 771–80.

Mehmood, Y. et al., 'Cost Benefit Analysis in Pakistan Public Hospitals', *International Journal of Pharmacy Practice and Pharmaceutical Sciences,* Vol 2, Issue 1, 2015.

Kalim, R. and Hassan, M. S., 2013, *Military Expenditure and Poverty in Pakistan,* Proceedings of 3rd International Conference on Business Management.

Kalim, R. and Hassan, M. S., 2014, 'Public Defense Spending Poverty in Pakistan', *Review of Public Economics,* 211, 93–115.

Kelegama, S., (2012), *Foreign Aid in South Asia: The Emerging Scenario,* SAGE.

Mandl, U., Dierx, A., Ilzkovitz, F., (2008), 'The effectiveness and efficiency of public spending'. *European Commission Economic Papers 301,* February 2008.

Pasha, H., Imran, M., Iqbal, A., Ismail, Z., Sheikh, R. and Sherani, S., 2011, *Review and Analysis of Pakistan's Public Investment Program,* International Growth Centre.

Pasha, H. A., (2014), *Progressive Fiscal Policy for Inclusive Growth.* Friedrich Ebert Stiftung, Pakistan.

Pritchard, A., (2002), 'Measuring productivity in the production of public services'. *Economic Trend No. 570,* pp.61.

PRIME, (2016), 'Circular Debt: State Incentives or Market Rules.' *PRIME Analytical Reports,* Issue 7, Vol: 1, Feburary 2016.

RAFTAAR, 2015, *Pakistan's Public Expenditure: Insights & Reflections,* Research & Advocacy for the Advancement of Allied Reforms.

Rehman, H. et al., 'Testing Wagner's Law for Pakistan: 1974–2004', *Pakistan Economic and Social Review,* Volume 45, No. 2, pp. 155–66.

SDPI 2013, *Managing Intra-Country Growth Disparities in South Asia,* 6th South Asian Economic Summit. Institute of Policy Studies, Sri Lanka.

Shahbaz, M., Afza, T. and Shabbir, M. S., 2013, 'Does Defence Spending Impede Economic Growth? Cointegration and Causality Analysis for Pakistan,' *Defence and Peace Economics,* vol. 24, No. 2, 105–20.

Trimble, C. et al., *Rethinking Electricity Tariffs and Subsidies in Pakistan,'* World Bank, 2011.

Speakman, J., 2012, 'SOE Reform: Time for Serious Corporate Governance.' *World Bank Policy Paper Series on Pakistan,* PK 04/12, November 2012.

Wahab, M. A., Ahmed, V. and Javed, A., 2013, 'Human Resource Development, Government Spending and Productivity of Human Capital in Pakistan,' *SAARC Journal of Human Resource Development,* vol. 9, No.1. pp. 32–48.

UNDP, 2015, 'Five Years of the 18th Amendment.' *Development Advocate Pakistan.* Volume 2, Issue 1, April 2015.

World Bank, '2014 Pakistan Country Development Landscape'. The World Bank, Pakistan.

Zeshan, M. and Ahmed, V., 2014, 'How Spending on Defense Versus Human Capital impacts Economic Productivity in South Asia?' *International Journal of Economics and Empirical Research.* 2(2), 74–83.

Notes

1. See also Kalim R and Hassan M S (2013) and Ali S (2010).
2. For example see Hussain F et al. (2003).
3. For details see PRSP progress reports.
4. See PRSP progress reports for details.
5. This interpretation of 'efficiency' makes this concept different from 'productivity' which is a ratio of output to input (see Pritchard 2002).

6. A point explained to the author by Pervez Tahir.
7. These enterprises are incorporated under various different arrangements including e.g., fully corporatized entities under the Companies Act, statutory entities etc.
8. Projects already approved however awaiting actual financing or pending instalments under the overall approved amount.

Chapter 5

Export Competitiveness

1. Background

At the time of the writing of this chapter, Pakistan's export of goods continues to be under severe pressure, facing a downward decline in terms of value and volume. Pakistan's share in the global export market has also dropped in the recent past, while peer economies, whose performance is exhibited in later sections, have experienced an increasing share in global exports, particularly in the export-oriented sectors of Pakistan.

At this juncture it is important to reflect and examine macro and micro level issues that influence production and exports competitiveness. These issues may include[1] (a) regulatory constraints[2] including those pertaining to tax and labour; (b) cost of doing business, including import tariff structure; (c) inability to participate in regional supply chains; (d) insufficient trade facilitation; (e) lack of coordinated support from provincial governments; (f) low credit provision for exports; and (g) an exchange rate regime that serves the pursuit of neither short-term export promotion, nor competitiveness.[3]

The management of the exchange rate left a lot to be desired. Recent literature suggests that the exchange rate cannot be used as an effective instrument for export promotion (McCartney 2015).[4] While theory may suggest that the balance of trade, the cost of doing business, total factor productivity, and inflation may be the principal factors in the determination of the exchange rate, however experience suggests that the exchange value of the rupee is also heavily influenced by workers' remittances from abroad and foreign aid linked with developments such as Pakistan being a partner in the war on terror. These factors have tended to appreciate the local currency significantly, allowing it to remain overvalued, in turn affecting the export competitiveness.[5]

This puts the private sector and those involved in longer term investment decisions in a difficult position. If there is further appreciation of the real effective exchange rate vis-à-vis the US dollar, this will imply a further eroding of export competitiveness. Furthermore, any slowdown in the growth of Pakistan's exporting destinations could also weaken exports demand. We also understand that with a higher debt to GDP ratio, the exchange rate is influenced by concerns about the budgetary impact of depreciating currency.

During the period July-May FY'16, the value of merchandise exports declined by 8.4 per cent and stood at US$ 20.1 billion. The government's own analysis of declining exports argues that the current export basket and markets abroad are limited. Cotton and cotton manufactures alone contributed 58 per cent exports during July-May FY'16 while leather and rice contributed 23 per cent during the same year. These categories include low value products that are vulnerable to shocks from global price fluctuations. Furthermore, Pakistan's textile, leather, and rice are only reaching a few traditional destinations which generally provide market access.

There has been little progress in the public or private sector to improve productivity and firm-level innovation that can help reduce costs and develop products and their variants with dynamic demand (Hussain and Ahmed 2012). As a consequence of lack of innovation, Pakistan continues to lose its share in the US textile market. A gradual shift in the preference of some western markets is observed, away from cotton products towards low cost substitutes such as man-made fibre. In the case of the crop sector, an example is the country's laxness to produce new varieties of Basmati rice in the past three decades, in turn resulting in India taking a lead in the global supply of high-yield varieties.

The management of sporadically announced export promotion measures was fragmented across federal and provincial governments. Under the IMF programme, stringent budget deficit targets reinforced the dominance of the Ministry of Finance (MoF) in the de facto trade policy execution. This resulted in the weakening of the authority and service delivery of most economic ministries, including the Ministry of Commerce (MoC). Due to the budgetary constraints, the MoF also held back Export Development Fund (EDF) for extended periods.[6]

Pakistan's ability to participate in regional supply chains and conduct regional trade has weakened over time. Some studies attribute this to fiscal policies that rely heavily on high import taxes and regulatory duties for increasing tax revenues[7], and the relatively high levels of protection[8] to some sub-sectors of the industry. The participation in supply chains was also not possible due to a lack of coordination between the MoC and the Federal Board of Revenue (FBR) resulting in contradictory trade and tax regime faced by potential value chain initiatives.

The reform of the regulatory regime faced by local businesses has slowed after the 18th Amendment as laws pertaining to labour, land, sub-national taxes, fixed assets, utilities, and environment are now in the provincial government's domain. Several recent frictions between the federation and the provinces have landed in the Council of Common Interests (CCI).[9] Some legal experts are of the view that it may take a substantially long time for CCI, and its secretariat, Ministry of Inter Provincial Coordination, to succeed in rationalizing the regulatory burden of the export sector. A broken regulatory regime also allows existing and large enterprises to influence the political process around de facto trade policy. This makes the markets less competitive. The lack of a level playing field for all implies a relationship-driven (rather than rules-driven) corporate milieu. This over the medium and longer run acts as a barrier for entry of new and innovative firms.[10]

The sectors that stand to gain from the market access arrangements such as European Union (EU) Generalized

System of Preferences (GSP) continue to face critical issues such as rising cost of necessary inputs, delays in sales tax refunds, and high customs and regulatory duties on import of raw materials used in the exporting sectors. The current free trade agreements (FTAs) were also shallow and could not promote competition in goods and the labour market, and product diversification.[11] Past FTAs were not accompanied by lowering of regulatory burden on industry therefore neutralizing the benefits of market access agreement.

The main objective of this paper is to look into the reasons that explain Pakistan's declining share in global exports, lack of product diversification, and missing product sophistication. Second, based on an extensive literature review, around three dozen key informant interviews with the leading exporting firms, nine focus group discussions (two in Lahore, Karachi, Peshawar, Quetta, and one in Islamabad) having participation of relevant government officials, and two national level seminars at Sustainable Development Policy Institute, we provide short and medium term policy recommendations for boosting export competitiveness. This assessment was carried out between January-September 2016.

The next section uses literature review and already published data through official sources to help explain Pakistan's overall and sectoral export performance. We also provide a comparison of cost structure and enabling environment faced by exporters in competitor economies like Bangladesh, China, India, and Vietnam. In Section 3, we give some key features of the recently launched Strategic Trade Policy Framework (STPF) 2015–18. We also discuss elements that may hinder implementation of some important trade promotion measures envisaged under this framework. We then go on to provide policy recommendations for federal and provincial administrations and relevant trade bodies. As suggested in the Conclusion, these recommendations cannot see the light of day unless trust and close collaboration with the private sector is developed.

2. Pakistan's Export Performance

Revisiting comparative advantage

A large part of literature on Pakistan's export performance deals with analysing sectoral comparative advantage. It is observed that Pakistan has revealed comparative advantage (RCA)[12] in textile vis-à-vis Bangladesh and India (Shahzad K 2015). In clothing, Bangladesh holds comparative advantage vis-à-vis India and Pakistan. Pakistan has held dynamic revealed comparative advantage in textile since 1980, however the country's share in global exports is decreasing. Bangladesh's comparative advantage in clothing has been on the rise since 1980s. Comparing with China, Yasmin B and Altaf S (2014) suggest for textile (and carpets), that the comparative advantage is steady for China and oscillating for Pakistan.

The removal of quota regime (faced by the textile sector) failed to substantially improve the competitiveness due to rising input costs and relative prices of per unit exports (Ahmad N and Kalim R 2014). EU and United States have maintained tariffs on textile and clothing goods (from time to time) and that is also contributing to increased cost faced by exporters. Similar issues faced by the garments and hosiery sector have led to declining productivity in these sub-sectors. Authors believe that the exchange rate could be used as a tool for short-term export promotion in these sectors.

Apart from textile, leather and leather manufactures provide a significant share of Pakistan's exports receipts. Pakistan has comparative advantage in the leather sector vis-à-vis China, India, and Iran (Sahab S and Mahmood M T 2013). Akhtar N et al. (2008) also show for footwear industry (having leather preparations) that between 2003 and 2006, technological improvements were experienced which strengthened comparative advantage vis-à-vis competitors. The value addition in this sector can still be enhanced through reduced or no custom duty for import of machinery used in tanneries, and exemption from Export Development Surcharge on value added exports.[13]

In the case of agricultural exports, rice occupies a substantial share. However, the share in global exports of rice and competitiveness decreased over time (Akmal N et al. 2014 and Akhtar W et al. 2007). Local producers did not look beyond the Middle East and China for exports of rice. With sanctions on Iran, the exports of rice had further plummeted. Enhancing production capacity and better infrastructure for rice supply chain was required to tap the benefits from high-earning and dynamic markets. Appropriate trade facilitation and marketing measures were needed to improve the competitiveness of Basmati rice.[14]

Apart from rice, Pakistan has sustained comparative and competitive advantage in the exports of cereal and horticulture (Akhtar W et al. 2013 and Riaz K et al. 2012). In fruits, Pakistan has comparative advantage in kinnow production which can be further strengthened by better production techniques, trade facilitation measures, and by controlling citrus diseases. A revealed comparative advantage is also seen for mangoes, dates, and vegetable exports (Riaz K et al. 2012, Akhtar W et al. 2009). In the case of dates and mangoes the revealed comparative advantage is increasing over time. However, the same is not the case for livestock products which have seen a declining productivity vis-à-vis competitors. Despite fiscal support packages for the minor crop sector Pakistan could not achieve strong comparative advantage, e.g., in the case of tomatoes during 1998–2008 (Tahir A et al. 2012). Literature attributes this to a lack of focus on increasing the area under cultivation of tomatoes. Currently, tomatoes are only marketed in Afghanistan and the Middle East.

There are also several items in the export basket for which Pakistan's comparative advantage is decreasing over time (Mamnoon D et al. 2011) vis-à-vis economies in the region. This includes ceramic goods, pharmaceutical items, fish and fish products, photographic products, and precious stones. Some of this loss can still be managed if Pakistan moves towards higher degrees of specialization within these products and intra-industry trade (IIT) is allowed to flourish in the region. IIT has greater probability of emergence over time with trading partners having similar demand preferences and patterns (Shahbaz M and Leitao N C 2010). Furthermore, IIT can be promoted through reduction in transport costs domestically and in the region.[15]

Studies have shown that Pakistan's maximum IIT potential lies with India, Malaysia, and Singapore (Zaheer R et al. 2013). For the specific case of India-Pakistan IIT, Taneja N et al. (2014) explains that the largest potential may be in clothing and apparels. India produces quality fabric which gives it a competitive edge in the manmade fibres segment (see also Akram A 2013). Whereas, Pakistan's cotton production is more competitive. Pakistan and India can develop value chain with Bangladesh and Sri Lanka for import of raw material used in textile and clothing production. Pant M and Pande D (2014) also highlight that IIT between Pakistan and India has potential in the pharmaceutical sector (see also Ahmed and Batool 2014). The study also stressed that IIT has positive correlation with increase in trade intensity. Low levels of research and development cooperation between Pakistan and India restricts IIT.

Regional trade agreement, if designed smartly, can also promote IIT. Ahmed S et al. (2010) while evaluating the FTA between Pakistan and Sri Lanka observed that welfare and efficiency has increased for both economies, whereas export goods remain the same even after the implementation of FTA. The IIT potential exists for both trading partners. Over time Pakistan has increased its specialization in iron and steel, live tree plants, bulbs, lime, and cement whereas specialization has decreased in cereal, flour, carpets, and other textile floor covering.

The evaluation of bilateral and regional trade agreements and their impact on export competitiveness has also received attention in the literature. It is observed that the comparative advantage for Pakistan vis-à-vis China and India changed considerably, and around 18 industries became uncompetitive vis-à-vis India (Memon N et al. 2014). The authors find that the trade concessions provided to China, under a free trade agreement (FTA) and flow of formal (and informal) trade with India may be affecting Pakistan's manufacturing sector's output.[16] Ahmed S et al. (2010) show for Pakistan-Sri Lanka FTA that the former has (post-FTA) comparative advantage in textile, clothing, electrical, and telecommunication equipment.

The trade in services has received inadequate attention in the literature on Pakistan's comparative advantage. Studies do however raise concerns regarding the setback in comparative advantage in bilateral trade for some of the services exported by Pakistan. Pakistan has comparative advantage in bilateral services trade with the UK in transport, computer, and IT-related services, financial services, government services, and personal, cultural, and recreational services. The comparative advantage of Pakistan with the USA lies in computer and

IT-related services, communication, and government services (Atif R M et al. 2016).[17]

Performance of key sectors

Pakistani exports are heavily concentrated in a small basket of commodities. The cotton-based textile products occupy the maximum share within the overall exports (Box 1). Within textile only the share of readymade garments has seen an increase with respect to overall exports of Pakistan. In the case of several value added sub-sectors, e.g., bed wear, cotton fabrics, and towels, the share in overall exports has in fact declined.

The US and the EU region remain the major buyers of Pakistan's goods. Pakistan's exports to China have risen, though still not in volumes anticipated in several scientific studies. Afghanistan, being a landlocked country, has also relied on Pakistan for its agricultural and food requirements, which has encouraged a growth in the export of wheat, rice, and other food items to the former.[18] In the case of imports, Pakistan is routing its imports from distant locations, which according to some increases import costs (Chatterjee and George 2012). Apart from China, most of the other leading countries of origin for imported items are outside of this region. The import savings could not be realized partially due to slow progress on South Asia Free Trade Agreement (SAFTA) and lack of political will to liberalize trade with India (Kaur and Nanda 2011).

Box 1: Pakistan's Trade Profile

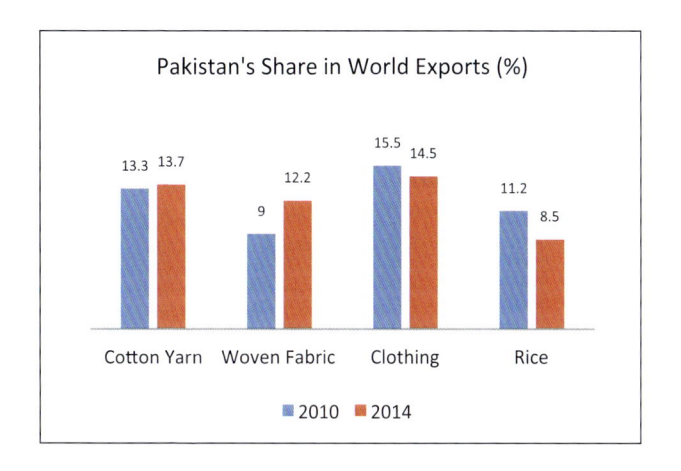

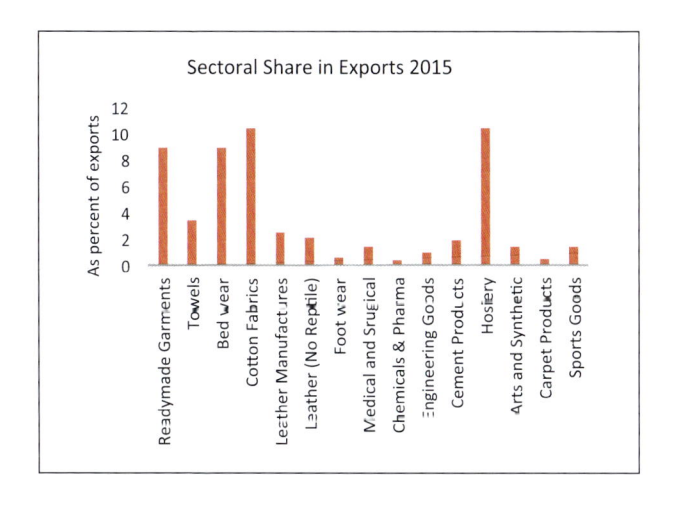

Pakistan's Share in World Exports (%)

	2010	2014
Cotton Yarn	13.3	13.7
Woven Fabric	9	12.2
Clothing	15.5	14.5
Rice	11.2	8.5

Sectoral Share in Exports 2015 (As percent of exports)

- Readymade Garments
- Towels
- Bed wear
- Cotton Fabrics
- Leather Manufactures
- Leather (No Reptile)
- Foot wear
- Medical and Surgical
- Chemicals & Pharma
- Engineering Goods
- Cement Products
- Hosiery
- Arts and Synthetic
- Carpet Products
- Sports Goods

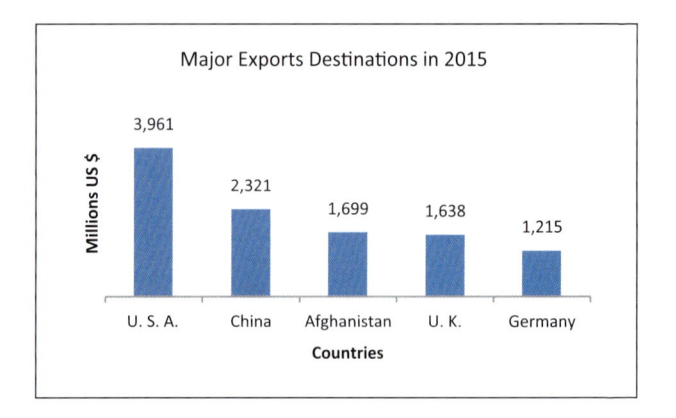

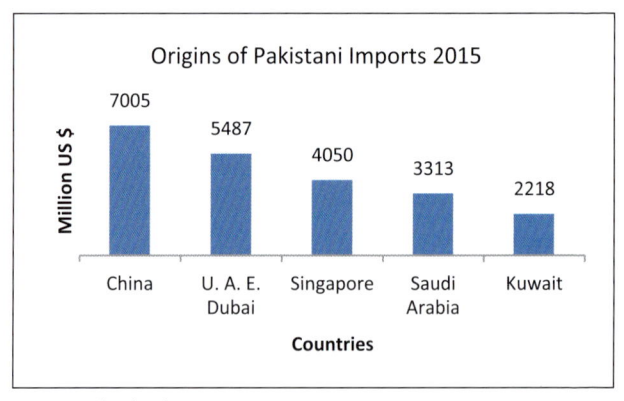

Major Exports Destinations in 2015 (Millions US $)

- U.S.A.: 3,961
- China: 2,321
- Afghanistan: 1,699
- U.K.: 1,638
- Germany: 1,215

Origins of Pakistani Imports 2015 (Million US $)

- China: 7005
- U.A.E. Dubai: 5487
- Singapore: 4050
- Saudi Arabia: 3313
- Kuwait: 2218

Source: State Bank of Pakistan.

As mentioned above, manufacturing sector's exports are dominated by textiles. Out of the total textile exports of USD 12.7 billion in 2014–15, the leading commodities included knit wear, bed wear, and cotton cloth. There are other manufactured exports including chemicals and pharmaceutical products, sports goods, and leather manufactures. In the food group, rice, fruits, fish, and fish preparations are the notable items. Some solid fuel and petroleum products have also seen foreign demand especially in Afghanistan.

Pakistan's export industries also rely on imported inputs. In 2015–16, Pakistan's imports mainly originated from China, UAE, Singapore, and Saudi Arabia and comprised mineral fuels and oil, machinery and appliances, chemicals and fertilizer, iron, steel, aluminium, cotton, and man-made fibres and man-made filaments. Pakistan can enhance import savings if more competitively priced inputs are allowed to come from Central and South Asia.

Cost of doing business: regional comparison

During 2015–16 Pakistan's textile industry's exports saw a decrease of USD 1.4 billion. Several factors were responsible for this decline. However, a rise in the cost of doing business was perhaps the single most important reason.[19] The major obstacles to businesses participating in trade include: lack of trade finance; dealing with taxes, licenses and permits; technological barriers; and strictly (at times distortive) regulated access to utilities such as power and gas.

During 2015–16, Pakistan's textile industry faced an electricity tariff of 11 cents/kilowatt hour. This was much higher in comparison to Bangladesh (7.3 cents), China (9.5 cents), India (9 cents), Sri Lanka (9 cents), and Vietnam (7 cents). The tariff was also high in case of gas which was at USD 8/

MMBTU in Pakistan compared with lower rates in Bangladesh (USD 3/MMBTU), China (USD 6/MMBTU), India (USD 4.2/MMBTU), and Vietnam (USD 4.5/MMBTU). See Waleed (2016) for a detailed analysis and perspectives from the local industry.

The textile industry also faced an overvalued exchange rate. For example, the Pakistani rupee during December 2013 and December 2015 witnessed an appreciation of 3 per cent against the US dollar. However, the economies in the region, Bangladesh, China, India, Sri Lanka, and Vietnam all witnessed a depreciation of 0.6, 5.1, 8.1, 9.3, and 5.6 per cent respectively. In view of the above-mentioned and the rising costs faced by the textile industry, Pakistan could not substantially increase the value of exports vis-à-vis competitor economies (Figure 1).

Figure 1: Regional Comparison of Textile Exports

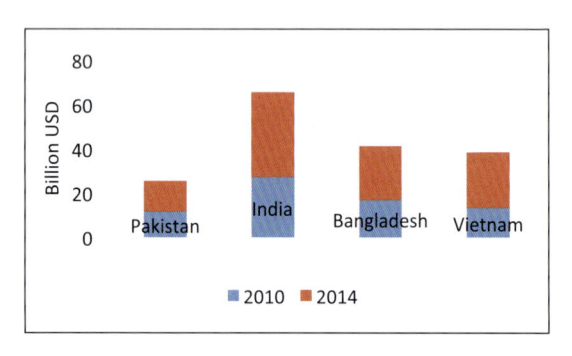

Source: UN Comtrade.

As the curve got steeper for local manufactures, the government also introduced new taxes and regulatory duties, which had economy-wide effects. The provincial governments in Khyber Pakhtunkhwa, Sindh, and Punjab introduced new taxes and levies which in turn altered exporters' own forecasts regarding their margins and working capital requirements. While Pakistani businessmen were complaining of double taxation at federal and provincial levels, the new goods and services tax law in India aimed at making processes easy for competitor firms, with new tax regime subsuming several forms of indirect taxes, and surcharges into a single tax levy. As argued earlier, tax and regulatory environment impact the cost of trading. This applies to both, cost of exports and imports. As Figure 2 exhibits, countries with lower costs of imports generally experience a higher export to GDP ratio.

Why has it been difficult to achieve competitiveness?

One of the answers to this question is Pakistan's excessive focus on short-term export stimulus and not addressing structural issues hindering competitiveness in real sectors. It is important to note that 'competitiveness' and 'growth in exports' do not carry the same meaning. It is argued in Ketels (2010) that a competitiveness-oriented approach may be conceptually more robust and that the effectiveness of an export-oriented approach may not be supported by the evidence. The author had also explained that competitiveness should be seen as the level of

Figure 2: Exports and Cost to Import

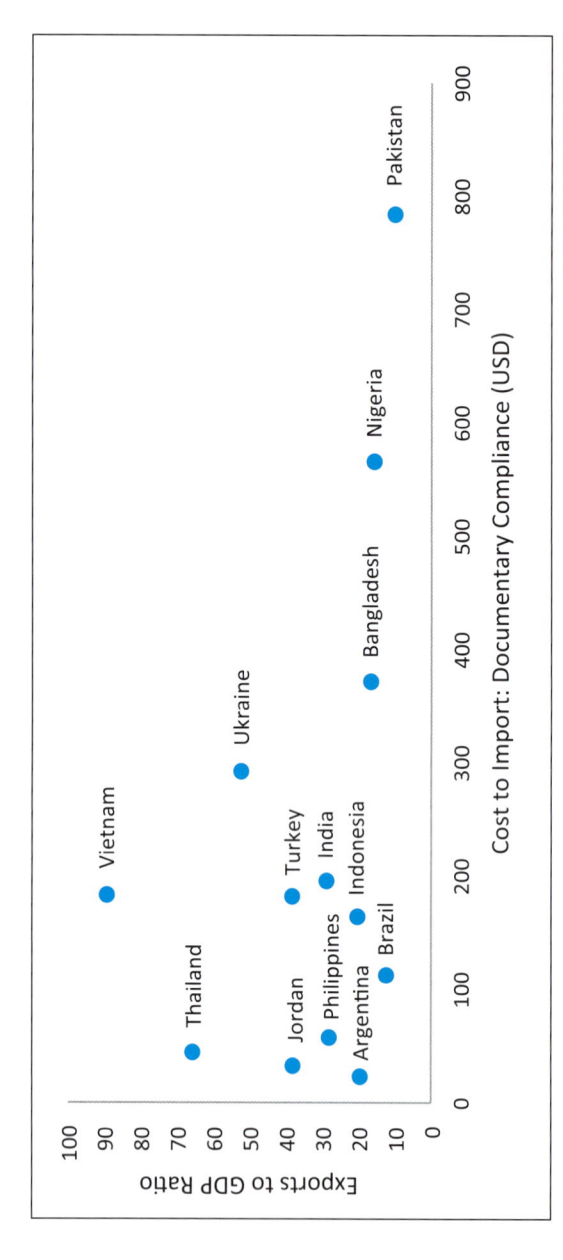

Source: World Bank Cost of Doing Business Indicators.

Note: As per World Bank, 'Documentary compliance captures the time and cost associated with compliance with the documentary requirements of all government agencies of the origin economy, the destination economy, and any transit economies. The aim is to measure the total burden of preparing the bundle of documents that will enable completion of the international trade for the product and partner pair assumed in the case study.' Source: World Bank, Doing Business Project (doingbusiness.org).

productivity that a firm may achieve given the underlying economic and business conditions. Competitiveness therefore is the structured approach for organizing business conditions and the relationships between such conditions, as also hinted in Porter et al. 2008. It may be argued that a focus on policies that increase competitiveness rather than exports per se may be more advantageous over the longer term period.

The recipes for achieving competitiveness are harder to deduce from econometric studies, which usually rely on three levels of indicators. There are firm-level characteristics: firm's size, location, and experience. Second, there may be indicators on firm behaviour which could include innovations, pricing policies, product line, outsourcing, licensing, quality certification, and use of technology. At a third level, there may be enabling environment indicators such as transport costs faced by the firm, customs procedures, access to utilities, access to physical premises, including land, level of competition, access to finance, exchange rate regime, tax and legal systems.

Such studies ignore an important focus on lessons from public choice theory i.e., the management of public decisions, governance of discretionary expenditures, and how the interaction between elected representatives, civil service, and citizens influences the way rules of production and trade are set. This approach may also help in answering why is it that trade liberalization reforms in Pakistan could not help declining competiveness, as indicated in Ahmad, N and Kalim, R (2014) and lack of diversification, explained in Yousaf, K M

(2009). Why was industrial policy not implemented to help the manufacturing sector move from low to high technology products over time? Similarly, another important question is why the exchange rate could not be effectively used in the recent past as a tool that supports export sectors.[20]

These questions have answers from public choice theory and most of these answers are interlinked. As McCartney (2015) argued that trade liberalization and exchange rate devaluation would have led to sustained gains in growth if: (a) it had been supported by a strategy to promote private investment, (b) loss in government revenues due to reduction in customs duties and other trade taxes had been compensated, and (c) if firms had upgraded their knowledge, skills, and technology.

The bilateral, regional, and multilateral agreements which were signed by Pakistan also had a political economy angle. Many were not negotiated on scientific basis using an appropriate level of rigour. However, these agreements that provide market access have the potential to influence competitiveness. The recipient country will need to position itself for receiving favourable outcomes. There now are conflicting conclusions from recent studies whether China-Pakistan FTA was useful for boosting competitiveness.[21]

Even in the case of Pakistan's market access through GSP Plus in EU markets, TRTA (2013) explains that the government needs to work extensively with the industry to improve the exporters' ability to comply with EU's regulatory framework on Sanitary and Phytosanitary Measures (SPS) and Technical Barriers to Trade (TBT) issues. There may also be sector-specific challenges which if not addressed can neutralize the potential benefit. For example, in the case of textile, the diversification towards synthetic and man-made fibre and moving towards value addition remains slow. In the case of seafood exports to EU, the suppliers still need to achieve compliance with EU's health and hygiene standards. In the case of footwear, exporters will require compliance in relation to labour and environmental standards.

The rampant informal trade in the recent past has also hurt competitiveness of formal enterprises. Such trade flows were allowed to happen between 2003–16 despite knowledge of government and security apparatus. As this merchandise was routed through Afghanistan, both countries did not have willingness (until August 2016) to set up trade gates and monitor inflow of goods.[22] Another reason for informal trade is high tariff rates and non-tariff measures. The list of items traded via Wagah-Attari border has a very narrow focus compelling some to use informal channels of trade. The government could increase the number of border openings (where trade may be allowed). Inaction on trade-related border management has hurt Sindh province the most, which remains the only province not able to trade with a neighbouring country through the land route.

The slow regional integration in both trade and investment terms may also have negatively affected competitiveness (Husain

2008). Political tensions with India and a volatile internal security situation may have prevented full implementation of regional agreements under SAARC. However, it is noteworthy that Pakistan could also not integrate fully with the ECO region where there were seemingly no significant political tensions. In this case a laxness of economic diplomacy and absence of long-term vision for regional integration is evident.

Nabi and Shaikh (2013) had also argued that lack of a supportive trade and transit policy, missing role of National Tariff Commission, weak investments in cross-border rail and road linkages, lack of trade facilitation (particularly customs clearance and warehousing), visa restrictions, and poor air connectivity with neighbouring countries is preventing integration of export oriented SMEs into organized production networks.[23] Pakistan was not able to source its imports from SAARC either (Iqbal et al. 2014). This in the longer run led to relatively larger costs for exporters using imported raw material and machinery.

The lack of a missing effective trade policy and possible lack of political understanding to give competitiveness agenda high priority was also discussed in TRTA (2015). The report advocates a focus on a less intrusive industrial policy (e.g., through revisiting or eliminating the role of Engineering Development Board in issuing concessionary statutory regulatory orders), and stronger Competition Commission of Pakistan (CCP). National competitiveness can also be helped through promotion of domestic commerce (see Haque and Waqar 2006) and trade in services (Kelegama 2009).[24]

A lack of trade policy which can effectively reduce trade costs for SMEs has played a role in discouraging potential exporters. An absence of a thick base of SMEs prevents intra-industry competition and in turn discourages export diversification (Reis and Taglioni 2013 and 2013b). A possible instrument for this could have been simplification of tariff code, and abolition of distortive regulatory duties. A focus on reducing sunk costs to start exporting could be possible through reduction in the fixed costs (e.g., land and building in SME export parks), and deepening of exporting relationships of the smaller firms outside of Pakistan.

Finally, despite a large urban and educated youth workforce, Pakistan continues to miss the opportunity to develop services sector exports. The lack of strategic coordination for services exports has given rise to gaps in data on services trade and lack of regularly published information and data as per international standards (TRTA 2015). There is no national inter-ministerial or inter-government mechanism to bring together relevant government organizations related to trade in services. The already announced tax incentives and business enterprise financing to facilitate services exporters has not been effectively launched and owned by the federal and provincial governments. The pre-2010 Service Export Development Strategy could not be put into action either. Pakistan's representation is often found missing in international services trade exhibitions.[25]

3. Constraints in the Implementation of STPF

The STPF 2015–18 sets a target of USD 35 billion by end-June 2018 and aims to improve export competitiveness, transition from a 'factor-driven' economy to 'efficiency-driven' and 'innovation-driven' economy, and also increase Pakistan's visibility in regional trade. To achieve these goals, the strategy aims to use key enablers including: (a) promoting competitiveness through quality infrastructure, improved labour productivity, access to electricity, gas, and other utilities, and essential technology development; (b) compliance to standards through greater convergence of local and international standards, protection of intellectual property, and dispute resolution mechanisms; (c) conducive policy environment through monetary policy, tax and tariff regime, industrial and investment policies; and (d) improving market access through multilateral, regional, and bilateral arrangements.

Given the above-mentioned enablers and the current challenges faced by export sectors, the strategy defines four key pillars of trade policy which include: (a) product sophistication and diversification through fiscal incentives, research, value addition, and branding; (b) enhanced levels of trade diplomacy; (c) restructuring and capacity-building of institutions responsible for trade promotion; and (d) trade facilitation through reduction in cost of doing business, standardization, and reduction in regulatory burden.

The STPF also has a section on short-term export enhancing measures. These measures are specifically focusing on: (a) products (Basmati rice, horticulture, meat and meat products, and jewellery), and (b) markets (Afghanistan, Iran, China, and EU). The focused support required by these sectors will include: warehousing and branding of Basmati rice, certification of citrus, meat, and rice. In the case of exports to EU, the government aims to support fisheries processing facilities, and certification of mango farms, and pack houses in compliance with SPS requirements.

The STPF has been criticized for not providing a bolder vision for competitiveness in Pakistan. More important is that the framework did not take account of the key issues due to which the previous STPF had failed to achieve its objectives. The implementation of trade policy continues to be undermined by the ad hoc sector-specific fiscal packages. For example, PML (N) in 2014–15 had announced a fiscal package for the textile industry.[26] The Budget 2016–17 also announced zero-rating for the textile sector. Notification is still awaited at the time of writing this chapter. During 2015–16, the government announced another fiscal package for the agriculture sector.

Critics also point out that the trade liberalization reforms under the previous policies were not accompanied by complementary reforms that could have ensured macro-level competitiveness, energy sector improvements, and lowering of regulatory burden on industry. After the Eighteenth Constitutional Amendment, several regulatory reforms (e.g., labour, tax, and environment) are now the responsibility of provincial governments. The trade policies fail to provide an inter-provincial and federal-provincial working mechanism that can coordinate regulatory reform. Experts have already advised the government to conduct a regulatory impact assessment (RIA) at both federal and provincial levels. This will provide updated estimates of transactions and compliance costs faced by businesses due to regulatory burden (which varies across sectors).

Since 2007 the previous and current governments have remained unable to consolidate the tax system across the country. According to the Board of Investment's own estimates, around 57 taxes, levies, and surcharges are faced by export enterprises in a single year.[27] Independent estimates vary however, but all point towards a large burden of tax documentation and filing. Simplification of tax regime faced by the exporters is also not a part of the STPF 2015–18.

The enabling infrastructure for exporters promised under previous STPF is still missing. An urgency for improvements in rail, road, port, and air connectivity promised in previous policies could not be created within the government. Smaller firms and potential exporters continue to face shortages of power and gas. While past and current trade policies realized this, however the energy deficit faced by the export sectors remains a key element in increased cost of doing business. Zero-rating of energy inputs as seen in neighbouring economies has not been allowed either. Most surprisingly, the current STPF completely ignores the discussion on how the government aims to leverage

China-Pakistan Economic Corridor (CPEC) and how this large Chinese investment in Pakistan could help trade-related infrastructure. The STPF is also missing linkages with Pakistan Vision 2025, formulated by the Planning Commission.

The lack of enabling infrastructure has even hurt the agriculture sector exports. The government continued various forms of untargeted subsidies which benefited the large-scale producers, usually servicing domestic demand. Pakistan lost Geographical Indication Bid for Basmati rice to India. The farming community was also not effectively helped in adoption of new technologies in various steps of the supply chain. Resultantly, Pakistan's rice exports plummeted in two key markets i.e., China and Iran. The producer price for rice also decreased in competitor economies such as India, making it more price competitive. It is understood that Pakistan is also struggling to match the overall level of per capita agriculture subsidies allowed in India.

The access to export financing and borrowing for working capital still remains inadequate. The borrowing conditionalities and application process for new and potential exporters is still cumbersome. Several potential exporting entities are not able to comprehend the due diligence procedures of formal financial institutions. Despite low levels of interest rates, export sectors continue to face liquidity crisis due to inability of the financial sector to lend on account of working capital and export financing.[28] A large part of trade and trade-led investment is compromised due to the lack of regional cooperation in the banking sector. Despite claims in previous trade policies, effective banking channels have not been established with India, Iran, and Central Asia. Banks have not been willing to increase long-term export financing, especially in case of trade with Central and South Asia region.

On marketing of 'Made in Pakistan', an independent evaluation of programmes and projects by Trade Development Authority of Pakistan (TDAP) is still missing. The organization remains unable to scale up exhibitions in China, EU, and US where Pakistan has formal market access arrangements. Even knowledge about US and EU's GSP Plus and provisions for SME exporters has not been disseminated. Help desks for engagement with the private sector are missing. The outreach activities by MoC and TDAP are usually reactive and ignore the various future challenges and opportunities on which business associations require high-frequency and interactive analysis. Examples of such behaviour include lack of knowledge among exporters regarding possible implications of Brexit, Trans Pacific Partnership, and Regional Comprehensive Economic Partnership.

MoC could also not fulfil its promise to persuade FBR for putting in place a tariff rationalization plan. The promised lowering of tariffs during SAARC ministerial meetings has not been delivered. Instead, regulatory duties were increased to meet revenue targets promised with International Monetary Fund (IMF). The earlier promised working group to assess the non-tariff measures faced by importers in Pakistan has also not been formed. While this is preventing import-savings, FBR and MoC remain unable to mitigate loss to the government's revenue and competitiveness of local producers due to weak border management which in turn is a cause of informal and illegal imports into the country.

The trade diplomacy efforts are being extended and new countries are being approached for bilateral trade agreements. However, this is being done without a comprehensive *ex ante* evaluation. It is also perceived by the local business community that partners of existing FTAs now have very different interests compared to when the previous FTAs were signed. For example, in the case of Sri Lanka, it is more interested in comprehensive implementation of SAFTA. Pakistan is currently more interested in enhancing bilateral arrangements. This could hinder future negotiations and revisions in FTA. Similarly, in the case of China, Pakistan's edge over competitor exporters to China has long vanished. Except for some agricultural products, nearly all imported items of China from ASEAN countries are at zero per cent customs duty. This has been the case since 2011 which renders Pakistan's exportable surplus uncompetitive in China despite the FTA. A key element of trade diplomacy should also be to secure long-term business visas for Pakistani exporters. Such a clause should be part of the future trade agreements.

The SBP was also not able to provide support to dwindling exports, through prudent exchange rate management. The currency remained overvalued during 2013 and 2016. Due to the ongoing IMF programme, Pakistan was unable to introduce a dual exchange rate which according to some experts, may have favoured exporting sectors (e.g., in the form of a more favourable rate for export sector inputs). The literature is however divided on the use and effectiveness of dual exchange rate regime.

Finally, STPF is silent on how important inter-ministerial and inter-governmental working relationships will be to deliver on the targets of export growth. Several past tax reform commissions have suggested to form working groups of: MoC and FBR (on tariff rationalization, non-tariff measures, and informal trade); MoC and MoF (on timely release of EDF); MoC and SMEDA (on designing and implementing capacity-building programmes for SME exporters); MoC and SBP (on prudential regulations that bind financial institutions to offer a portion of overall lending to new exporters); and MoC with provincial governments on implementation of conventions promised under EU GSP Plus conditionalities.

4. Reforms to Boost Competitiveness

Some constraints to the implementation of trade policy in Pakistan were outlined above. We also emphasized the importance of RIA which can help in prioritizing key policy corrections at federal and provincial levels. Until such RIA is made available, we offer the following policy recommendations, mainly related to governance of trade policy and the required institutional capacities to deliver the targets under STPF. These recommendations are a result of extensive qualitative assessment explained in the introductory section.[29]

Restructuring of MoC for better delivery of STPF objectives

It is now being proposed by various government and non-government quarters that MoC needs to focus on its core tasks as defined in Government of Pakistan's Rules of Business 1973. This implies for example shedding the responsibilities of managing public sector entities such as State Life Insurance Corporation—an entirely unrelated subject. This can then allow the ministry to focus strictly on the objectives of STPF. The restructuring of this ministry can also make way for a more targeted utilization of the EDF. According to the business community, this fund for incentivizing exports should be protected for using towards promotion of 'Made in Pakistan' brand and supporting the marketing efforts of the private sector. The trade related assistance to Pakistan can be clubbed with the EDF to provide support to 'GSP Plus Support Mechanism Unit' at MoC. This unit in turn can provide technical and capacity-building services to the provincial governments and business associations. MoC should also pursue an expansion of EDF and expand funding lines through other revenue sources of the federal government.

The restructuring of MoC should receive internal ownership as MOC has hinted during recent years its inability to accomplish core responsibilities under the realm of export promotion.[30] With growing grievances of the exporting community, the medium-term goals for the ministry should be to focus on developing the appropriate in-house skill-set to achieve objectives under

STPF. A key in-house deficit is that of research and evaluation. We are therefore proposing a permanent research and evaluation unit for this purpose to provide timely analytical evidence for informed policymaking.[31] The key analyses demanded by the ministry (around which necessary capacities need to be augmented) include quantitative and qualitative analysis on FTAs, SROs, and impact of regional agreements by Pakistan's competitors.

The MoC Yearbook 2015–16 explains that the ministry has the mandate to assess and provide actionable advice to the other government entities on both foreign trade and domestic commerce. The ministry is also tasked to look into how to increase the productivity in the real sectors with a view to ultimately boost exports. Given this vastly spread mandate, it is therefore recommended that a working group, comprising high-level sectoral experts be formed to look into possible merger of the Ministry of Textile Industry, and the Ministry of Industries and Production, with the Ministry of Commerce. A possible move in this direction, besides saving the recurrent expenditure on these ministries will result in improved coordination on already announced export promotion measures under STPF and Textile Policy (2014–19). At the time of writing this chapter, the Federal Minister for Commerce is also holding the charge to look after the Ministry of Textile.

A key missing unit within the MoC is strategic communications. This aspect has immense significance as the ministry often struggles to develop a common ground with the provincial governments, private sector, and consumer associations. A dedicated strategic communications unit at the MoC can also help in collecting feedback from the stakeholders and incorporate the same in trade policy revisions.

RESTRUCTURING OF CABINET COMMITTEE ON EXPORTS AND PRODUCTION

The reforms towards enhancing competitiveness require a 'whole of the government approach', it is therefore necessary that the Prime Minister should take sincere ownership of this agenda and convene the meetings of the Cabinet Committee on Exports and Production (CCEP) on priority. However, it is also proposed to restructure the CCEP and only have six key members. Agenda-specific members can also be co-opted for a particular meeting if there is a need. The six members should include the Federal Ministers for Commerce, Finance, Textile, Petroleum and Natural Resources, Water and Power, and the Governor, State Bank of Pakistan. After the restructuring of CCEP the current inter-ministerial committee, headed by the Commerce Minister, may be abolished to avoid any multiplicity of directives.

CCEP should meet on a monthly basis, and receive a detailed presentation by MoC on monthly export numbers, perspectives of relevant business associations, consumer groups, and development partners. A frequent meeting of this committee will also reduce the bureaucratic discretion in the implementation of export promotion measures, and also enable a more objective accountability of institutions responsible for the revival of exports.

To ensure linkages with provincial governments, it is recommended that the Federal Secretary, Ministry of Commerce should meet with all Chief Ministers in the provinces and debrief them regarding the meetings of CCEP and desired support from the provincial governments, within a week after CCEP meeting. This will also be an opportunity for the Chief Ministers to inform the Secretary regarding any specific facilitation required from the federal government with regards to production and exports.

The above-mentioned inter-ministerial and inter-government approach is essential for implementation of no duty no refund scheme, announced in Budget 2016–17.[32] The Committee referred to above will ensure implementation of the scheme. Furthermore, MoC being the secretariat for the committee should have the task of appraising the members regarding ongoing and anticipated challenges facing Pakistani exports. For example, Brexit and the aftermath require a policy response from Pakistan so that the trading interests with EU are not negatively influenced.

The committee's oversight is also important in the context of the review of EU GSP Plus scheme and to ensure that Pakistan is able to ratify conventions required by EU. The compliance with EU's framework on SPS and TBT will also be an essential component in the review of GSP. The committee will seek progress on the National Certification Centres aimed to facilitate SPS and TBT compliance, and the work of TDAP, responsible to increase its frequency of exhibitions in EU. The committee should communicate a clear message to all relevant departments and provincial governments that the renewal of market access will be contingent upon the favourable findings of GSP reviewers. An unfavourable review could affect Pakistan's negotiations with bilateral trade partners in the context of FTAs.

Supporting improved competitiveness of SMEs

Some short-term measures that can help the private sector should focus on reducing the trading costs, especially for the SMEs.[33] The federal government can start from support towards the necessary product compliance and standard certifications required to enter and remain in a foreign market. Usually the costs and procedures towards these certifications are time consuming and expensive for SMEs and act as a barrier to their entry in the export markets.

SMEs have also complained of higher inland transportation costs vis-à-vis competitor economies. The Ministry of Finance, using EDF, can incentivize containerisation via railways for SMEs in export sectors. EDF can also be used to cover partial costs of transportation e.g. transit levies especially in the case of trade with regional neighbours and transit trade. This could be a time-bound incentive. The investments under CPEC and Central Asia Regional Economic Cooperation (CAREC) programme can also be aligned with this goal.

The small and medium scale exporters have weak access to policymaking quarters and hence suffer from a deficit of information on incentives available under STPF. It is therefore recommended to expedite outreach and implementation of other measures announced under STPF, aimed at enhancing knowledge and capacity of current and potential exporters. The collaboration of the Chambers of Commerce and Industries may be invited for outreach programmes.

Equally important is to focus on gaps in capacities of SMEs that may be preventing product sophistication. A key intervention could be to use the available EDF for creative industries. These industries have recently attracted interest of foreign firms, who see potential in Pakistan's copyright-based industries including local arts, crafts, drama, and film productions. A focus on this industry will involve modest costs on the part of the government given the indigenous knowledge and skills already available with communities. The creative industries can also help in the promotion of a soft image for Pakistan.[34]

On the same topic, in 2015, it was reported that creative industries contribute 4.5 per cent and 3.7 per cent in Pakistan's overall output and employment respectively.[35] The local arts and fashion schools have produced innovative graduates with a larger share of women. These graduates are now seen across visual and performing arts industry. The local craftsperson and publishers are also gradually moving towards greater value addition and more sophisticated technologies. The provincial governments specially stand to gain through supporting local communities in boosting production in creative industries. Targeted export promotion measures (through provincial governments) for communities with indigenous knowledge, can help these prospective exporters realize their potential.

The MoC is also receiving recent support from the World Bank (Pakistan Trade and Investment Policy Programme), USAID (Pakistan Regional Economic Integration Activity), and European Union (Trade Related Technical Assistance Programme) in improving capacity in the key areas of trade policy and diplomacy. It is proposed that the support received by MoC through development partners should be strictly focused at: (a) export industries with highest concentration of SMEs and potential new exporters, and (b) creative industries with vast potential for value addition, as well as product and geographical diversification of the export basket. With improved government revenues and a larger public sector development programme, it is expected that the flow of resources to the MoC will improve.

Engagement between provincial governments and local exporters

The provincial governments for promotion of local exports will need to establish low-cost and internationally accredited testing laboratories. The aspects around accredited testing can also be undertaken in collaboration with internationally reputed labs, with proven record of technology and knowledge transfer. This will further strengthen the compliance with quality standards in line with the requirements of importers.

Furthermore, provincial governments will need to help the local exporters with expanding vocational and technical training centres in line with the desired export demand. Support for such capacity-building is already available under EU's assistance to Pakistan. The management of some of the existing vocational and technical training centres, for sub-sectors in which Pakistan has a comparative advantage, could be considered for transfer to private or non-governmental entities having experience in providing skilled workers with recognized certifications.

Deeper agreements for greater regional integration

The revised regional and bilateral trade agreements should go beyond the usually negotiated market access. In order to ensure trade-led investments, these revisions can now focus on specific clauses allowing investment in goods and services, and increasing the list of services for trade. Regional agreements could also carry provisions for transit arrangements for people, goods, and natural resources (e.g., gas and electricity) and one-stop border posts, which can reduce travel time for goods, and expedite the establishments of supply chains across the region. MoC should initiate the next round of trade negotiations with

India and offer deep forms of integration at the next heads of state SAARC Summit. This will also help in expediting the overall integration process under SAFTA. Similar revisions to Pakistan's preferential trade agreement with Iran is long due.[36]

It is also important to learn from the past that implementation of existing FTAs has been delayed due to lack of coordination between MoC and FBR. It is therefore recommended that MoC should take timely initiatives for regular and official liaison with FBR and the private sector at the revision and negotiation stages of trade agreements. FBR also needs to have a senior-level position, preferably equivalent to a member FBR, responsible to liaise with the MoC and act as a focal person for removing any hurdles in the implementation of existing and future FTAs. The MoC should include FBR and business association representatives in meetings with counterparts from partner countries to negotiate framework agreement for FTAs. During the same meetings, reputed policy research think tanks may be invited as observers and also to provide technical support. It is anticipated that FBR's presence during the various rounds of negotiations will help in ensuring a better understanding of inter-ministerial perspectives.

Comprehensive package to support SMEs cost of doing business

In order to help the private sector in moving away from a subsidy-led growth model, it is important that the federal government should help in providing a comprehensive technical support package for SMEs. Some mention of this is already in the STPF which aims to provide greater knowledge-based inputs to the value addition in SME sector. We also propose supporting the SMEs in making their production processes more energy efficient through timely energy audits. Any costs incurred by the federal government will be offset by future (tax) revenue gains.[37]

The two-slab tariff structure faced by the manufacturing sector has resulted in the smaller entities facing a relatively greater average industrial (tariff) rate. This anomaly needs correction. The NEPRA determined rate should ideally be capped for a pre-announced period in consultation with the small business associations. NEPRA may also review the incidence of energy tariffs through a detailed quantitative and economy-wide evaluation.

Furthermore, refinance under the Export Finance Scheme (EFS) needs to be made more inclusive. SBP's independence should be respected by the federal government in implementing this measure. MoF will need to be more accommodative in creating space for increasing loanable funds under EFS. The current enterprises benefiting from EFS predominantly include the large-scale entities. There is a strong case for widening the coverage of EFS.

A significant portion of both EFS and long-term financing facility (LTFF) may be dedicated for SMEs and new exporters. The larger exporter entities with greater credit worthiness should be incentivized to access the commercial banks for their borrowing requirement, especially during times when interest rates are historically low. The EFS and LTFF for agriculture and manufacturing sector's plant and equipment may be made available at Treasury Bills and PIB rates respectively. For small-scale exporters, the documentation under EFS will need to be rationalized in order to bring down the costs of accessing these facilities. The federal government can also increase the credit worthiness of small scale exporters through time-bound guarantees to the banks.

Upgrading technology in warehousing is also long due and particularly important for Pakistan's crop sector, livestock, and fisheries exports. There has been a demand for a common bonded warehousing. If allowed by the government, this facility may even be completed without financial contribution from the public sector. There are reputed global enterprises that will be willing to perform this function on build-operate-transfer basis. Several of these entities are providing warehousing services in the region and ports close to Pakistan. Second, having foreign firms to perform this function will also lead to much desired knowledge and technology transfer in the warehousing sector.

Administrative measures for curtailing informal and illegal trade

Research studies e.g., Ahmed et al. (2015) highlight the existence of Pakistan's informal trade with Afghanistan, China,

India, Iran, and the United Arab Emirates. During recent years the losses to the exchequer due to these informal flows have increased. Furthermore, the manufacturing sector has complained regarding the unfair competition posed by the informal flow of merchandise, which usually avoids the full payment of customs and other levies.

It is therefore proposed to form an inter-ministerial group including MoF, Ministry of Interior, Ministry of Commerce, FBR, and SBP. The group should come up with the short to medium term measures for formalizing the currently informal flows of inward and outward trade. A couple of immediate steps that can be taken by the group include: extending the integrated border management systems to land routes which currently do not have this facility; monitoring by security authorities on a monthly basis, of any gaps in the trade-related border management systems; expediting the development and complete implementation of Integrated Transit Trade Management System (ITTMS); acquiring land to expand the operations of ITTMS; bolstering the security apparatus at all land route trading gates (particularly at Chaman and Torkhum), deputing officials of FIA, customs, and intelligence agencies at the gate complex; and fencing of all border areas through which illegal trade can take place. A successful model that can be replicated for other land route border posts is the one now seen at Wagah-Attari border.[38]

Tariff reform can also help curb informal trade. A high incidence of smuggling is particularly witnessed in tradable commodities which face higher relative tariffs, para-tariffs, non-tariff barriers, and transit fee. Higher tariffs also curb the diversification of the export basket. We discuss this in more detail below.

Reform of tariff regime faced by exporting sectors

Since 2007 the earlier gains in trade liberalization have been reversed through high tariff and non-tariff barriers in the country. Currently, customs duties are seen as a key pillar of the revenue growth plan, which is creating an anti-export bias. Several recent studies recommend a revenue-neutral, tariff rationalization plan.[39] This reform can start with the gradual removal of regulatory duties, which were imposed during 2014–15 as part of revenue targets agreed with the IMF. In the second step and after a careful assessment, tariffs faced by the five export oriented sectors should be phased out. This step should also include reducing the dispersion seen across average nominal tariff rates. In the third step, in line with recent studies, a move towards a uniform tariff regime should be encouraged. It has already been demonstrated that a uniform tariff regime will increase government revenues.

It is recommended that a committee co Chaired by the Federal Secretary, MoC, and the Chairman, FBR should formulate a time bound-plan for review and approval of the Cabinet Committee on Exports and Production (CCEP). While doing so, the committee should be helped by a team of experts who can offer analysis based on a tax incidence study, as to how such a tariff rationalization plan can be made revenue-neutral, efficient, and fair.

Facilitation to integrate with regional and global supply chains

Pakistani businesses, particularly in agriculture and manufacturing sectors, remain unable to integrate with foreign supply chains due to: (a) high levels of protection to traditional sectors which incentivize a focus on monopolizing the local demand, and (b) distortions in the tax and regulatory regime which make exports, particularly new types of exports, uncompetitive in price terms. The federal and provincial budgets in 2016–17 increased the scope of indirect taxes at a time when the exporting sector was faced with the introduction of transport and transit levies, gas cess, and infrastructure cess.

As the regulatory easing will require an ownership from the provinces, therefore it is proposed that MoC should review the tax and regulatory issues curtailing the enterprise-level capacities and give a detailed presentation at each NFC Award Monitoring Committee, chaired by the Finance Minister. The committee can then brainstorm institutional arrangements for removal of such constraints on regional and global supply chain integration.

Enhanced trade facilitation which includes simplification of trade procedures, can also help in creating regional production networks involved in parts and components trade, with reduced inventories and delivery periods. Harmonization of tariff codes with the Central and South Asian economies can reduce tariff related transactions and compliance costs.

It is proposed that a separate section for trade facilitation should also be allowed in the future FTAs after careful review by the parties involved. Specific trade facilitation measures can complement other arrangements within the FTA e.g., rules of origin, non-tariff barriers, SPS measures, services, and investment provisions.[40] There is an absence of evidence-based evaluation regarding the role of provincial governments in trade facilitation. Several key issues related to commercial trade and transit, including security of cargo, are now under the jurisdiction of provinces. A detailed study may be commissioned by MoC on this subject and findings disseminated to all provincial governments. It is important that this study should be survey-based, account for firm-level responses, and be conducted by local experts.

A market gap analysis can help in identifying some low-end value chains in services sectors where Pakistan can readily participate due to a young labour force, with low wage rate, and having proficiency in frequently demanded skills in services sectors. Once skills and technology transfer take place, then Pakistani firms can easily catch up with more value added services.[41]

In order to facilitate the above-mentioned, market-gap and demand analysis (particularly with reference to regional markets e.g., China and Central Asian economies), will be required. A technical team at MoC will need to gather data, in line with international definition and standards, on regional services trade. As the governance of services trade in the country is fragmented across various government bodies, therefore it is recommended that an inter-ministerial and inter-governmental working group may be convened by the MoC on a quarterly basis, to discuss challenges in the way of promoting regional value chains in services sectors. The composition of this working group may be approved by the CCEP, which should also receive updates regarding proceedings of this committee. FBR can inform this working group regarding the incentives provided by the government to promote IT-based services in Pakistan.[42] Similarly, SBP can streamline the business enterprise financing through scheduled financial institutions that can facilitate services sector exports.

The Services Export Development Fund proposed under Strategic Trade Policy Framework 2009–10 should now be fully rolled out in consultation with sector experts. This will also help in the implementation of the under formulation Service Export Development Strategy at MoC. Similarly, facilitation from TDAP will be required to enhance Pakistan's presence in services trade exhibitions held abroad. If TDAP currently lacks capacity, a new unit focusing on promotion of services exports may be raised.

INSULATING THE EXPORT-ORIENTED SECTORS FROM ENERGY COSTS AND STOPPAGES

While this matter of high energy costs deserves a separate discussion, it is noteworthy that energy costs in the country remain high, despite a period of low global energy prices. This is attributed to expensive fuel-mix used in power generation, high operational costs incurred by the power generation companies and gas distribution companies, various types of taxes and levies imposed on energy usage, and technical losses in both power and gas sectors for which surcharges are levied. Several of these issues will require a medium to longer term energy reform plan. However, there are some short-term measures which could provide respite to the exporters.[43]

First, until the time a downward trend in Pakistan's exports is not reversed, federal and provincial governments may reduce their rates of taxes and levies on oil, power, and gas sectors. NEPRA and OGRA should ensure that the reduced prices faced by the generation, transmission, and distribution sector is in fact transferred to the end consumers—both bulk (manufacturing sector) and residential consumers. Similarly, the energy tariff structure is prone to misuse, at least in the small-scale manufacturing sector, as bulk and residential consumers face different rates. Second, a time-bound priority should be given in the allocation of power and gas to export-oriented sectors. Third, a gradual move towards equalizing the energy tariffs with a basket of peer economies should be considered.

Updating research on export competitiveness

There remains a need to update data and information on three key aspects of Pakistani exports, which in turn can help in better planning of future policy interventions. First, an urgent study is required at the federal and provincial level to assess the regulatory regime faced by agriculture sector exports. The entire supply chain in agriculture exports suffers from a lack of coordination for which a new evaluation may propose mechanisms keeping in view the post 18th Amendment governance framework. The coordination between federal, provincial, and sub-province administrations will be of immense importance in implementing any plans to improve competitiveness in the crops sector, livestock, or fisheries. For example, we observe that while issues of fertilizers, seeds, and pesticides remain the responsibility of the federal government, issues of impurities in these farm inputs and their subsidized supply remains in the domain of provincial governments. A two-tier regulation leads to several distortions which have not been evaluated in recent years.

Second, a detailed audit of trade documentation and processing is required with clear guidelines on how the relevant authorities can reduce time and cost overruns faced by traders. A good start by MoC could be to use elaborate information under World Bank's Cost of Doing Business database to negotiate with provincial governments a more conducive trading regime. MoC should use the findings of this audit to persuade CCEP towards advising the provincial governments to conduct RIA every three years, in line with the cycle of STPF.[44]

Third, an updated study on the formulation and effective implementation of services export strategy is required. In the current services export framework there are few working linkages across various relevant ministries, federal, and provincial board of investment, and accreditation authorities. Such a study will aim to propose the various vertical and horizontal working arrangements that are needed to implement the services export framework.

MAINSTREAMING GENDER IN POLICIES FOR COMPETITIVENESS

Only recently MoC and the World Bank in Pakistan have initiated some work on this subject. Initial policy recommendations advocate for a fixed percentage of the EDF for women-led export enterprises—having women as Chief Executive, or more than 50 per cent women in the senior management cadre. A fixed quota should also be ensured by TDAP, incentivizing women's participation in national and international trade exhibitions. Those women-led enterprises, which have been set up during the past 36 months, and have yet to realize economies of scale, should be eligible for special discounts for reservation of exhibition centres and stalls.

To help organizational development and capacity-building, SMEDA may customize training programmes in consultation with MoC, FPCCI, PBC, and reputed think tanks working on women entrepreneurship. These trainings should have a focus not just on improving internal operations but also on helping to market exportable surplus outside of Pakistan. In order to gauge the demand for such a capacity-building exercise, MoC, through CCEP, may advise Pakistan Bureau of Statistics to modify all existing survey tools to help in the collection of gender disaggregated data by industry, occupation, education, and region on self-employed and wage-employed women.

MoC will also need to approach the SBP for making appropriate amendments to the relevant prudential rules that can bind the financial sector to find and lend to women borrowers, who in turn may require customized financial products.

5. Conclusion

Pakistan, like several other developing economies, has a history of pursuing import substitution and safeguarding only the interests of large exporters in select sectors. The exporters from the SME segment are often neglected. We have, in this chapter, tried to explain several reasons for such behaviour. These reasons include the missing capacity to implement trade policy, measures, and instruments for boosting across-the-board competitiveness.

Going forward, the federal government will need to focus on implementation of STPF and reconsider the working arrangements at the federal and provincial level for bringing down the cost of doing business. The implementation of measures under trade facilitation is long overdue. A critical component here is the desired improvements in trade-related infrastructure. This can now also benefit from investments being made under CPEC, and transit trade cooperation under CAREC. MoC can better deliver on the governance of trade policy if it sheds the non-core tasks identified in this chapter.

The federal government will require more focused support from bilateral and multilateral development partners in improving the country's business image, optimally utilizing GSP and other available market access arrangements, ensuring compliance with SPS and TBT, strengthening dispute resolution mechanism, and putting in place policies and measures which can help Pakistani firms to become part of regional supply chains. For this, MoC may prepare and revise on a biannual basis, a matrix for seeking technical and financial support from development partners. A Partners' Trade Group could be chaired in rotation by leading bilateral and multilateral partners in Pakistan. The MoC will also need to institutionalize methods and mechanisms for internal monitoring and evaluation of its operations. A permanent evaluation unit with capacities in quantitative methods and skills in negotiating trade agreements can be a good way forward.

The private sector will also need to get better organized. There are high quality and experienced exporters who can play a mentoring role for SMEs and their back-end suppliers. To some extent this has happened in Sialkot, Gujranwala, and Sukkur. The Chambers of Commerce and Industries in other cities may like to follow the assimilation of knowledge and skills in these cities through better and more organized business associations.

References

Acharya, L. and Marwaha, A., *India-Pakistan Economic Relations*, Federation of Indian Chambers of Commerce and Industry, 2012.

Ahmad, M., 'Improving Regional Trade to Support Pakistan's Economic Growth', *The Lahore Journal of Economics*, 19: pp. 461–69, 2014.

Ahmad, N. and Kalim, R. 'Implications of Export Competitiveness, and Performance of Textile and Clothing Sector of Pakistan: Pre and Post Quota Analysis', *Pakistan Journal of Commerce and Social Sciences*, Vol. 8 (3), 696–714, 2014.

Ahmad, N. and Kalim. R, 'Implications of Export Competitiveness, and Performance of Textile and Clothing Sector of Pakistan: Pre and Post Quota Analysis', *Pakistan Journal of Commerce and Social Sciences*, 2014.

Ahmed, V. and Ahmed, S.S. Trade—low hanging fruit in Af-Pak ties. Daily Times, 27 May 2017.

Ahmed, S. et al., 'Trade agreements between developing countries: a case study of Pakistan-Sri Lanka free trade agreement', *Pakistan Institute of Trade and Development*, 2010.

Ahmed, V et al., 'Informal Flow of Merchandise from India: The Case of Pakistan.' Editors: Taneja, N., and P. Sanjib; *India-Pakistan Trade: Strengthening Economic Relations*, Springer, 2015.

Ahmed, V., 'Capacity-Building of Human Resources and Services Sectors: Improving Education and Technical Skills, Using Innovation and ICT.' Report titled *Building Knowledge-based Economy in Pakistan* by Islamabad Policy Research Institute, 2016.

Ahmed, V., 'Contours of Pakistan's Power Crisis', Editor: Z. I. Cheema, *Energy Crisis and Nuclear Safety and Security of Pakistan.* Strategic Vision Institute, 2013.

Ahmed, V. A, Suleri, Q., Wahab, M. A., Javed, A., *Informal Flow of*

Merchandise from India: The Case of Pakistan, Editors: Taneja, N. and S. Pohit, India-Pakistan Trade. Springer, 2015.

Ahmed, V. et al., 'Public Infrastructure and Economic Growth in Pakistan: A Dynamic CGE-Microsimulation Analysis.' Editors, Cockburn, J. et al., *Infrastructure and Economic Growth in Asia.* Springer, 2013.

Ahmed, V., Suleri, A. Q., Wahab, M. A., and Javed, A., *Informal Flow of Merchandise from India: The Case of Pakistan,* Springer, 2015.

Ahmed and Batool., 'India-Pakistan Trade: A Case Study of the Pharmaceutical Sector.' Working paper 293, Indian Council for Research on International Economic Relations, 2014.

Ahmed and Batool., 'India-Pakistan Trade: Perspectives from the Automobile Sector in Pakistan.' *Working paper* 293, Indian Council for Research on International Economic Relations, 2015.

Akhtar, N., Zakir, N. and Ghani, E., 'Changing Revealed Comparative Advantage: A Case Study of Footwear Industry of Pakistan', *Pakistan Development Review*, 47 (4), pp. 1–17, 2008.

Akhtar, W. et al., 'Export Competitiveness of Pakistani Horticultural Products', *Pakistan Journal of Agriculture Research,* Vol. 26 No. 2, 2013.

Akhtar, W., Sharif, M. and Shah, H., 'Competitiveness of Pakistani Fruits in the World Market', *The Lahore Journal of Economics*, 14: 2 (Winter 2009): pp. 125–33.

Akhtar W., Sharif. M. and Akmal, N., 'Analysis of Economic Efficiency and Competitiveness of the Rice Production System of Pakistan's Punjab', *The Lahore Journal of Economics*, 12:1, pp. 141–53, 2007.

Akmal, N. et al., 'The Structure and Competitiveness of Pakistan's Basmati Rice Exports', *Asian Journal of Agriculture and Rural Development,* Volume 04, Number 04, April 2014.

Akmal, N. et al., 'The Structure and Competitiveness of Pakistan's Basmati Rice Exports', *Asian Journal of Agriculture and Rural Development*, Vol 4 (4), pp: 304–12, 2014.

Akram, A., 'Pak-SAARC Intra-Industry Trade', *PIDE Working Papers*, 93, 2013.

Amir, S. S. and Hyder, D., *An Assessment of the Pakistan-Sri Lanka Free Trade Agreement*, The Pakistan Business Council, 2015.

Atif, R., Haiyun, M. and Naveed, Z., 'Patterns and Dynamic Positioning of

Pakistan's Revealed Comparative Advantage in Services Trade', *European Online Journal of Natural and Social Sciences*, Vol. 5, No. 1, pp. 220–33, 2016.

Bashir, F., Andleeb, F. and Fatima, R., 'Intra Industry Trade, Fiscal Policy and Terms of Trade of Pakistan: A Long Run Analysis Using ARDL Technique', *Pakistan Journal of Humanities and Social Sciences* (PJHSS), Jan–June 2016, Volume 4, No. 1, Pages 1–16.

Chatterjee, B. and George, J. (2012) Consumers and Economic Cooperation: Cost of Economic Non-cooperation to Consumers in South Asia. CUTS International.

Competition Commission of Pakistan, 'Competition Impact Assessment Report on the Automobile Industry of Pakistan', Government of Pakistan, 2013.

De, P., Raihan, S. and Ghani, E., 'What does MFN trade mean for India and Pakistan? *Policy Research Paper* 6483, World Bank, 2013.

De, Prabir, *Strengthening Regional Trade and Production Networks Through Transport Connectivity in South and South-West Asia,* UN Economic and Social Commission for Asia Pacific, 2014.

GoP 'Framework for Economic Growth, Planning Commission,' Government of Pakistan, 2011.

Haque Ul, N. and Waqar S. I. (2006) editors: Domestic Commerce—The Missing Link. Ministry of Commerce, Government of Pakistan.

Husain, I., 'Pakistan's Export Competitiveness in Global Markets' A Paper Presented at the Seminar on Export-Led Growth Strategy. Export Promotion Bureau, Lahore. Available online at www.iba.edu.pk, 2008.

Hussain, S. S. and Ahmed, V., 'Experiments with Industrial Policy: The case of Pakistan', Sustainable Development Policy Institute, *Working Paper* 124, 2012.

Iqbal, N., Ghani, E., Din, M., 'Pakistan's Dependency on Imports and Regional Integration', *The Lahore Journal of Economics,* 19: SE September 2014.

Kardar, Shahid, *South Asia—Intraregional Cooperation: The Way Forward,* Asian Development Bank, 2011.

Kaur, S. and Nanda, P. An Analysis of Actual and Potential Exports of

Pakistan with SAARC Countries: A Panel Data Analysis. Pakistan Journal of Applied Economics, Vol. 21 Nos. 1 & 2, (69–91), 2011.

Kayani, U. J. and Shah, S. A., *Non-Tariff Barriers and Pakistan's Regional Trade*, International Growth Centre, 2014.

Kelegama, S. (2009) editor: Trade in Services in South Asia: Opportunities and Risks of Liberalization. SAGE Publications.

Ketels, C., *Export Competitiveness: Reversing the Logic*, Harvard Business School, weblink: http://hbswk.hbs.edu/item/export-competitiveness-reversing-the-logic, 2010.

Khalid, A. R., *The Economic Contribution of Copyright-Based Industries in Pakistan*, World Intellectual Property Organization, 2010.

Mamnoon, D., Paracha, S. A., Mughal, H. and Ayesha, A., *Pakistan's Trade Competitiveness and Complementarities in South Asia,* Pakistan Institute of Trade and Development, 2011.

McCartney, M., 'The Missing Economic Magic: The Failure of Trade Liberalization and Exchange Rate Devaluation in Pakistan, 1980–2012', *The Lahore Journal of Economics* 20: SE (September 2015): pp. 59–86.

Memon, N., Rehman, F. and Rabbi, F., 'Should Pakistan Liberalize Trade with India against the Backdrop of the FTA with China? A Comparative Advantage Analysis for the Manufacturing Sector', *The Lahore Journal of Economics*, 19, pp. 327–48, 2014.

Nabi, I. and Shaikh, N., 'Pakistan Business Council: Regional Trade Report', *International Growth Centre, Working Paper*, 2013.

Pant, M. and Pande, D., 'India-Pakistan Trade: An Analysis of the Pharmaceutical Sector', *Indian Council for Research on International Economic Relations (ICRIER), Working Paper* No. 275, 2014.

PBC, *Preliminary study on Pakistan and China trade partnership post FTA,'* Pakistan Business Council, Karachi, 2013.

Porter et al., 'Moving to a New Global Competitiveness Index', *Global Competitiveness Report 2008/2009,* 2008, Geneva: World Economic Forum: 2008.

Porter, Michael, Takeuchi, E. H. and Sakakibara, M., *Can Japan Compete?,* Basic Books and Perseus Publishing, New York: 2000.

Pursell, et al., *Pakistan's trade policies: future directions,* International Growth Centre, 2011.

Quddus, M. A. and Mustafa, U., 'Comparative Advantage of Major Crops Production in Punjab: An Application of Policy Analysis Matrix', *The Lahore Journal of Economics*, 16:1, pp. 63–94, 2011.

Reis, J. G. and Taglioni, D., 'Determinants of Export Growth at the Extensive and Intensive Margins: Evidence from Product and Firm-level Data from Pakistan', *Policy Research Working Paper* 6341. World Bank, 2013.

Reis, J. G. and Taglioni, D., 'Pakistan: Reinvigorating the Trade Agenda.' *Policy Paper Series on Pakistan* PK 15/12, March 2013' World Bank, 2013.

Riaz, K., Jansen, H. and Malik, S., 'Spatial Patterns of Revealed Comparative Advantage of Pakistan's Agriculture Exports', *Pakistan Economic and Social Review*, Volume 50, No. 2, pp. 97–120, 2012.

Sahab, S. and Mahmood, M. T., 'Comparative Advantage of Leather Industry in Pakistan With Selected Asian Economies', *International Journal of Economics and Financial Issues*, Vol. 3, No. 1, 2013, pp.133–39, 2013.

Shabbir, S. and Ahmed, V., 'Trade & Transit Cooperation with Afghanistan' *Working Paper* 153, Sustainable Development Policy Institute.

Shabbir, S. and Ahmed, V., 'Trade with Iran,' *Criterion Quarterly*, December 2015.

Shah, A, Mehboob, I. and Raza, S. H. 'The Impact of the Exchange Rate Fluctuations on Pakistan's Export Sectors: An Empirical Analysis Based on the Sectorial Data', *Asian Economic and Financial Review*, Vol 2 (6): 658–77, 2012.

Shahbaz, M. and Leitao, N. C., 'Intra-Industry Trade: The Pakistan Experience', *International Journal of Applied Economics*, 7(1), pp.18–27, 2010.

Shahzad, K., 'An RCA Analysis of Textile and Clothing in Pakistan, India and Bangladesh', *The Lahore Journal of Economics*, 20:1, pp. 157–68, 2015.

Tahir, A. et al., 'An Overview of Tomato Economy of Pakistan: Comparative Analysis', *Pakistan Journal of Agriculture Research*, 25 (4), 288–94, 2012.

Taneja, N., Ray, S. and Pande, D., 'India-Pakistan Trade: Textiles and Clothing' *Indian Council for Research on International Economic Relations* (ICRIER), 2014.

Trade Related Technical Assistance Programme, 'Policy Reform Agenda for Promotion and Development of Trade', European Union, 2015.

Trade Related Technical Assistance Programme, 'Enhancing Pakistan's

Trading Benefit from the Proposed EU GSP Plus Scheme', European Union, 2013.

Trade Related Technical Assistance Programme, 'Strategy for Export Development of Services for Pakistan', European Union, 2014.

UK Trade & Investment Department, 'Doing business in Pakistan: Pakistan trade and export guide', Weblink: http://ow.ly/3M9M302s5oF, accessed on 22 September 2015.

Waleed, H., 'Competitiveness on regional matrix: Textile exports Drop', *Business Recorder*, 16 September 2016.

World Bank 'Impact of China-Pakistan FTA on Pakistani Exports', Unpublished, 2016.

World Bank, 'Mainstreaming Gender in Trade', Unpublished, 2016.

Yasmin, B. and Altaf, S., 'Revealed Comparative Advantage of Carpets and Textile Floor Covering Industry in Pakistan, India and China', *Journal of Economic Cooperation and Development*, 35, 4, 113–34, 2014.

Yousaf, K. M., 'Towards a Vision 2030 and the Challenges of Openness to Pakistan's Economy: Export Competitiveness of Pakistan's Manufacturing Sector, Past Trends and Future Prospects', *Institute of Developing Economies, Japan External Trade Organization, V.R.F Series No. 443*, 2009.

Zaheer, R., Nizami, U. and Niazi, M. F., '31 Years Intra-Industry Trade of Pakistan', *European Journal of Business and Management*, Vol. 5, No. 31, 2013.

Notes

1. This is not a comprehensive list as we will discuss later in this chapter.
2. Processes for initiating or expanding a business activity, permits for construction, procedures in getting access to electricity, gas, and other necessary infrastructure.
3. The existence of these issues may also help in explaining why Pakistan could not derive benefit from GSP Plus status provided by the US and EU and bilateral and regional trade agreements with other trade partners.
4. McCartney (2015).
5. This Dutch disease-like phenomenon is also explained in Ahmed et al. (2013).
6. According to legislation on EDF, this funding window is to be utilized for capacity-building of exporting entities, subsidizing delegations and sale missions

going abroad including participation in trade exhibitions, establishment of offices abroad of the Federation of Pakistan Chambers of Commerce and Industry, research and development in the private sector, strengthening of Pakistan Trade Offices abroad, and support to export services.

7. This also resulted in the reversal of the trade liberalization reforms undertaken during the period 1996–2003.
8. In the form of a negative list and relatively high tariffs.
9. For example, issues related to overlapping administrative powers in taxation system can be seen in 2015 Tax Reform Commission Report.
10. See Competition Commission of Pakistan (2013) and (2015).
11. On evaluations of past FTAs see: Ahmed, S. et al. (2010) and PBC (2013).
12. As per the World Bank 'the RCA indicates whether a country is in the process of extending the products in which it has a trade potential'. For details: http://wits.worldbank.org/wits/wits/witshelp/Content/Utilities/e1.trade_indicators.htm.
13. The establishment of a Leather Board is also being suggested by some quarters.
14. Also see Quddus M A and Mustafa U (2011).
15. Also see Bashir F et al. (2015), Ahmed et al. 2015, De Prabir (2014).
16. Also see Ahmed et al. (2015).
17. Khalid, A. R. (2010) makes a case for export potential of copyright based industries in Pakistan.
18. More recently deterioration in political relations is hampering trade cooperation (see Ahmed and Ahmed 2017).
19. Pakistan saw deterioration in its position on World Bank's Cost of Doing Business ranking.
20. As explained in Shah et al. (2012) currency depreciation can improve short-term growth of Pakistani exports.
21. In the case of China-Pakistan FTA, PBC (2013) had suggested revision to this agreement. The study proposed that one way to gain greater access to the Chinese market can be attained if concessions are equal to or more than those given to other suppliers of similar products, such as those available to exporters from ASEAN regions. Getting Pakistani products in larger quantities in China can strengthen possibilities of future supply chains.
22. Ahmed et al. 2015 estimated for 2013 that the inflow of goods arriving from India could be in the vicinity of USD 1.8 billion annually. This adversely affected Pakistan's auto, pharmaceutical, and textile sectors.
23. On studies specific to India-Pakistan and Pakistan-Sri Lanka trade see Acharya, L. and Marwaha, A. (2012) and Amir, S. S. and Hyder, D. (2015) respectively. For India-Pakistan's case also see De et al. (2013). For intra-regional trade

in South Asia see Ahmad, M. (2014), and Kardar (2011). On trade with Afghanistan and Iran, see Shabbir, S. and V. Ahmed (2015b) and Shabbir and Ahmed (2015). On non-tariff barriers in the region see Kayani, U. J. and Shah, S. A. (2014).

24. The report also highlighted the high regulatory burden on export sectors (e.g., tariff structure, sales tax cascading), complexity of tax code, lack of export insurance mechanisms, missing awareness about Trade-Related Aspects of Intellectual Property Rights (TRIPS).
25. Pakistan's representation was missing from recent such exhibitions e.g., World Medical Tourism and Global Healthcare Congress, International Transport Forum's Summit, and Global E-commerce Summit.
26. Could not be fully financed by the government due to a resource constraint.
27. Interview of Chairman, Board of Investment, Government of Pakistan on Capital TV, dated 7 July 2016.
28. The liquidity is already under strain as FBR refuses to release refunds within the promised timelines.
29. The author acknowledges the efforts of Mr Shahid Kardar and Mr Wajid Rana in reviewing and providing comments and inputs on some key reforms mentioned in this section.
30. Ghumman, M., 'Commerce Minister Criticizes Import Tariff Regime' http://www.brecorder.com/top-stories/0/59084/Business Recorder, 10 July 2016.
31. This unit should work under the supervision of the permanent Economic Consultant already in place at MoC.
32. Exporters still have concerns that in the past, input adjustments were an integral part of the GST regime. However, after the budget 2016–17, zero rating difficulties, failure in getting GST adjustments on inputs like ginned cotton, packaging, and provincial GST paid by the services sector, may result in delayed refunds.
33. Includes costs related to manufacturing, marketing, transportation, warehousing, and distribution.
34. This recommendation is in line with Khalid (2010).
35. UK Trade & Investment Department (2015).
36. As discussed earlier, future trade agreements should allow for long term visas for Pakistani business persons particularly current exporters.
37. A deeper cost and benefit analysis of this recommendation can be commissioned by MoC.
38. Measures such as integrated border management, scanners, and dry ports can be made available at all land border trading posts. Similarly, a timely establishment of, and autonomy to Land Port Authority, can streamline processes across

regulatory agencies, including immigration, terminal operator, security, customs, quarantine, banks, shipping agencies, and freight forwarders.

39. GoP (2011) and Pursell et al. (2011).
40. As part of the WTO Doha Development Agenda meeting, Pakistan had agreed to be part of the negotiations on trade facilitation which will include: (a) increasing the transparency of trade regulations; (b) simplifying, standardizing, and modernizing import, export, and customs procedures; and (c) improving the conditions for transit.
41. Relevant institutions within the federal government have been advised on a long-term strategy for improving regulatory environment for services sectors, see Ahmed, V. (2016).
42. According to our consultations with the IT and telecom industry representatives, domestic taxes need to be rationalized for ensuring export competitiveness.
43. Ahmed, V. (2013).
44. SECP's 2014 Annual Report had asked the federal government to make regulatory impact assessment exercise a regular feature. Ideally this assessment update should come before each year's Finance Act is updated.

Chapter 6

Economic Corridors, Investment Diplomacy, and Transit Cooperation

1. Brief Context

After attending Track-II meetings for around a decade (since 2005), I realized during 2016 South Asia Economic Summit in Dhaka, how feelings towards Pakistan were fast evolving in the region. I will leave the India-Pakistan relationship out of this discussion and look at the rest of wider South Asia's perceptions and feelings towards Pakistan. My definition of wider South Asia includes China and Iran, currently not members of South Asian Association for Regional Cooperation (SAARC).[1]

At the start of the previous decade, the geographically smaller and least developed countries in South Asia looked towards Pakistan for balancing the power of India in SAARC. Around the mid of this decade and with faster economic growth in India, these states realized the potential gains that could accrue by having trade and investment cooperation with India. This led to an inner tension within these states, regarding how to get closer to India and yet keep their reservations alive given the baggage of history in this region. During the same time, their perceptions regarding Pakistan changed and it was felt that Pakistan had its own problems grounded in law and order and regional security issues before which it could be seen, once again, as a regional power that could balance India's position in the region to some extent. Such a perception greatly reduced Pakistan's relevance for the geographically smaller states in wider South Asia.

By the end of 2016, Pakistan was entirely out of the new geopolitical developments in South Asia. Bangladesh, Bhutan, India, and Nepal went ahead with sub-regional cooperation framework for trade and connectivity. India and Sri Lanka initiated negotiations on Economic and Technology Cooperation Agreement and had already signed bilateral free trade agreement. Afghanistan and Iran were inviting investment from both China and India. Both felt that due to the fragile security situation in Pakistan, the connectivity arrangements between Afghanistan, Iran, China, and India may bypass Pakistan. Subsequently, China initiated a cargo train arrangement, which started bringing agricultural goods to Afghanistan via Central Asia. India also found a route to Afghanistan through Iran's sea ports.

While Pakistan was gradually falling behind the cooperation moves between other SAARC countries, several Central Asian countries and Iran expressed their interest in piggybacking on the proposed Chinese investment in China-Pakistan Economic Corridor (CPEC), however they did not have a clear idea regarding how soon the benefits of CPEC would materialize in integrating Pakistan with the region. Therefore, Pakistan's cooperation during 2014–16 with the region essentially remained limited to signing ceremonies for various CPEC projects and trans-boundary energy agreements such as Tajikistan-Afghanistan-Pakistan-India gas pipeline, Iran-Pakistan gas pipeline, and electricity transmission under Central Asia-South Asia power project (CASA-1000) initiative.

It was around this time that India and some members of SAARC framed Pakistan as an irritant in the regional integration process and pulled out of the proposed Islamabad, Heads of SAARC States meeting, which was due to be held during October 2016. While Afghanistan and India wanted this action as a move to isolate Pakistan and highlight security issues which Pakistan should first address before integrating with the rest of the region, the geographically smaller member countries in the region were clear that Pakistan's relevance for the foreseeable future had declined and they must look into ways in which they could meaningfully engage with India.

As a Pakistani economist, my own assessment was that a perception of wider South Asian community, rooted in the above-mentioned developments, is certainly not painting a good image for trade and investment prospects in Pakistan. A country having volatile relations with neighbours will always be the least preference for local and foreign investors. A plausible way forward, as being advised by some analysts in Pakistan was: (a) to counter propaganda from India regarding Pakistan being a country keeping the region unstable (Khan 2016), (b) winning minds and hearts in wider South Asia, including India, once concrete actions to address security concerns of our neighbours, including Afghanistan, China, and Iran had been addressed, and (c) making decent technical and financial aid contributions in geographically smaller and land-locked South and Central Asian economies, particularly Afghanistan, in order to showcase and offer Pakistan's endowments in science and technology, including defence technology.

While the above-mentioned is a medium to longer term agenda, and best left to the diplomats representing Pakistan, one major short term-measure that could enhance intraregional economic interdependences in wider South Asia is enhancement in trade, transit, and investment cooperation (Rehman and Ahmed 2016). This will have a two-pronged influence: first, Pakistan's business community will get a chance to participate in value chains in agriculture, industry, and services across the wider South Asia. They will act as ambassadors of Pakistan with strong ability to change perceptions in the region. Second, enhanced people-to-people interaction will give a two-way chance for countries in the region to see how Pakistan is breaking away from the past.

This paper builds on two arguments. First, Pakistan has an opportunity to use assistance provided by China to the benefit of its own people and the people in wider South Asia to forge interdependencies and win over the prevalent pessimism and non-cooperation in the region. Second, strategic location of Pakistan can enhance its relevance for the region if economic corridors inside the country result in regional value chains for the benefit of business community and consumers of the region. To seize both these opportunities, major reforms related to trans-boundary energy cooperation, transportation, trade, and transit are required. This chapter points towards some of these much needed reforms.

Our methodology in this chapter has relied on five in-depth interviews with thought leaders across each of the wider South Asian (as defined above) countries. In total, forty interviews were conducted. Second, we also relied on focus group discussions (FGDs) held on the sidelines of the Eighth South Asia Economic Summit, held in Islamabad during December 2015. In total, 4 FGDs were organized having participation of private sector, academia, and policymakers. Third, inputs were also received from senior-level government and non-government participants during moderated sessions (at the summit) on the regional cooperation potential of Pakistan. The officials debriefed regarding minutes of recent meetings on CPEC, Central Asia Regional Economic Cooperation (CAREC), Afghanistan-Pakistan Joint Economic Council, and related regional cooperation forums discussed later in this chapter.

The next section takes stock of some ongoing regional integration efforts, and how Pakistan may benefit through timely improvements in the quality of infrastructure. Section 3 then explains how benefits of CPEC can be offered to neighbouring economies and ultimately create enhanced interdependencies. This is followed by a discussion on how Pakistan's energy crisis can be helped through proactive energy diplomacy. Before concluding we argue in favour of expansion of transit trade and its potential gains for the private sector and local communities in the western provinces of Pakistan. We point towards reforms for increasing transit trade with Afghanistan, China, and Iran.

2. Making Pakistan Regionally Relevant

This section makes an argument that regional connectivity has the potential of increasing Pakistan's economic relevance across the region and beyond. An effective and efficient connectivity can be achieved through continuous improvements in road, rail, port, and aviation infrastructure, supplemented by a conscious effort to become part of the regional and bilateral transit transport agreements and accession to international conventions. Pakistan's relevance in the region as a reliable partner in supply chain can further increase if timely harmonization of trade, customs, and transport regulatory framework is undertaken, along with trade facilitation reforms and removal of any tariff and non-tariff barriers to trade faced by own and the region's private sector.[2]

After the global financial crisis in 2007, Asia was termed as a key driver of economic recovery as it was able to grow and maintain high levels of domestic demand. Much before this period, Asia started to benefit from intra-regional integration and there was a clear conclusion that more open and connected Asian economies were able to grow faster than those which were less integrated in regional value chains. Alongside the integration of markets for goods and services, effort towards physical connectivity within the region also increased. An example of this is the Asian highway network, and linked economic corridors in East and South Asia (Woodburn et al. 2008).

Pakistan, due to its ongoing political frictions with Afghanistan and India, and a not so proactive economic cooperation with Iran, has struggled to make itself relevant in Economic Cooperation Organization (ECO), South Asian Association for Regional Cooperation (SAARC), and regional trade agreements such as South Asian Free Trade Area (SAFTA) and ECO Trade Agreement (ECOTA). While a bilateral agreement between China and Pakistan to pursue physical connectivity under China-Pakistan Economic Corridor (CPEC) programme is encouraging, however the progress on connectivity with other countries in the wider region remains sluggish.

Let us first take the case of ECO. Pakistan's business community has been demanding for greater rail linkages with ECO member countries including: Afghanistan, Azerbaijan, Iran, Kazakhstan, Kyrgyz Republic, Pakistan, Tajikistan, Turkey, Turkmenistan, and Uzbekistan. Most of these countries had already signed Transit Transport Framework Agreement (TTFA) for providing access to inward and outward merchandise of land-locked countries in the ECO region. Apart from rail, the agreement also covers provisions dealing with the road connectivity, inland water transportation, motor vehicles, third party insurance, customs control, and a Transit Transport Co-ordination Council (TTCC) for smooth implementation of policy decisions.

The Islamabad-Tehran-Istanbul (ITI) rail and road corridors also need to be operationalized. The rail operations which had initially been started are on a halt currently. This is attributed to technical difficulties which are currently being addressed by the Railway Authorities in Pakistan, security issues (e.g., in the case of Iran-Pakistan freight service), and low volumes of trade activity, in turn not allowing the authorities to recover costs. The lack of intra-regional and inter-industry trade is a reflection of Pakistan's manufacturing and services sector not being integrated with the region. Perhaps a revised PTA with Iran and FTA with Turkey could help stimulate trade volumes and demand for ITI rail operations.

Due to political tensions with Afghanistan, Bangladesh, and India, Pakistan has also not been proactive in connectivity related agreements within SAARC. During the 2014 SAARC Heads of States Summit, held in Kathmandu, Pakistan excused itself from signing SAARC Motor Vehicles Agreement and demanded more time for review. This prompted Bangladesh, Bhutan, India, and Nepal (BBIN) to move forward with a sub-regional agreement. The operations under BBIN sub-regional arrangement started in 2016.

Pakistan has also not been able to extend timely support on the ongoing infrastructure projects, aimed at strengthening transit and trade cooperation with Afghanistan. Pakistan had promised support for reconstruction in Afghanistan in 2003 under the Technical Assistance Programme initiated by the Ministry of Planning, Development, and Reforms. Under this programme

NESPAK started work on 24 infrastructure projects out of which several are still ongoing.

To sustain and promote bilateral trade between Afghanistan and Pakistan, the first phase of Torkham-Jalalabad road (75 km) was completed in 2006. With further help from the National Highway Authority the 222 km long Kabul-Torkham-Jalalabad road was completed in 2011. Phase II of the same project, Torkham-Jalalabad Additional Carriageway was started in January 2007. More than 50 per cent of the project had been completed until November 2008 before it was suspended. The Government of Pakistan is now making efforts to remobilize the contractor.

The National Highway Authority had also proposed a Peshawar-Kabul motorway under which the PC-II (i.e. survey and feasibility study) has already been prepared for carrying out the feasibility study and design. Both the countries are also looking into an additional transit-trade corridor through Bannu-Ghulam Khan-Khost road and rail link. In the road sector, Afghanistan has also offered the CAREC corridor from Pakistan to Tajikistan. In 2015 both Afghanistan and Pakistan had completed the feasibility study of the new link road between Jalalabad and Torkham. International financing agencies have offered a loan of USD 1.5 million for its construction.

Any delay in the above-mentioned projects can also mean a loss of political capital currently needed to bring energy to Pakistan through Afghanistan. For example, CASA-1000 is considered a landmark initiative in terms of the beginning of economic cooperation between Central and South Asia. The agreement has been signed by Kyrgyz Republic and Tajikistan from Central Asia, and Pakistan and Afghanistan from South Asia. It is expected that it will lead to an investment of US $1 billion. It will be helpful for exporting countries i.e., Kyrgyz Republic and Tajikistan in terms of export earnings, and it will help Afghanistan and Pakistan to overcome power supply shortages. Hence, a win-win situation is expected from this initiative.

The CASA-1000 project more specifically includes: (a) 500 kV AC line from Datka (in the Kyrgyz Republic) to Khudjand (477 kilometers away, in Tajikistan), (b) 1300 megawatt AC-DC convertor station at Sangtuda (Tajikistan), (c) 750 kilometer high voltage DC line from Sangtuda to Kabul (Afghanistan) to Peshawar (Pakistan), (d) 300 megawatt convertor station at Kabul (with import and export capability), and (e) 1300 megawatt DC-AC convertor station at Peshawar.

Similarly, another immensely important energy project, Turkmenistan, Afghanistan, Pakistan, and India (TAPI) gas pipeline project aims to bring natural gas from the Yoloten-Osman field and adjacent gas fields in Turkmenistan to Afghanistan, Pakistan, and India. The feasibility study funded by ADB, proposed a design of the project that includes a 56-inch diameter 1,735 km pipeline with design capacity of 33 billion cubic meters of gas per year from Turkmenistan through Afghanistan and Pakistan up to Pakistan-India border. The capital cost of the project was originally estimated at USD 3.3

billion, however, it was revised to USD 7.6 billion, taking into account change in prices of steel and construction costs. As per the revised estimate, the first flow of gas may start from 2018.

Pakistan's own infrastructure deficit is also preventing the country from becoming part of the regional supply chains (World Bank 2015). The infrastructure quality indicators highlighted in Table 1 have contributed to less than potential trade with the region and missed transit opportunities (Ahmed et al. 2015).

Table 1: Transport Infrastructure: A Cross-country Comparison

Country	Quality of Roads Rank	Quality of Roads Score	Quality of Railroad Infrastructure Rank	Quality of Railroad Infrastructure Score	Quality of Port Infrastructure Rank	Quality of Port Infrastructure Score	Quality of Air Transport Infrastructure Rank	Quality of Air Transport Infrastructure Score
Bangladesh	113	2.9	75	2.5	93	3.6	121	3.2
India	61	4.1	29	4.1	60	4.2	71	4.3
Pakistan	77	3.8	60	2.8	66	4.1	79	4.1
South Africa	34	5.0	42	3.6	36	4.9	14	5.9
Turkey	36	4.9	53	3.1	53	4.5	33	5.3
China	42	4.7	16	5.0	50	4.5	51	4.8
Thailand	51	4.4	78	2.4	52	4.5	38	5.1
Kenya	60	4.2	72	2.6	63	4.2	49	4.8
Poland	76	3.8	51	3.1	67	4.0	83	4.1
Indonesia	80	3.7	43	3.6	82	3.8	66	4.4

Source: Global Competitiveness Report 2015–16.

Rank/140

Score: 1-7 (best) 1 = extremely underdeveloped—among the worst in the world; 7 = extensive and efficient—among the best in the world] | weighted average.

Box 1: Governance of Infrastructure in Pakistan

Pakistan: Quality of Infrastructure

Indicator	Ranking
Quality of Air Transport Infrastructure	79
Quality of Port Infrastructure	66
Quality of rail road Infrastructure	60
Quality of roads	77
Quality of Overall Infrastructure	98

Pakistan: Logistics Performance

Indicator	Score
Timelines	3.5
Tracking and Tracing	2.9
Logistics Competence	2.8
International Shipments	2.9
Infrastructure	2.7
Customs	2.7
Overall LPI	2.9

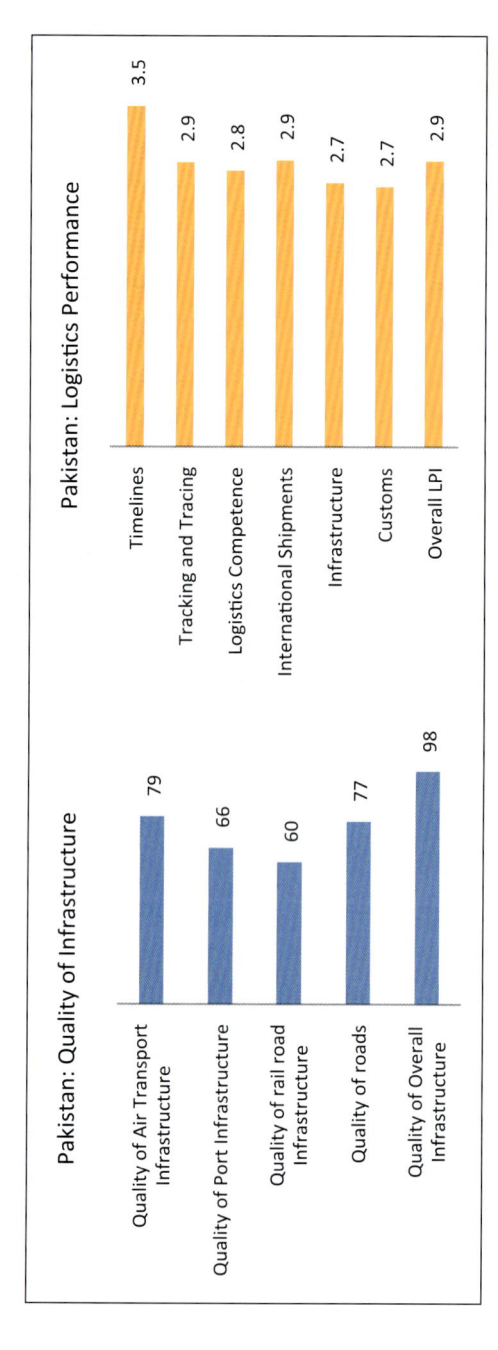

Note: For quality of infrastructure, data labels provide ranking out of 139 countries. Source: Global Competitiveness Report 2015–16. Logistics performance scores given in data labels range between 1 to 5; very low = 1, and very high = 5, Source: World Development Indicators, 2016.

Even in the case of logistics performance the efficiency of transport and trade facilitation processes has room for improvement (Box 1). The Logistic Performance Index (LPI) measures the challenges and opportunities a country faces in the performance of trade logistics and ranks each country out of a total sample of 160 countries. In 2016 Pakistan ranked 68 compared to India at 35 and China at 27. Pakistan was placed at the same rank in 2007. A comparative analysis of LPI explains that Pakistan has been relatively slow to improve efficiency of customs and border management clearance, ease of arranging competitively priced shipments competence and quality of logistics services, ability to track and trace consignments, and the frequency with which shipments reach consignees within scheduled or expected delivery times.

Despite of the above-mentioned gaps, Pakistan has pursued China and multilateral partners for technical and financial help toward improving trade and transport related infrastructure. China also realizes that the rail and road links through Pakistan will provide freight access to the Arabian Sea, Middle East, and European countries. China has pledged investment to expand the Gwadar Port and invest in linking this port through Pakistan's existing and new rail and road connections with the Chinese border (Haider 2005). The land route links between Gwadar, Khunjerab, and Urumqi save Chinese merchandise almost seven trading days in comparison to the current route via Shanghai and Malacca Straits. For example, there is a reduction of 4,300 miles, if goods from China are coming from Urumqi passing through Gwadar and Dubai to reach London. Likewise, from Dubai to Shanghai via the Indian Ocean, the distance is almost three times more if compared with Dubai to Khunjerab. A trial run of freight via CPEC road link reached Gwadar during November 2016. The containers were sent off to Europe and Middle East.

Plugging the infrastructure gaps in Pakistan will be important in view of the country's desire to become an active player in the CAREC programme, which aims at promoting development through regional cooperation and integration in order to accelerate economic growth and poverty reduction. Ten countries are participating in this programme, which is being supported by multilateral development partners. The countries include Afghanistan, Azerbaijan, China, Kazakhstan, Kyrgyz Republic, Mongolia, Pakistan, Tajikistan, Uzbekistan, and Turkmenistan. The Asian Development Bank is serving as secretariat to this project. Priority areas of the project include transport, trade facilitation, trade policy, and energy.

Since 2001, the programme has mobilized over $22.4 billion in the transport, trade, and energy infrastructure investments. To guide the CAREC Programme in the next decade, ministers of all CAREC member countries endorsed the CAREC 2020—a strategic framework for the Central Asia Regional Economic Cooperation Programme. CAREC 2011 was formed at the 10th Ministerial Conference in Baku, Azerbaijan in November 2011. A year later, to ensure effective and timely achievement of the strategic objectives, the 11th CAREC Ministerial Conference held in Wuhan, China in 2012, endorsed the Wuhan Action

Plan. The action plan emphasized three themes: operational priorities under each sector, the CAREC Institute Work Plan 2013–17, and the Transport Facilitation Action Plan.[3] According to a performance appraisal of the CAREC programme, transport and energy sector indicators seem on-track while trade facilitation and trade policy related indicators call for expedient action.[4]

3. Leveraging CPEC for Regional Integration

CPEC has the potential to increase Pakistan's economic relevance. Such corridors can be game changers only if they lead to improved trade, investment, job-creation for the poor, and people-to-people engagement. It is these interdependencies that can ensure future peace inside and outside of Pakistan (Samad and Ahmed 2014).

A seamless transit in the region will also boost intra-regional trade. Furthermore, the Strategic Trade Policy Framework 2015–18, formulated by the Ministry of Commerce, points out that benefits from investments in connectivity will result in shared gains for the region once Pakistan undertakes: (a) resolution of pending issues in Afghanistan-Pakistan Transit Trade Agreement (APTTA), (b) negotiation and implementation of trilateral Afghanistan, Pakistan, and Tajikistan Transit Trade Agreement, (c) implementation of Transports Internationaux Routiers (TIR) Convention, and (d) reactivation and effective implementation of Quadrilateral Transit Trade Agreement (QTTA) among Pakistan, China, Kyrgyz Republic, and Kazakhstan.

While there is significant political will towards implementation of CPEC projects and a strong follow-up by Chinese state-owned enterprises, however Pakistan's own capacity to design, manage, and reform existing and new infrastructure is far from satisfactory. This was a key lesson seen in the evaluation of unsuccessful National Trade Corridor Project in 2005. The civil service reforms which can help enhancement of design and management capacities have still not been undertaken. This laxness in improving governance of infrastructure also led to less than anticipated outcomes of bilateral trade agreements.

Such agreements were also unable to increase on a sustained basis the engagement between private sector and its associations in the region. A sense of frustration was expressed by the President of SAARC Chamber of Commerce and Industries at the inaugural of 2015 South Asia Economic Summit in Islamabad. This lack of private sector engagement adversely affects the rate of return of infrastructure projects. Another evolving opportunity for Pakistan for increased private sector engagement, if supported by the public sector, is under the CAREC programme. This is only possible if Pakistan is able to identify and put aside the constraints which resulted in weak progress towards promises made during past ECO and SAARC interactions. A supplementary opportunity comes from Iran, which has recently expressed its interest in integrating with CPEC. Iran is also an important partner in CAREC which has in total six corridors, including the three routes to the Arabian Sea i.e., Karachi, Gwadar, and Bandar Abbas.

It will also be important to link CAREC and CPEC with other regional connectivity arrangements. This includes QTTA, which if implemented in a timely manner, can enhance transit and provide cross border movement for merchandise of neighbours, and reduce the number of trans-shipment and intermediary stopovers. Furthermore APTTA should be extended to a maximum number of Central Asian countries and this will require Pakistan to fulfil its promise of building the promised infrastructure including additional transit trade corridors and the Peshawar-Kabul Motorway. In this regard, it has already been over a year since January 2015 that the Government of Tajikistan had requested Afghanistan and Pakistan to extend APTTA so that Dushanbe could secure alternate routes for its merchandise via Pakistani seaports. As of now there is no progress on this subject given the deterioration in political relations between Afghanistan and Pakistan.

On the eastern borders, for its own interest and exercising soft power, Pakistan should express its interest in making use of South Asia Motor Vehicle Agreement to connect with the corridors under South Asia Sub-regional Economic Cooperation (SASEC). These road corridors are also part of the Asian Highway-2 (connecting Nepal and Bangladesh via India), and the Asian Highway-48 (connecting India, Bhutan, and Bangladesh). In due time, and once political tensions ease, Pakistan should also look into benefiting from the Bangladesh-

China-India-Myanmar (BCIM) Corridor by transporting goods through this road access via Indian highways that connect Wagah Border (Aiyer 2014). Over time BCIM could also get connected with Quadrilateral National Highways in India which will enable the merchandise to flow between India's western seaside to the ports in Gujarat and Mumbai.

Again, once political tensions ease and if Pakistan is in a position to offer India transit facility for goods passing through Pakistan going to Afghanistan, Iran, and Central Asia, India could then be asked to provide access to the North-South-East-West Corridor. This corridor runs from Srinagar to Kanyakumari and has another highway running from Silchar to Porbandar.

As of now Pakistan has apprehensions that there may be elements in some neighbouring countries, which may be involved in sabotage activities against CPEC projects. Pakistan also feels that such elements try to exploit the youth and population in impoverished areas of Pakistan, possibly through financial and material support. If this is true, then it is important to consider that regional corridors can become peace corridors if local communities have a stake in such projects and the poorest of the poor in the impoverished areas see tangible benefits.

In this regard, local communities, particularly from Balochistan, Federally Administered Tribal Areas, and Gilgit-Baltistan need to be politically and economically engaged. Both regions are currently confused about their gains from CPEC and they should be assured regarding direct economic gains. Moreover, they should also receive regular official communication regarding special economic zones and energy generation and transmission projects—long demanded by Balochistan's business community. Confidence-building at the community level will also require the provincial governments in larger provinces particularly Punjab and Sindh to assure the smaller provinces that gains and prosperity resulting from infrastructure growth and connectivity will be shared. Such assurances could take the form of changes to the National Finance Commission and the award mechanism.

A key outcome of the 15th Ministerial Conference of CAREC in Islamabad was in the form of the highest political leadership in Pakistan committing to position the country to play a major role in enhancing economic cooperation between member countries across four areas of CAREC i.e., energy, trade policy, trade facilitation, and transportation. This political resolve now needs to be backed by strengthened capacities and reform of institutions involved in each of these four areas at the federal and provincial government levels.

4. Energy Diplomacy

At the time this chapter was written, Pakistan was facing a shortage of 5000MW in the power sector. This is being attributed to policy and regulatory uncertainty, technical losses, electricity theft, and over time increasing cost of generation, transmission, and distribution (Ahmed 2014). In quantitative terms, the Pakistan Economic Survey explains that power sector deficits trim the annual growth of national income by at least 3 per cent.

Despite a large-scale effort to diversify energy supplies in the country, Pakistan remains dependent on imported petroleum crude and products—now amounting to a third of the overall imports of Pakistan. It is due to this heavy dependence that in times of price and exchange rate volatilities, the country is often found in a Balance of Payments crisis (Ahmed and O' Donoghue 2010).

The circular debt in the energy sector, largely arising on a recurrent basis due to lack of governance reforms and slow progress on prudently managing or privatising the loss making energy sector entities, is also creating a cash flow problem for the entire electricity and gas supply chain. The government usually provides for the circular debt through distortive subsidies borrowed from the central and commercial banks, in turn leaving lesser loanable funds for the private sector. In the past, particularly after 2008, excessive borrowing to fund losses of the energy sector also led to higher levels of inflation and reduced liquidity with the banking sector. The persistently high levels of expenditure on debt servicing leaves little room for maintenance expenses required to repair and augment transmission and distribution networks. Furthermore, the fiscal space for investment towards new capital projects is also squeezed. It is due to this reason that the economic managers are forced to look towards multilateral partners or charge higher levels of infrastructure taxes (e.g., Gas Infrastructure Development Cess) for financing of CASA-1000, Turkmenistan-Afghanistan-Pakistan-India (TAPI) Pipeline, and Iran-Pakistan Gas Pipeline. Ultimately, both modes of financing (i.e., debt or taxes) lead to a higher burden on the producers of power and gas, and the consumers (Ahmed et al. 2013).

The constituency that advocates for alternate and renewable sources of energy in Pakistan is still weak and lacks power to balance the narrative of vested interests. The government's own pursuit of exploring shale resources, soon lacked in persuasion as oil prices came down drastically after 2013. Nevertheless, it remains to be seen how Pakistan can benefit from its domestic endowments including: 18000 MT of coal, 33 trillion cubic feet of natural gas, 324 million barrels of fossil oil, and 50000 MW of hydropower.

While the above-mentioned constraints may have a solution in the medium to longer term, however in the short term these will result in at least three foreseeable outcomes i.e., increased energy tariffs given the growing costs of generation, transmission, and distribution; government having to bail out the generation and distribution companies through grants, and hidden and cross subsidies; and continued high levels of technical losses and theft in turn prompting load shedding of power and gas (Ahmed 2013).

This section argues that the government can still improve its supply side if regional energy cooperation is pursued. There are lessons from the Eastern African sub-region, the Latin American, and Gulf region where energy-deficient countries were able to bridge the demand and supply gap through regional energy sector integration.

Even in the case of South Asia, Nepal is gearing up to supply hydro power to India. Similarly, the supply of hydropower from Bhutan to India remains a key source of stable supply to the latter. Bangladesh has now signed an agreement with India to pursue grid connectivity and joint investment in Bangladesh Power Development Board and its initiatives. In the case of Sri Lanka, the Ceylon Electricity Board in Sri Lanka is undertaking construction of submarine cables to put in place transmission of electricity in collaboration with Power Grid Corporation of India.

Pakistan's eastern neighbour, India, now has long-term contract with Qatar for the supply of gas and oil resources. A long term arrangement also exists with Russia and the US for supply of LNG. It is engaging with China for the possibility of a pipeline originating from Russia and entering northern India. Similarly, a sea gas pipeline is being negotiated between Iran, Oman, and India.

In Pakistan's western neighbourhood, Kyrgyz Republic, Uzbekistan, Kazakhstan, and Tajikistan have proven energy surpluses. Afghanistan has long been importing power from Tajikistan and Uzbekistan. Afghanistan is already using seasonal power surpluses from Iran and Turkmenistan. Similarly, despite sanctions on Iran, Turkey continued to import oil and gas from Iran. Likewise, Armenia and Iran have decided to construct a joint hydro-electric power plant. To increase the mobility of petroleum crude and products, North-South railway line between Armenia and Iran is under consideration. This environment of regional cooperation in energy resources has promoted peaceful ties between Central Asian countries, China, and EU.

In the case of Pakistan, the government, in the past, has been reluctant to pursue liberal energy ties with Iran due to fear of opposition from the US and Saudi Arabia. While the former may not oppose such moves now as the sanctions against Iran are being gradually phased-out, however in the case of the latter, its relationship with Iran will determine if Pakistan is able to openly pursue higher levels of energy cooperation with Iran. Pakistan's largest province in geographical terms, Balochistan, already receives 100MW of power and Iran has been offering to increase this volume. Pakistan has yet to complete 781 kilometres of gas pipeline under Iran-Pakistan Gas Pipeline Programme. According to several news reports, Iran has completed the infrastructure on its side.

In the case of TAPI, Pakistan has yet to seek guarantees from Turkmenistan and transit countries which could ensure the supply of gas. Pakistan will need to move fast, given the already placed intent of Chinese and Turkish government for purchase of gas from Turkmenistan. Currently, given its interests in the region, the US is backing TAPI. However, as time passes and with gradual withdrawal of the US from the region, this interest may fade and finding financial support may get even more difficult.

With existing gas reserves in Pakistan only projected to last 15 more years and no new mega discoveries in sight, the current domestic gas production will come down from 4 billion cubic feet per day (bcfd) to 2.53 bcfd by 2020 (RAFTAAR 2015). This could affect supplies to both industry and residential consumers, in turn affecting the overall competitiveness of Pakistan's productive sectors (Ahmed 2016). Such statistics further strengthen the argument to urgently pursue and complete existing regional energy cooperation negotiations.

At this point it is also important to discuss the recent progress on CASA 1000 project, under which Kyrgyz Republic and Tajikistan will export 1300MW of electricity to Afghanistan and Pakistan. The World Bank, Asian Development Bank, and Islamic Development Bank are in agreement to provide support for this project. However, even in this case, at the time of writing this chapter, there are no secure guarantees from Kyrgyz Republic and Tajikistan. Any attractive proposal from other neighbours can prompt a change of stance from these governments. There are local interest groups in Kyrgyz Republic advocating for enhanced energy cooperation ties with China, India, and Russia given a more stable domestic security milieu in these countries. These larger economies have also expressed willingness to support in financial terms, towards development of energy supply facilities in Kyrgyz Republic. The Dataka-

Kemin electricity transmission arrangement can help China in receiving electricity from Kyrgyz Republic. The former is also interested in energy resources of Tajikistan. Both countries have also signed an arrangement for a gas pipeline and this could be an early possibility given Beijing's existing investments in Tajikistan's mining sector.

The multilateral development partners, notably the Asian Development Bank and World Bank Group, have explained that countries and institutions willing to support Pakistan in integrating with regional energy hubs wish to see quick progress on: (a) mitigating security threats to infrastructure projects, and (b) early reforms to improve governance of the energy sector in Pakistan, including reforms related to regulation, management, and pricing of oil, power, and gas. They have also recommended greater independence for all three energy regulators in the country. Furthermore, they wish to see a more balanced public investment diverted towards transmission and distribution networks, which in turn are expected to carry the enhanced energy supplies to end-consumers. Any failure to deliver on these reforms will result in multilateral partners and private sector shying away from such programmes due to apprehensions regarding the uncertain rate of return and payback.

5. Pakistan's Transit Trade Opportunity

As part of our background research for this chapter a series of interviews with the private sector representatives involved in the transit and commercial trade with Pakistan's neighbouring countries was conducted during November 2016. In the case of transit, the respondents were from wholesale and retail trade, transport, distribution, and storage sub-sectors. To validate this information and acquire related information on the subject, we also conducted interviews with MoC, FBR, Ministry of Interior, and development partners supporting Pakistan in transit and regional commercial trade including World Bank Group, Asian Development Bank, DFID UK, and USAID. We have grouped this discussion into current challenges and policy recommendations, discussed below.

Current challenges

The existing Afghanistan-Pakistan Transit Trade Agreement (APTTA), signed in 2010, now requires revision due to the need to comply with Transports Internationaux Routiers(TIR), decisions of Pakistan-Afghanistan Joint Economic Commission (JEC) which need to be provided a legal cover, adoption of a liberal visa regime for business persons in transport and warehousing related to transit, improved insurance mechanisms for merchandise trade, possible extension of APTTA to other countries, and strengthening of dispute resolution mechanisms (Shabbir and Ahmed 2016).

Currently, the agreement allows Afghan-bound goods to reach Karachi, Port Qasim, and Gwadar seaports and thereafter get transported through land route to Afghanistan via Chaman and

Torkhum customs posts. Under the agreement, Afghanistan should also allow Pakistan's merchandise to reach Central Asia, not permitted yet by the Afghan government. Pakistan has also not entirely fulfilled its commitments, as per past JEC meeting minutes, regarding timely completion of improved transit trade infrastructure projects which in turn could increase the flow of transit goods and reduce overall time taken for the goods to reach Afghanistan.

On Pakistan's side, completion of road, rail, and port-related transit facilitation projects will require significant inter-ministerial coordination at both federal and provincial government levels. With regards to Afghanistan's demand for providing enhanced security for the movement of goods through Balochistan and Khyber Pakhtunkhwa, the federal government will need to liaise proactively with relevant security agencies.

The government in Pakistan has to be mindful that for offering efficient transit services to Afghanistan and beyond, it will now have to compete with competitors including Iran (through Chabahar Port), Kazakhistan, and Uzbekistan—providing access to Chinese goods to reach Afghanistan seen by Afghan traders as relatively more secure and efficient routes, despite higher number of days. Furthermore, Afghanistan, India, and Iran, during May 2016 reached an agreement which will enable Indian goods destined to Afghanistan and Central Asia to pass through Chabahar Port. Similarly, Afghanistan's merchandise will also be able to access the Indian Ocean.[5]

To increase competitiveness in provision of transit to Afghanistan, Iran, Tajikistan, and other Central Asian countries, homework related to reducing the compliance costs of transit-related documents, and putting in place systems which prevent frequent policy and procedural changes in customs regime is missing. In the case of both of these issues, coordination between trade-related governance institutions, including the Ministry of Commerce and FBR, is weak.

The Afghan traders during our survey complained regarding: Chaman and Torkhum terminals awaiting necessary funding from Islamabad for upgradation, multiple costs borne by Afghan importers which are usually not part of conventional trade, including tracker costs for monitoring movement of goods and insurance. We also understand that no Pakistani financial institution currently provides insurance cover to Afghan-bound merchandise. The customs authorities process multiple containers of a single importer all at once. In the event where one of the containers goes missing, there is a high probability that the entire consignment will be stopped. The traders also informed that the online clearance system (WeBoC) is not synchronized with the software installed by Afghan authorities, which is more sophisticated. This has significant time cost, and danger of damage and decay in the case of perishable goods. Senior Afghan officials were also of the view that they were promised that Afghan trucks could go up to Wagah. However in current practice they are only allowed to go till Peshawar. The off-loading of goods at Peshawar and reloading on Pakistan trucks often leads to damage of goods.

The business community on both sides was also of the view that complex scanning and screening of goods and related procedures invites rent-seeking. Furthermore, the goods dispatched from Karachi and Gwadar, destined for Chaman and Torkhum, can be examined at multiple points on the route, again leading to the possibility of damage. In the event of any grievance, most traders refrain from registering any complaints under APTTA. According to a firm-level survey by SDPI (Shabbir and Ahmed 2015), only 15 per cent of the firms had filed a complaint and out of these firms, 80 per cent never received acknowledgement of their complaint. In this regard greater efforts will be required from FBR to minimize the dwelling time for goods in transit, put in place a more efficient grievance redressal mechanism, and ensure a smooth public-private communication on transit issues.

A major opportunity for Pakistan can be the desire of several Central Asian economies to use Pakistan's seaports for transport of their goods in transit. In this regard Tajikistan has already been proactive during trilateral meetings to discuss extension of APTTA to Dushanbe. However, Pakistan needs to find alternate ways for goods to reach Tajikistan, in case Afghanistan does not allow transit of goods through its territory. CPEC and ratification of TIR convention may provide some entry points, as connectivity to Tajikistan via Kashgar will boost the prospects of transit trade with Central Asia. Furthermore, Pakistan also needs to find a way by which it can offer similar arrangements to other central Asian countries.

There are also issues which will require an inter-ministerial and inter-government (i.e., matters where both federal and provincial governments are involved) response. An updated assessment regarding the roles and perspectives of government institutions involved in the governance of transit trade is required. Similarly, the current *de facto* policy and practice of transit trade needs to be aligned with modern standards.

Second, inter-ministerial and inter-governmental response will also be required for improving road linkages, integrated border and custom management, and coordination across security bodies for strengthening law and order. Specifically on land route linkages, more expedient upgradation of rail and road connections between Quetta and Zahedan and Quetta-Taftan road need to be pursued. The demand from the business community in Iran and Pakistan for opening up new land routes for transit and trade should be evaluated on priority (Shabbir and Ahmed 2015b). The constraints on funding of these connections can either be addressed through engaging with a multilateral partner or offering these projects on public-private partnership and build-operate-transfer basis.

Third, the federal government will need enhanced understanding of how synergies can be created across various connectivity commitments under APTTA, CPEC, CAREC, ECOTA, and QTTA. Furthermore, synergies should not be limited to merchandise trade, but also look into creating the enabling environment for transit of natural resources and energy supplies. Transit- and trade-led interdependencies in the region can strengthen the political will to expedite work on CASA-1000, TAPI, Iran-Pakistan Gas Pipeline, and other such possibilities.

6. Recommendations to Improve Transit Trade

While the above-mentioned challenges will require a response in the form of a coherent and certain policy on transit trade, it is equally important to put in place urgent measures which can alleviate the current constraints of those involved in the trade, transport, distribution, and warehousing sectors. In this sub-section we only document recommendations provided by our respondents, which may have the likelihood of implementation within 8 to 12 months.

As a starting point, Pakistan needs to refine and strengthen its follow-up mechanism on transit trade with Central Asia and ECO member countries. For this it will be wise to move the secretariat for CAREC affairs from the Economic Affairs Division to MoC, as the latter has relatively greater knowledge and understanding on technical issues related to transit. This should be complemented by strengthening of relevant Central Asia desks at MoC and the Ministry of Foreign Affairs (MoFA), particularly to enable the former to conduct quantitative and qualitative analysis on the potential of transit trade. Pakistan is also a full Member of ECO and Shanghai Cooperation Organization (SCO). Therefore, a joint working group of Economic Affairs Division (EAD), Ministry of Foreign Affairs

(MoFA), MoC, FBR, and State Bank of Pakistan (SBP) should regularly meet to see how synergies across Pakistan's contribution towards each of these forums could be strengthened.[6] To strengthen Track-II diplomacy in the region, it will be important to help Pakistani think tanks establish liaison with CAREC Institute and counterparts in other countries with whom Pakistan could strengthen transit linkages.

Second, in order to enhance confidence-building measures with Afghanistan, Pakistan will need to ensure a speedy implementation of JEC decisions. It was already recommended in the past that JEC should meet bi-annually and the schedule of the meetings should be pre-determined. It will also help if representation from Afghanistan-Pakistan Joint Chamber of Commerce and Industries is part of all JEC meetings and ministerial working groups. For a more certain and strengthened follow-up, a senior official can be deputed in the Finance Minister's office to ensure timely coordination on JEC decisions awaiting implementation.

Third, the concerns of industry within Pakistan regarding APPTA leading to increase in trade of illegal and informal inflow of goods need to be addressed. A large part of this problem should stand resolved if effective operationalization of integrated border management system and trade gates at Chaman and Torkham border is guaranteed. Support from security agencies will also be required to curb illegal flow of persons and merchandise through other possible border crossing points. The cost of such illegal flow can be minimized through reduction in tariff and non-tariff barriers on the Pakistan side, and rationalizing the transactions costs involved in securing a valid long-term business visa for Pakistan. While integrated border management systems with Afghanistan can help improve the efficiency of scanners and one-window operations, another related proposal by some experts is to follow the example of Bangladesh-India 'border haats' which will provide decent means of livelihood to the people living across the borders and reduce their temptation to get involved in illegal activities (Shabbir and Ahmed 2015b).

Fourth, the roadblocks in the way of establishing Land Port Authority should be removed. Ideally this authority should function under the Ministry of Interior given the security concerns involved in transit operations. However, a coordination committee of this authority should meet every month and have participation from MOC and FBR. As the government considers early launch of new trade routes at Tari Mangal and Angoor Adda, the operationalization of this authority should be placed on priority.

Fifth, the already initiated rail and road linkages which are facing delays due to fiscal austerity should be prioritized. Most notably, Jamrud-Torkham, Peshawar-Torkham, and Quetta Chaman roads are awaiting upgradation and appropriate security measures. In case the government believes that it will be difficult to mobilize its own resources in the short term, it may consider private sector participation in these projects. Similarly, in the case of the rail infrastructure, the Chaman-Spin Boldak

Link, should be completed at the earliest. This rail link in its later phases is planned to connect with Central Asia via Spin Boldak, Kandahar, Herat, and into Turkmenistan.

Finally, updated research is required in some areas of transit trade cooperation to help evidence-based decisions. This may start from conducting a more recent assessment on missing logistics facilities at all border posts. This could also include an evaluation of which new border posts can be opened with neighbouring countries (Ahmed et al. 2015). Taking the lead from Chirundi One Stop Border Post (OSBP) in Zimbabwe and South Africa, the government may look into the feasibility of establishing OSBP at select border points. Such initiatives lead to reduction in supply chain transaction costs and increased revenue for the government. The efficiency of such initiatives is enhanced through expanded land crossing points, scanner machines, and Electronic Data Interchange Systems. These studies will also provide inputs to the government's desire for promotion of intermodal freight transport.

7. Conclusion

While the pursuit of connectivity-related infrastructure is important for future economic growth prospects in Pakistan, this also has favourable implications for poverty. For example, evidence suggests that transit trade with Afghanistan benefited a significant portion of the population in Balochistan and Khyber Pakhtunkhwa provinces of Pakistan, particularly those working in wholesale and retail trade, transport, communication, and warehousing (TTCW) sectors (Shabbir and Ahmed 2015c). The employment in TTCW sectors increased sharply after 2004 with the increase in the supply of goods for NATO. The increase was seen particularly for the poorest income quintiles. The real incomes of households associated with these sectors also increased, and relatively more than non-trade sub-sectors. The data also suggests that between 2004–2011, the gaps between incomes of trade and non-trade households increased in favour of the former. The secondary data already indicates a higher mean income for households associated with the trade sector vis-à-vis non-trade sectors.

In view of the above-mentioned macro and micro level benefits of transit and regional trade, it is important for Pakistan to put in place a cogent foreign policy which gives attention to trade promotion, transit, investment, and energy cooperation. For this, Pakistan may formally request China to play a role in convincing Afghanistan to allow Pakistan transit to Central Asia. Furthermore, the government should move quickly to engage with Iran and extend to them linkages through CPEC. Pakistan's role in CAREC can also be enhanced though timely implementation of QTTA. This could link several Central Asian capital cities with port cities in Pakistan, creating significant future interdependencies in the region.

Specifically, in terms of the efficient governance of transit trade, this chapter recommends stronger follow-up mechanisms for smooth implementation of JEC minutes, and decisions under

CPEC, CAREC, and related ministerial meetings. Furthermore, modern border trade infrastructure such as installation and operationalization of electronically integrated scanning system (see Ali 2015), minimization of customs processing, improved en-route monitoring, full implementation of TIR, and multi-modal transit should be developed on a priority basis.

References

Ahmad, V. Suleri, A. Q. and Javed. A., 'Strengthening South Asia Value Chain: Prospects and Challenges', *South Asia Economic Journal*, Vol. 16, No. 2, 2015.

Ahmed, V., 'Contours of Pakistan's Power Crisis' (ed.), *Energy Crisis and Nuclear Safety & Security of Pakistan*, Strategic Vision Institute, 2015.

Ahmed, V., 'Overcoming Fragmented Governance: The Case of the Energy Sector in Pakistan', *Social Science and Policy Bulletin*, Volume 5, No. 1, 2014.

Ahmed, V., Abbas, A. and Ahmed, S., 'Public Infrastructure and Economic Growth in Pakistan: A dynamic CGE-Micro Simulation Analysis' *Springer*, 2013, pp 117–43.

Ahmed, V. and O Donoghue, C., 'External Shocks in a Small Open Economy: A CGE-Microsimulation Analysis', *The Lahore Journal of Economics,* 15: 1, 2010, pp. 45–90.

Ahmed, V. and Shabbir. S, 'Trade & Transit Cooperation with Afghanistan: Results from a Firm-level survey from Pakistan', *Sustainable Development Policy Institute, Working Paper No. 153,* 2016.

Ahmed, V. et al., 'Strengthening South Asia Value Chain: Prospects and Challenges', *South Asia Economic Journal*, 16(2S) 55S–75S, 2015.

Ahmed, V. Focus on the gas sector. The News, January 24, 2016. Web link: http://tns.thenews.com.pk/focusing-gas-sector/#.WTmokZCGPIU.

Aiyer, S., 'BCIM corridor versus Gwadar-Kashgar Corridor', *Business

Recorder. Weblink: http://ow.ly/2D1j3068rAF, accessed on 14 November 2016.

Ali, S., 'Transit trade through Pakistan: Practitioner's Perspective', Presentation at Eighteenth Sustainable Development Conference, Sustainable Development Policy Institute Islamabad, 2015.

'CAREC (2020): A Strategic Framework for the Central Asia Regional Economic Cooperation Program 2011–2020' Asian Development Bank, Manila.

Haider, Z., 'Balochis, Beijing, and Pakistan's Gwadar Port', *Geo. J. Int'l Aff., 6(95)*, 2005.

Khan, I. A., 'New committee to hammer out India policy', DAWN, 23 November 2016.

RAFTAAR., 'Energy in Pakistan: Chronic Shortages, Concrete Solutions', *Research and Advocacy for the Advancement of Allied Reforms*, Islamabad, 2015.

Rehman, A. and Ahmed, V., 'CPEC and regional cooperation', *The News*, 2 October 2016.

Samad, G. and Ahmed, V., 'Trade Facilitation through Economic Corridors in South Asia: The Pakistan Perspective', Chapter in book, edited by Prabir De and KavitaIyengar *Developing Economic Corridors in South Asia*, Asian Development Bank, 2014.

Shabbir, S. and Ahmed. V., 'Trade with Iran', *Criterion Quarterly*, Volume 10, No. 4, 2015.

Shabbir, S. and Ahmed. V., 'Welfare Impacts of Afghan Trade on the Pakistani Provinces of Balochistan and Khyber Pakhtunkhwa', *International Journal of Security & Development*, 2015.

Notes

1. Although China, Iran, Mauritius, and Myanmar from the near-region attend SAARC meetings as observers.
2. Major trade facilitation reforms will include increased transparency of trade-related regulations; simplifying, standardizing, and modernizing customs procedures; and improving the regulatory conditions for transit.
3. http://www.carecprogram.org/.

4. http://www.carecprogram.org/index.php?page=carec-development-effectiveness-review.
5. Chinese goods have also recently reached Afghanistan through Kazakhstan and Uzbekistan.
6. The Government of Pakistan hosted 15th CAREC Ministerial Meeting in Islamabad on 25 October 2016.

Chapter 7

Job Creation and Decent Work

1. Background

There is a consensus across most long-term development plans by the federal and provincial governments in Pakistan, and manifestos of political parties in the country that a key outcome of economic success should be sustained job creation. This is in line with goal eight of Sustainable Development Goals (SDGs) which aims to 'promote sustained, inclusive, and sustainable economic growth, full and productive employment, and decent work for all'.

The government's own analysis highlights that low economic growth in the recent past was a key factor in a less than desired increase in jobs. For Pakistan to absorb the annual increase in the labour force, the economy will need to grow by at least 7 per cent per annum over the medium to longer run (GoP 2011). Furthermore, there is a realization that labour market efficiency needs to be increased by streamlining the currently fragmented labour market regulations. The skills base of potential and new labour market entrants also needs to be expanded through a reformed programme for technical and vocational education and training (TVET) (GoP 2014).

While the recognition of prevalent issues is important, Pakistan's labour market, like several other developing economies suffers from various forms of inefficiencies and inequalities arising from several underlying characteristics. These include: a large proportion of workers in informal employment; a less than desired share of workers in industry and services; and barriers for youth and women to access labour market opportunities. These among other characteristics are accentuated due to low levels of growth in agriculture and industry. Another key reason is continued prevalence of 'decent work' deficits e.g. terms of employment in the agriculture sector are insecure, giving rise to several vulnerabilities (ILO 2013).

The quality of employment is less highlighted in the mainstream discourse on Pakistan's labour market dynamics. The above-mentioned lack of decent work can arise from insufficient opportunities for all, missing social protection or social safety nets, inadequate worker's rights and entitlements, and a weak state of voice and dialogue in the labour market (Webster 2011, ILO 2001). A weakening of the quality of employment also arises because of volatile economic activity resulting in a reduced demand for labour over the medium to long term. This may be seen, for example, around and after the period of global financial crisis. In case where economies continue to remain in low economic growth milieu, employers prefer temporary or short term-contracts. As the bargaining power erodes during times of low productive activity, employees would end up accepting such contracts especially in economies where social safety nets are inadequate.

As concerns of social responsibility in business operations gain limelight, the pressures on Pakistan to demonstrate effective compliance of the ILO conventions have increased. This is already seen in European Union's award of Generalized System of Preferences (GSP) plus status to Pakistan, which will allow duty-free exports in select categories to EU markets conditional upon Pakistan's ratification and compliance of twenty seven human and labour rights conventions (Pasha 2014). These conventions include: Forced Labour Convention 1930, Abolition of Forced Labour Convention 1957, Freedom of Association and Right to Organize Convention 1948, Right to Organize and Collective Bargaining Convention 1949, Equal Remuneration Convention 1951, Discrimination (Employment and Occupation) Convention 1958, Minimum Age Convention 1973, and Worst Forms of Child Labour Convention 1999. Effective compliance with these conventions will require political will and capacity at federal and provincial government levels to strengthen capabilities of workers, safeguard their rights, and provide them with a progression path that helps in building a motivated workforce.

Box 1 illustrates that during 2003–04 and 2014–15 there was an increase in the size of the labour force and the employment-to-population ratio. A large part of these new entrants were absorbed in the non-agriculture sub-sectors and within this segment informal employment grew more than in the formal. The labour force participation rate (LFPR) decreased in recent years between 2012–13 and 2014–15. The LFPR measures the labour force to the working age population and this rate is regarded as a measure of the extent of working-age population that is active. The decrease in LFPR was seen for both female and male labour. A cursory look at the employment share by sex indicates that women are found in traditional sectors including agriculture and social services. In the manufacturing sector they are concentrated in apparel production. The non-traditional services e.g., communications, trade, warehousing, and transport have not witnessed much increase in female share of employment.

Box 1: Pakistan: State of Workforce

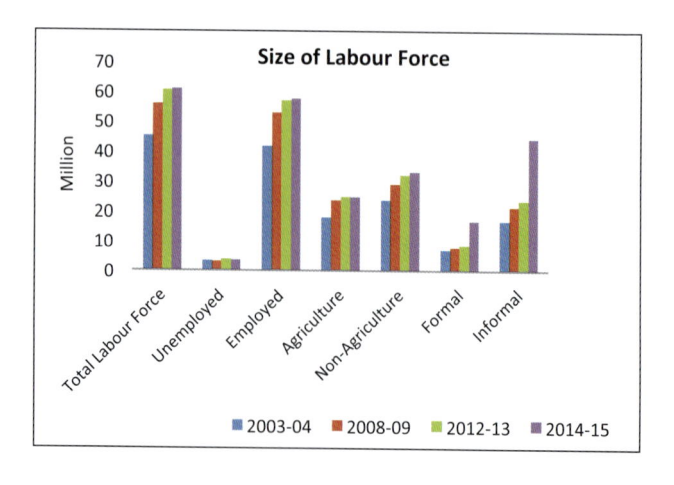

JOB CREATION AND DECENT WORK 297

Labor Force Participation Rate

Employment to Population Ratio (15+ Age)

Employment Share by Sex (2015-16)

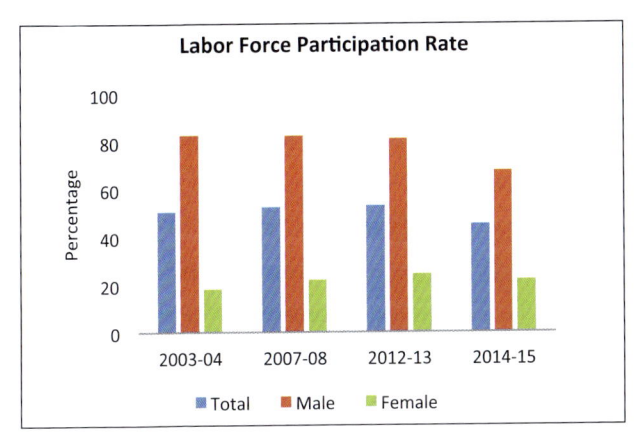

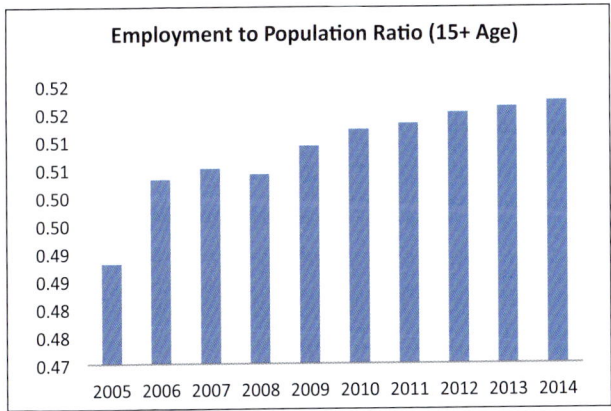

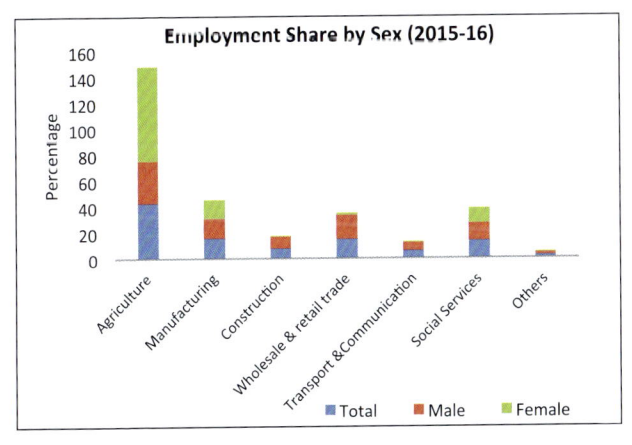

Source: Economic Survey of Pakistan (various issues). The employment to population ratio is based on modelled ILO estimates.

Figure 1 indicates that the unemployment rate increased between 2004–05 and 2014–15 for ages 15–34 years. However, the unemployment rate declined for all other age groups. This trend may indicate a lack of productive and decent employment for youth and particularly women (within the youth category). Given the relative improvements in health and physical well-being standards, the labour force already in work is willing and able to perform for longer tenures. However, this coupled with low growth witnessed since 2007–08 have resulted in squeezing of opportunities for new entrants in the market.

The next section provides a literature review focusing on: various forms of inequalities in the labour market, lack of effective social protection, and the need to harness the demographic dividend. Section 3 briefly describes ongoing employment generation schemes in the public sector, followed by a brief discussion on efforts by bilateral and multilateral development partners to help skill development and employment potential in Pakistan. In Section 5, we provide policy recommendations to accomplish decent and full employment. These recommendations are based on an extensive qualitative research exercise explained in the same section.

2. Pakistan: State of Labour Market

This section draws from existing studies which highlight various sources and types of distortions in Pakistan's labour market. Such distortions can arise due to missing information regarding

Figure 1: Unemployment Rate

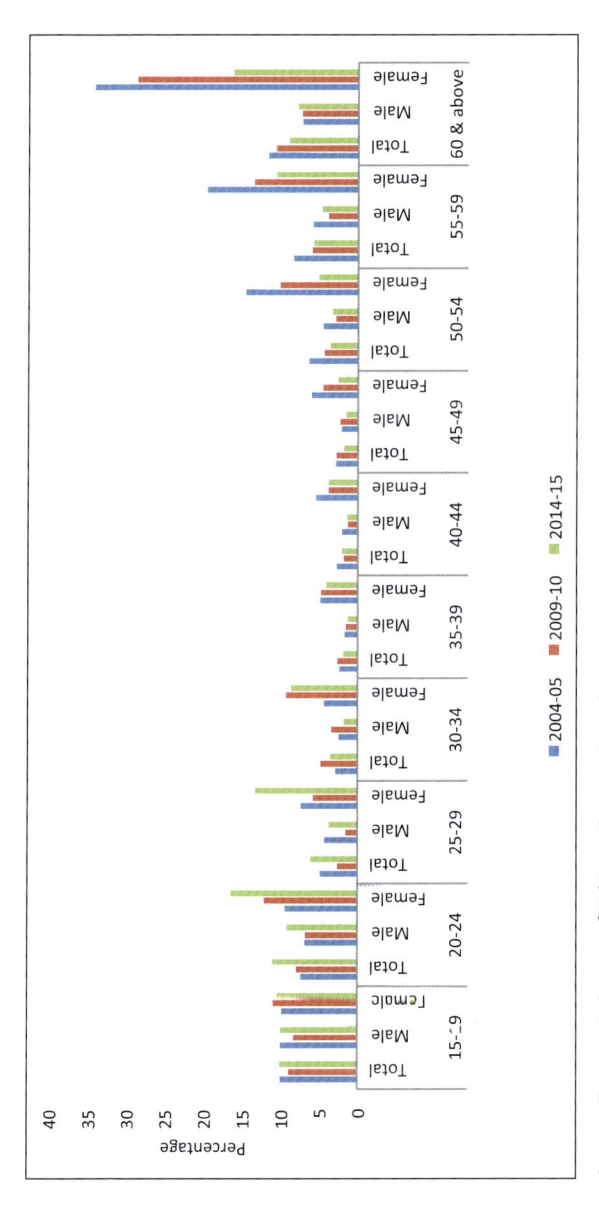

Source: Economic Survey of Pakistan (various issues).

vacancies, skills required by employers, mismatch of supply and demand of labour, and discrimination and inadequate regulation and safeguards in the labour market (GIZ 2012).

INEQUALITIES IN THE LABOUR MARKET

Lack of inclusive economic growth has been an issue in the recent past and prevented labour force absorption, giving rise to both underemployment and unemployment phenomenon. Robalino D and Cho Y (2012) indicate that the labour market in Pakistan is not generating enough jobs to absorb the new entrants. In addition, the jobs are inadequate in highly productive sectors. The female labour force participation rate remains almost stagnant in the medium term and there also exists a disparity among rural and urban earning prospects. The study recommends that the government needs to put in place policies that reduce the cost of doing business for the private sector, which in turn can absorb youth and new entrants in the labour force (see also GoP 2011).

The literature also provides evidence regarding various forms of inequalities in the labour market. Yasin G et al. (2010) examined the wage disparities among men and women in Punjab province and found that the job availability scenario is different for both. The efficiency of both groups is quite similar and women can compete with male counterparts at every level of operations and management. The inequality is severe in rural areas as compared to urban areas. The study pointed out that socio-economic and cultural constraints are affecting the female participation rate in the labour market (see also Nazli N 2004).

Similarly, Ali L and Akhtar N (2014) scrutinized the earning differential among men and women in Pakistan. The education variable tends to enhance the earning level of both; however, the returns are higher for women. Apart from this, profession, job status, and marital status are important factors that establish the earning gaps. Married men are earning more as compared to singles whereas single women are earning more than married women. Farooq M and Sulaiman J (2009) also stress upon the need to pay attention to female education at all levels, in order to minimize the wage difference.

Aslam M (2009) also noted that education provides higher returns to females as compared to males. However, in contrast, the total earning of males is more than that of females. The study indicates the possibility that returns to a girl's education are attained more by her in-laws and husband than her parents, so parents decide to invest in the education of their son with whom they may live in the future. By considering the opportunity cost of educating girls, the investment in their schooling remains low as compared to that of boys.

At a district-level, Maqsood R et al. (2005) pointed out that in Faisalabad, the general behaviour of considering the male as a superior member of society and the workplace is the root cause for disparity between the male and female workforce. The study points towards various social norms preventing women from participating actively in the public spaces (see also Abbas and Ahmed 2016). However, the restrictions are declining with the passage of time.

Looking through the lens of private versus public sector employment, Aslam M and Kingdon G (2009) highlighted that earnings are higher in the public sector as compared to the private sector. This divergence is more acute for women. The majority of women are in professional occupations; however their wages are lower than those of their male counterparts in both public and private sectors. Irfan M et al. (2013) also pointed out that gender segregation exists in all occupational sectors in Pakistan, particularly in managerial, elementary, and skilled professions. It is observed that with an increase in age, the difference between earnings tends to decline, whereas with an increase in education the difference between the earnings of males and females increases.

Hassan M U and Noreen Z (2013) recommend the need for diversity and related aspects in the curricula. The behaviour of economics students in Punjab was studied and the results reveal that there is an observed difference in the skills of male and female students as well as across same-batch students. Two key factors that contribute to this difference (apart from the attained grades) are lack of customized and demand-driven skills, and communication abilities. This also highlights the lack of training around life skills which needs to be embedded at both university and vocational training levels (See also Hou X 2011). Life skills usually take the form of knowledge acquired through learning or experiences enabling somebody to manage daily life challenges. According to the British Council these skills may include 'creativity, critical thinking, problem-solving, decision-making, the ability to communicate and collaborate, along with personal and social responsibility that contributes to good citizenship'.[1]

Social Protection: Key challenges

Pakistan's framework of social protection is not effectively bridging the existing gaps in the labour market. Currently, the modes of social protection include Zakat, Baitul Mal, citizen's damage compensation, provincial labour market programmes, and Benazir Income Support Programme (BISP) (SDPI 2013). The already established social assistance programmes are available for public and private sector employees at the federal and provincial levels. However, even these interventions suffer from some operational inadequacies. For example, complex procedures to apply and demonstrate eligibility make it challenging for the vulnerable, including women and the elderly to access education, health and unemployment, and disability or old age-related benefits. This is particularly true for the informal sector.

While social insurance dominates the overall social protection framework, this leaves limited funds for active labour market programmes e.g., grant for work and assistance for skills development. The resource constraints which limit such programmes have implications for youth. The potential and new entrants in the labour market are endowed with inadequate skills and training, hence they find it difficult to enter the formal sector.

Ahmed et al. (2013) studied the poverty and social impact of the Workers Welfare Fund (WWF) Programme. The authors argue that the documentation process, delays in disbursement, and distance of school from home were key hurdles in accessing education facilities under the fund. The promised housing schemes for the labour were marred by the slow pace of construction work, with frequent stoppages in release of funds in turn affecting the quality of buildings and delayed repair and maintenance. The existing labour colonies face acute sanitation and sewerage issues creating health and environmental hazard. Furthermore, instances of reported discrimination in access to healthcare in turn implies that those entitled but excluded end up exhausting their own savings for private healthcare.

Harnessing demographic dividend

Studying the job mismatch problem, Farooq S (2011) highlights that the educated are finding it hard to search for jobs in the labour markets that match the acquired qualification. The graduates are either over or underqualified in most cases. It is observed that women faced more mismatches as compared to men. In order to address these and similar issues, Mazhar Z A and Gill J (2014) recommend developing labour market information systems (LMIS). This tool, if implemented correctly and regularly updated and used in the development planning process, can reduce information deficits in the labour market which may emerge from: missing information about job openings, choice of professions, and information regarding potential employees available with potential employers (GIZ 2012).

Taking the banking sector as a case study, Amen U (2014) inspects the variance between the performance of the educated and the anticipation of employers. Results revealed that a significant gap exists between the anticipation of employers and the qualities possessed by the applicants. The author questions the skills imparted by the universities which are not meeting the employers' expectations. Analyzing the same subject, Mirza F M et al. (2014) used a survey of industry employers and graduates from Gujrat-Sialkot-Gujranwala. A skills gap exists in terms of communication and related interpersonal traits. There is a wide disparity in skills of students from IT, engineering, and computer science. There is also lack of professional and life skills in students from economics, business administration, and commerce. The study recommends that internship programmes, curriculum related to labour market requirement, and training courses can bridge the gap between the skills mismatch.

In Khan et al. (2016) we had made an effort through a semi-structured inquiry from key informant interviews across South Asia to understand factors constraining productive and decent employment in South Asia. First, the mandate for youth engagement and within this a core area of youth employment suffers due to overlapping institutional roles and responsibilities at the policy level. The public sector institutions responsible for youth engagement, which include: (a) skills and start up assistance, (b) community service including peer education, (c) counselling including mentoring, guidance towards capacity-building, exchange visits, fellowships, and (d) greater voice for youth in mainstream discourse on community mobilization, are not operating under one roof or in an integrated manner. Several of these functions are being performed by provincial departments across all four provinces. Despite clear constitutional provision, there exists no arrangement which can provide a more coordinated implementation of youth engagement and employment initiatives across the country.

Second, there exists a lack of results-based management and weak monitoring and evaluation across most youth employment programmes implemented by the public sector. Current monitoring arrangements have a large focus on (monitoring of) outputs and a weak focus on (monitoring) outcomes and impact. The linkages across various activities under the programme mandate and its outcomes and impact are also weak.

Third, there are ineffective official accountability measures[2] which can ensure transparency in the financial and physical implementation of programmes. The anti-corruption measures at the sub-province level are still inadequate. This gives rise to alleged financial irregularities and rent-seeking for which verification means are weak. This also links with a related point of lack of outreach and a weak grievance redressal mechanism in turn reducing public confidence in public sector efforts. Most programmes which manage grants for the provision of skills or micro finance operate without a documented or active complaint management mechanism.

Fourth, weak community-based social accountability mechanisms imply that there is minimal feedback from the local stakeholders to the relevant institutions regarding issues, challenges, and ideas for future improvement. This is particularly a challenge for rural areas where youth and communities will require guidance from civil society organizations to self-organize and participate in improvement of programme activities. Possible collaboration between relevant public sector institutions and non-government organizations specializing in youth and community engagement needs to be ensured and strengthened.

Fifth, the lack of partnerships across the public and private sectors and civil society organizations also endangers programme sustainability. There are examples of youth employment initiatives which were shut down by the administration as their sustainability after the donor's exit could not be ensured. A more recent example is around initiatives started for social entrepreneurship which have a job creation element (Ahmed 2016). The failure to establish horizontal and vertical partnerships with peers, the financial sector, and community based organizations led to gaps in implementation and programme success.

Sixth, despite demands from the private sector and potential employers outside of Pakistan, the federal and provincial governments have not been able to reach a consensus around establishing minimum standards for skills certifications. This has allowed continuity of trainings without compliance with minimum quality benchmarks. Another private-sector recommendation to establish a national skills standards authority to fill the above-mentioned gap is still pending.

Seventh, the currently available programmes for youth employment are not reaching the youth in informal sectors of the economy. The informal activities remain the incubators for a large portion of the youth coming from economically backward regions. Due to issues related to access, information availability, and weak counselling services, it is difficult for the youth to fully understand their scope in the formal economy. This compels them to remain in the informal sector for prolonged periods and without any formal social protection. Like other developing economies where the private sector is facilitated through fiscal measures to help attract the youth towards formal businesses in rural areas, such measures are found missing across all provinces. The private sector is also not rewarded for ensuring a quota for various marginalized segments of the population.

Finally, the lack of regional integration particularly with respect to 'trade in services' has limited the scope of skilled youth to offer their services in, for example, South Asian Association for Regional Cooperation (SAARC) and Economic Cooperation Organization (ECO) regions. While Central and South Asian economies have a significant share of the services sector in the overall GDP, yet the share of services in intra-regional trade remains low. The qualified youth in Pakistan who is proficient in foreign language as well as the use of information technology is least integrated with the regional value chains. It has been recommended in past studies that Pakistan should include a services trade clause for its professional and highly skilled workers in existing and future free-trade agreements and move towards effective implementation of regional arrangements such as SAARC Agreement on Trade in Services (Ahmed 2013; Ahmed and Batool 2014).

3. Public Sector Employment Generation Schemes

The general elections in 2013 witnessed three leading political parties clinching provincial governments in Punjab, Khyber Pakhtunkwa, and Sindh provinces. This started a new wave of development competition in the country where each of these political parties, Pakistan Muslim League (Nawaz), Pakistan People's Party Parliamentarians, and Pakistan Tehreek-e-Insaf designed labour market interventions in line with their manifestos with the primary ambition to demonstrate that their welfare programmes would lend greater relief for the population within their jurisdiction.

The post-18th Amendment political milieu also witnessed greater politically motivated ambitious programmes to appeal to various segments of the population including the youth and women. While evaluation of such programmes is difficult without a publicly available baseline data and annual midline surveys, however, it is still important to discuss the various initiatives designed and currently being managed by the federal and provincial governments. For ease of comparison, we will only discuss here those employment generation schemes which have been designed as part of the overall youth mobilization strategies.

National Vocational and Technical Training Commission (NAVTTC): This is described as the apex entity for designing skills development and training in Pakistan. The organization works through apprenticeship interventions in collaboration with the private sector. The key objective is to offer certified training to around one million people annually. This initiative is helped by the National Training Bureau (NTB) which is supporting forty affiliated institutes. NTB aims to increase training to 3,000 individuals every year in various skills with market demand. The training is aimed to cater for both formal and informal activities. In the recent past, NTB's graduates have found their way into labour markets in the Gulf region.

Prime Minister's Programme for Youth: This initiative intends to minimize the prevalent youth unemployment and has a national focus. The programme specifically targets the deprived groups of the society and provides them an opportunity to enhance their employment prospects. Youth Business Loan Scheme, Interest Free Loans Scheme, Youth Training Scheme,

Skills Development Programme, and Fee Reimbursement Scheme are included under the Prime Minister's Programme for Youth.

Punjab Youth Internship Programme (PYIP): The Government of Punjab initiated PYIP for unemployed youth to provide them an opportunity to gain experience of working for a limited term within a public sector department. The successful applicants are placed in various offices in accordance to their educational qualification for three months. During this time they are awarded a stipend of PKR 10,000 per month. The expected outcome here is that having a PYIP certificate at the end of the three months internship will enhance the probability of these candidates getting more stable jobs elsewhere in the public and private sectors.

Skilled Labour Market Information System (SLMIS): The system is implemented by Technical Education and Vocational Training Authority (TEVTA) in Punjab. The programme has three components focusing on: online information system, online and offline placement system to assist graduates of TEVTA and related institutes, and skills mapping of all the districts of Punjab. The information system presents comprehensive information regarding the labour market of Punjab, market tendencies, database of job seekers, and sector-specific opportunities by industry and skill-type.

Khyber Pakhtunkwa Youth Employment Programme: This programme aims to enrich the skills among the youth and facilitate them in getting productive employment within and outside the province. The programme targets unemployed and underemployed youth currently residing in the province. Through provision of necessary skills and online job opportunities, the programme also integrates them internationally, for example, for freelance work. During the first phase of this programme the Government of Khyber Pakhtunkwa intends to provide employment to 21,000 unemployed youth. The programme particularly encourages youth entrepreneurs through training, funding, and incubation, and enables them to initiate their business.

Benazir Bhutto Shaheed Youth Development Programme: This programme was started by the Government of Sindh in 2008 and has provided training to almost 292,000 youths, and enables them to find productive employment in 389 trades across 89 sectors of the economy. The key objective here is to eradicate poverty through job creation and address the unemployment issue on a sustainable basis. Representatives from private sector are also invited for any reforms related to this programme and possible selection of highly skilled human resource.

Apart from the programme-specific interventions, there is also a realization at the provincial level of the importance of initiating province-level legislation around a comprehensive labour policy. In this regard, Punjab Labour Policy (PLP) 2015 aims to establish a mechanism to safeguard the rights of workers, along with creating a social protection system which gives basic securities and safety nets to labourers and their families. It also envisages bringing about a favourable environment to promote industrial growth through peace and harmony across both employers and employee cadres. Other objectives of this policy include: (a) decent working conditions where labourers get appropriate wages, working hours and minimum wages are defined and health and safety measures are properly enforced; (b) equal job opportunities for males and females, promoting employability on the basis of skills and education, and elimination of bonded and child labour; (c) health insurance, compensation, pension, education and training, and maternity benefits for laborers and their families; (d) coordination among concerned departments for enterprise growth and productivity; (e) establishing dispute and alternate dispute settlement systems; (f) enhancing fair labour practices; (g) consistent policies for trade, industry, investment and FDI, women empowerment, youth, and TVET.

As mentioned above, there is usually limited real time data in the public domain which can allow poverty and social impact analysis of such programmes. However, studies on past programmes are certainly available from which lessons may be drawn. For example, Shaheen S (2008) had pointed out that National Internship Programme was initiated to provide graduates a useful opportunity to apply their skills in the industry relevant to their academic qualification. Some students were intended to be retained by employers after the completion of their internship. Students rated the internship programme quite useful and said that it made them familiar with the working procedures in the public sector. It was advocated by the then government that the internship programme should continue regardless of any government in office. The author pointed out that National Internship Programme in 2007 was neglected by the political government which came into power in 2008. Even after one year, students were not able to get certificates of completed internship activity. It was only verbally communicated to the interns after a year that their services were no more required and there was no documentation as part of the employees' separation. Even the appreciation letters promised to the high performing interns where not provided despite repeated reminders by the candidates.

A more recent evaluation of Benazir Income Support Programme (BISP) highlights the potential of such programmes under specific conditions to spur job creation. Launched in 2008, the programme aimed at mitigating the impact of slow economic growth and lack of jobs in the economy. BISP now is the largest social safety net programme in Pakistan's history. The number of beneficiaries under this programme had grown from 1.7 million households in 2008–09 to 4.7 million by end December 2014. During the same period, annual disbursements increased from PKR 16 billion in 2008–09 to PKR 65 billion in 2013–14. The traditional social safety net interventions are complemented by interventions towards: education for all; health, accidental, and life insurance; interest-free returnable financial assistance; and vocational and technical training.

OPM (2016) explains that BISP contributed in reducing

reliance of beneficiaries on casual labour. The transfers under the programme have led to an increase in the proportion of men engaged in the agricultural sector or livestock. Similarly, these transfers 'led to a reduction in the proportion of women engaged in unpaid family help'. BISP also supported at the household level procurement of small-scale livestock related assets, and increased formal savings.

Some of the labour market interventions were also rooted in the provincial youth policies. For example, Punjab Youth Policy (2012) intends to provide a conducive environment and equal prospects to all young individuals in the province. The key goals include economic empowerment of youth, enhanced investment in skills training, and encouraging youth entrepreneurship. The policy also provides for vocational training and cash programmes. Other initiatives promised include: job banks, youth venture capital fund, micro finance, and internship programmes.

Similarly, Sindh Youth Policy (2016) also aims to foster the employment and livelihood prospects for youth along with increasing the entrepreneurial skills and opportunities. The policy focuses on establishing youth venture capital fund, annual innovation competition, establishing incubation centres at universities, training of entrepreneurs, and promotion of programmes of Sindh Small Industries Cooperation. Some sectoral initiatives promised under the policy include: encouraging local craft-based enterprises in order to promote skills development among youth. A Youth Development

Commission is envisaged for better coordination across all youth-related institutions in the province.

4. Role of Development Partners

The role of development partners can be observed during design, implementation, and evaluation of employment generation interventions. While most donors have as a key target in their output manuals in the form of 'number of jobs created' and 'number of persons trained' as a key indicator of programme success, we only discuss interventions by select development partners, based upon our interaction with their field offices.

Decent Work Country Programme (DWCP) of ILO: This programme is aimed for implementation during the ongoing period 2016 to 2020. The key objectives are to encourage the decent work in rural economy, develop jobs for the youth and deprived segments, promote international standards in the domestic labour market, and support the social protection in the country. The programme is also helping the Balochistan and Sindh governments to bring about legislation regarding improvements in conditions for the agriculture labour force.

Technical and Vocational Education and Training (TVET) Reform of GIZ: This programme aims to increase access to technical vocational education and training in the country. The programme is supported by the German Federal Ministry for Economic Cooperation and Development (BMZ) and the European Union. Apart from this, the Embassy of the Kingdom of the Netherlands and the Royal Norwegian Embassy also provided support for various projects within the overall programme. The initiative helps in developing skills among the labour force all over the country. Around 1200 TVET programmes work under the first National Vocational Qualification Framework of Pakistan. The Vocational Counselling Centres throughout the country and two job placement centres in Swat and Peshawar were also established.

Punjab Skill Development of the World Bank: The project aims to enhance the quality and access to skills training along with improving the labour market conditions in major economic sectors of the Punjab province. The project was started in 2015 and expects to increase the employment prospects for young graduates. It is estimated that approximately 70,000 people will benefit from this project out of which 15 per cent will be female. Young graduates will be assisted to enhance their skills with the help of training and coordination specialists and entrepreneurs.

Sindh Skills Development Project of the World Bank: This project was initiated in 2011 for promoting skills development across Sindh province. The project intends to enhance the quality and spread of vocational training, develop the skills base of the existing labour force, develop new opportunities for unemployed youth to get suitable jobs, and encourage reforms in existing training organizations. The project aims to target around 50,000 unemployed youth in the province to help them in getting a reasonable job through providing technical and demand-driven courses.

5. Reforms for Productive Employment and Decent Work

This section draws from recent qualitative research which used in-depth interviews with federal and provincial government officials, elected representatives including some members of the Standing Committee on Overseas Pakistanis and Human Resource Development; key informant interviews with labour market stakeholders, including employer and employee associations and civil society organizations involved in youth and community mobilization; and focus group discussions held with recent graduates of TVET institutions. Through several rounds of key informant interviews during 2015–16 we had provided recommendations to ensure productive and decent employment for youth in Ahmed (2016) and Khan et al. (2016). These have been summarized below under four sub-sections. The first focuses on fiscal interventions while the second explains institutional reforms required for youth engagement within which employment is a key aspect. We then also look at specific reforms for increasing women's participation particularly through a self-employment lens, followed by key design reforms required in a vocational training setup.

Using fiscal policy as a tool for employment generation

According to several independent experts, low economic growth over the medium term was a key factor in slower job creation. This milieu was accentuated by the post-devolution increase in the number of taxes at the federal and provincial levels and high energy- and security-related costs which further dampened medium-term growth prospects (Ahmed and Naqvi 2016, Jamali and Ahmed 2016).

The instruments under the fiscal policy i.e., taxation, non-tax revenue measures, and government spending provide important tools to spur short to medium term growth and jobs. The fiscal policy is particularly effective in reducing cyclical unemployment in times of uncertain economic activity. The fiscal policy also has its limitations e.g., an expansionary policy perhaps through domestic borrowing, if continued over a prolonged period, has the tendency to crowd out private investment which in turn could have created more sustainable jobs.

For fiscal policy to be effective, the first and foremost measure may be to revisit the regulatory environment faced by the businesses—primary creators of jobs. Every possible measure should be taken to keep the cost of doing business minimal so that a level-playing field is ensured locally, foreign investment is lured, and local firms remain competitive abroad.

Second, a revenue-neutral change in the overall tax collected from the corporate sector may be designed so that indirect taxes on labour-intensive formal businesses may be reduced. Several progressive taxes under the federal and provincial domain can be used to make up for any revenue loss to the government. These include excise duty on luxury items, property taxes, motor vehicle tax, and environmental taxes. Those taxes which are rendering low revenue and have relatively high administrative costs may be consolidated. This will reduce the compliance costs of formal businesses. For example, currently, small and medium enterprises face more than three dozen levies in the form of taxes, cess, surcharges, and license fees collected at various levels of the government.

Third, all tiers of the government need to design their youth development and employment programmes in a manner that enhances the self-employment potential of the young and marginalized segments. In the formal sector, some dynamic incubators have provided the youth an opportunity to realize their entrepreneurial potential.[3] However, sustaining start-up initiatives and their growth over the medium term continues to remain a challenge. Second, because of several limitations such programmes are still not able to reach to the youth in the informal sector (SDPI 2016).

Fourth, increased participation of women in the workplaces can significantly increase productive capacities. This is possible through enhanced coverage of social safety nets and promotion of women-led micro, small, and medium enterprises including social businesses. While several public sector entities may be interested to champion this cause, however, there is an urgent need to remove any duplication across federal and provincial programmes.[4] For women to be more confident about initiating a business enterprise they will need to be assured regarding simplification of procedures to start a firm, minimal intrusion by tax and regulatory authorities during the initial phases, and certain access to funding and technical support (Yaseen and Ahmed 2016).

As increased participation of women requires providing them with a balance between their responsibilities at work and in the home, therefore established enterprises in rural areas which hire an increased number of women and provide them with flexible schedules, childcare, offsite work facilities, and prospects for promotion to senior management levels, should be encouraged through tax credits.

For women-led businesses to graduate into larger entities and possibly also participate in trade, appropriate fiscal policy measures including: targeted funding for entering regional and global value chains, free participation in exhibitions organized by Trade Development Authority of Pakistan, and subsidies that contribute to costs of branding may be considered. The provincial governments may also look into subsidizing part of the outreach costs of microfinance institutions and Small and Medium Enterprises Development Authority (SMEDA) which in turn can help in building capacities of new entrepreneurs and their staff.

Reform of labour market institutions

The above-mentioned fiscal policy measures may not deliver unless accompanied by efforts of all provincial governments to strengthen labour market institutions. This could start with improvements in LMIS, revival and enhanced coverage of employment exchanges, deeper apprenticeship programmes that also lead the candidate to wage or self-employment, and encouraging the private sector (through provincial annual development plans) to develop its own training facilities. A well-developed and integrated LMIS (Figure 2) could ensure greater availability of data and information regarding: demand and supply of labour by skill set and location, demand and supply of technical vocational education training, quality of training, and gaps in communication of job request and job offers by employers.

The measures under fiscal policy are limited in their effectiveness in times of structural unemployment. This happens when workers lack the knowledge and technology-related skills required by the fast evolving labour market. This is where supply-side measures focusing on improving productivity and mobility of workers can help. This can partially happen if private sector-led technical and vocational education and training is facilitated by the government. Improvements in the overall labour market regime will also call for appropriate changes in the laws which allow for more conducive labour-employer relations (see PWC 2015), flexibility of wage determination, and hiring and exit laws.

JOB CREATION AND DECENT WORK 323

Figure 2: How LMIS helps in Studying Growth of Employment

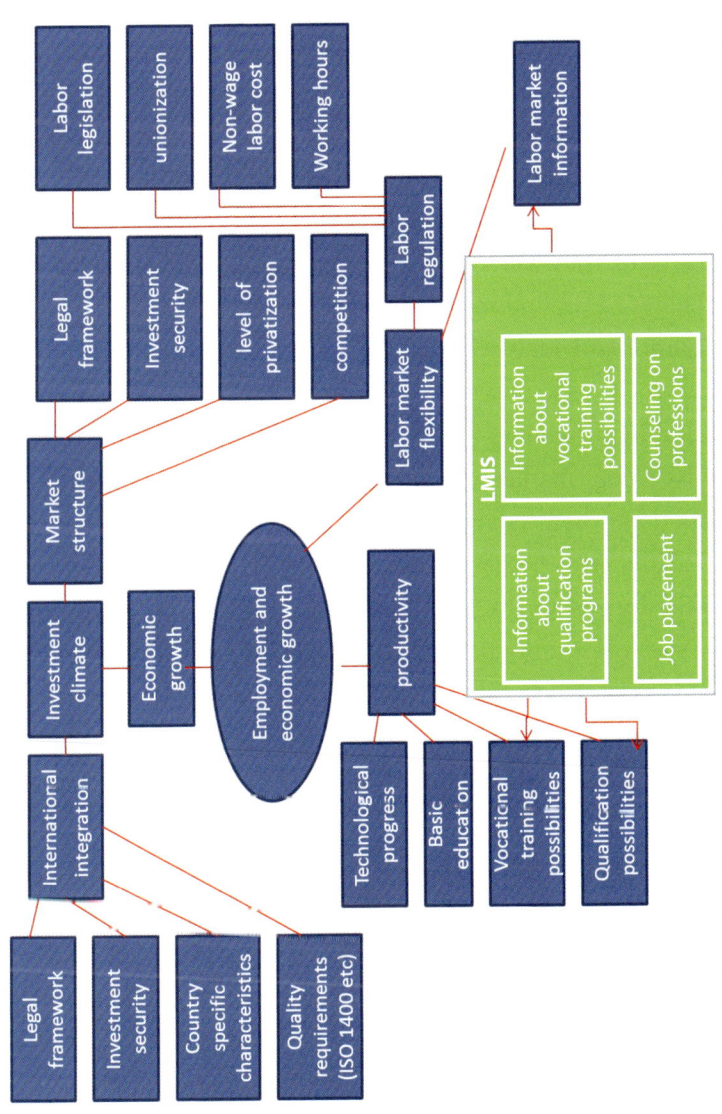

Source: GIZ 'The Labor Market Information System as an Instrument of Active Labour Market Policies' Internationale Zusammenarbeit (GIZ), 2012.

As institutional change is an ongoing reform, therefore provincial governments may look into a high-level Advisory Council at their labour departments which will ensure implementation of active and passive labour market programmes without any political interventions. The same council, having participation of relevant think tanks, non-government organizations, and representatives of labour unions and Chambers of Commerce and Industries will also see that new employment generation schemes are in line with the overall development strategy of the province and skills required by the private sector.

Relevant provincial government institutions can also design active labour market programmes such as public works initiatives which can help facilitate the entry of informal workers and gradually provide them with soft skills which allow a graduation to the formal sector. Well-designed public works programmes having community participation, can help in keeping informal workers at work during times of economic downturn and can also help economically backward districts of Balochistan, Federally Administered Tribal Areas, and Khyber Pakhtunkhwa.

Targeted social protection schemes are also required to address child labour and facilitate transition of the young from school to work (Mete and Jamil 2013). Schemes that integrate part-time work and schooling, provision of conditional cash transfers that help the household in deciding to send their child to school, and vocational training for older children can bring the out-of-school children to the mainstream, eventually helping those who end up doing labour under pressing circumstances.

Improved planning, implementation, and evaluation

During our interviews, several experts and organizations involved in youth and social mobilization had informed us regarding weaknesses in public programmes to deliver productive employment. The key issues which were highlighted included:

- multiplicity of similar employment generation schemes at the federal and provincial levels.
- weak needs-assessment exercises before initiating such schemes.
- weak results-based management across publicly funded employment generation programmes.
- ineffective official accountability measures.
- weak grievance redressal mechanisms particularly for groups which remain excluded from these schemes.
- lack of public support to non-governmental organizations which can increase awareness about social accountability in turn improving feedback mechanism.
- lack of partnerships with the private sector, corporate social responsibility initiatives within the corporate sector and philanthropists.

The improvements in planning, implementation, and evaluation of, for example, youth employment schemes will need to start with a clear mapping of unemployed and underemployed youth by region and community. It is these youth which will require targeted social safety nets. At this point the federal government will need to play coordination and monitoring role so that the 'leave no one behind' agenda is at the forefront of youth employment programmes, and so that such initiatives are designed in a manner which contributes to a reduction in various forms of horizontal and vertical inequalities.

A coordinated effort between the national-level Planning Commission and provincial planning and development departments will also be required to make changes in the overall domestic regulations, taxes, and subsidies to incentivize skill development across the country. It will be best if tax and subsidies regimes can be designed to incentivize the business community to mobilize its own resources for skills building. In provinces or regions where the private sector may not find it lucrative to locate and provide such capacity-building, it may be appropriate to look into public-private partnership (PPP) models, for example, matching grants for the private sector by the public sector.

In cases where even PPP has less traction, local community-based organizations and non-government entities may be facilitated through a targeted grants programme which encourages skills that spur self-employment, particularly growth of social enterprises. Such grants can be designed and implemented through development partners or local resources under BISP. However, it will be important that some such programmes allow the trained youth to serve their own communities, perhaps through social enterprises and community service. For this purpose, forums which strengthen youth advisory services including mentoring progammes, and youth media platforms which help amplify the voices of youth should be institutionalized under the provincial youth and information departments respectively.

Reforms for women entrepreneurship

In our survey described in Yaseen and Ahmed (2016) we had explained that a majority of women-led micro, small, and medium enterprises were home-based. With very little fixed overhead costs, these enterprises have a lot of potential to generate employment, particularly at a local level. The single most important challenge faced by self-employed women is acquisition of working capital. Another key issue is the market structure or the state of competition in markets, which favours male counterparts. Other challenges include recruitment of relevant and skilled staff, putting in place systems for managing cash flows as the volume of business increases, and inventory management, particularly in case of agriculture where it is not easy to access storage facilities.

Over half of the respondents in this survey had identified rising cost of doing business in recent years as a key hurdle in growth. The costs have increased due to uncertainty of energy supplies, poor road connectivity particularly in rural and peri-urban areas, missing building infrastructure facilities, and corruption faced in dealing with tax and other regulatory bodies. The lack of women-friendly marketing and distribution channels in the case of small-scale manufacturing and cottage industry was also identified as a key reason for weak outreach.

Our key informants had highlighted that a national-level effort to revisit the potential of women entrepreneurship should start with a rapid assessment regarding the effectiveness of programmes such as the Prime Minister Youth Loan Scheme and Benazir Waseela-e-Haq Programme for women. The Central Bank and the banking sector need to be approached to inquire why they remain reluctant to lend to women as compared to men of similar risk profile. The Ministry of Commerce will need to evaluate why there are only a few (twelve in 2016) women chambers of commerce and industries across Pakistan. This number is very low compared to women's overall share in Pakistan's population. Women should also be encouraged to join mainstream Chambers of Commerce and Industries, and opportunities should be provided for them to progress to senior office bearers within these chambers. One way to increase the membership of women may be to lower the registration and annual renewal fees by chambers and other associations.

The security of women entrepreneurs in some regions was a key concern highlighted by several Women Chambers of Commerce and Industries. For this, the Ministry of Interior will need to send a clear directive to municipal-level administration to identify security gaps in consultation with women business groups and implement urgent measures which can ensure the safety of the lives and assets of women-led enterprises.

Reforming technical and vocational education and training

A national standard in TVET which has recognition locally and abroad can only come about through: regularly updating LMIS which can track clusters of labour demand and supply; strengthening linkages between public sector TVET initiatives and employers; regularly revisiting quality of TVET curricula and teaching methods; having market rules which encourage TVET provision in the private sector; and also targeting the poorest of the poor, perhaps through a combination of capacity-building programmes and public works programmes which provide jobs (Sánchez-Triana et al. 2014).

Taking a lead from our interviews on this subject and the above-mentioned guiding principles, it is important to understand that the roles of federal and provincial governments should be clearly identified so that there are no administrative overlaps and wastage of resources. We propose that the Ministry of Overseas Pakistanis and Human Resource Development should do a clear mapping of roles and responsibilities of all federal, provincial, and private sector players in the skills development supply chain. This mapping will then inform the revamping of the TVET provision at all levels of the government.

For example, NAVTTC will need to focus on curricula development and modernizing teaching methods. This should be a consultative process where representatives of industry and labour may be involved. NAVTTC should also be responsible for tracking labour demand in countries where Pakistani workers can be placed for decent and productive jobs. While the government also receives a demand formally, for example, Malaysia had requested for Pakistani trained paramedic staff at one point, however, a more scientific analysis can lend important insights into future demand, for example, a boom in the hospitality industry in United Arab Emirates will imply a rise in demand for staff skilled in restaurant and hotel operations.

Second, skill development funds may be effectively operationalized in all provinces and districts. This can be done in partnership with the private sector or in cases where the private sector is reluctant, this may be undertaken by the provincial government. Ideally, the boards of these funds should be led by the private sector with representation of public officials. Qualified professionals having private sector experience should be selected to lead teams that manage funds. Some portion of the proceeds from workers' welfare funds may also be transferred to skills development funds.

Third, the provincial governments may look into expanding the internship programmes particularly in skills required by the private sector. Ideally, all TVET trainees should be allowed short-term placement in internship programmes. However, the scope will need to be broadened particularly for regions with high underemployment and unemployment, and for informal youth. For the informal workers a cost effective and short-term solution may be to increase the number of vocational training centers at primary and secondary schools.

The apprenticeship is a key mode through which TVET-related knowledge can be delivered. However, the provincial governments need to move towards effective implementation of apprenticeship related laws (e.g., The Apprentice Ordinance, 1962). A buy-in from employers and their associations is still missing and this is a key hurdle in the revival of the apprenticeship system. Sánchez-Triana et al. (2014) had proposed a review of the entire system to see why there are low levels of registered apprenticeships; and to learn from experiences in the region and beyond regarding incentives which can be provided to encourage employers, trainers, and trainees involved in the apprenticeship schemes.

All TVET related institutions and branch offices of skill development funds should house employment exchanges. As the sources of vacancy-related information such as newspapers and online job search portals have their limitations in rural areas and the informal sector, therefore, employment exchanges have the potential to bridge this gap and also to help the labour market in conducting due diligence of the potential employee.

5. Conclusion

The SDG-8 demands all UN member countries to 'promote sustained, inclusive, and sustainable economic growth, full and productive employment, and decent work for all'. The pursuit of this goal will require inclusive economic growth, increase in productivity, and reforms which strengthen competition, innovation, and entrepreneurship. This goal is of particular importance for Pakistan, currently endowed with a demographic dividend which can push economic growth in agriculture, industry, and services to new heights in relatively less time.

Pakistan also has this opportunity to learn from East Asian economies regarding the benefits of increasing women's labour force participation. Currently, women face geographical and occupational mobility constraints which can be eased through more inclusive education and TVET and social mobilization efforts that ease discriminatory cultural norms, and provide more inclusive access to working capital.

This paper uses a review and qualitative approach to discuss constraints to productive employment in Pakistan and recommends policy actions at federal and provincial levels that are needed to prioritize SDG-8 and particularly youth employment. We also highlight the need for learning from case studies from the region and beyond to take stock of the determinants of successful employment generation schemes abroad.

Our findings suggest that the policies for youth employment ought to be grounded in a broader framework of youth and community engagement.[5] All political parties and provincial governments will need to make a stronger commitment backed by budgetary proposals and allocations to improve the quality of human resource through education, health, and social safety nets. To achieve this, the chapter recommends: (a) using fiscal policy as a tool for employment generation, (b) reforming labour market institutions at both national and sub-national levels, (c) improving planning, implementation, and evaluation of public sector employment generation schemes, (d) promoting active and passive programmes to spur women's self-employment, and (e) improving resources and technologies for TVET.

References

Abbas, M. H. and Ahmad, V., (2016), 'Challenges to Social Accountability and Service Delivery in Pakistan', *Social Change*, SAGE Publications 46 (4), 560–82.

Ahmad, V., Zeshan, M. and Wahab, M. A., (2013), 'Poverty and Social Impact Analysis of Workers Welfare Fund', *Public Policy and Administration Research*, Vol. 3, No. 7.

Ahmad, V., (2016), 'A Budget for Jobs' *The News on Sunday*, 20 March 2016.

Ahmed, V. (2016), *Social Enterprise Landscape in Pakistan*, Sustainable Development Policy Institute.

Ahmed, V. and Naqvi, A., (2016), 'Tax Reforms in Punjab' *Sustainable Development Policy Institute, Policy Brief No. 53*.

Ahmed, V., (2013), Presentation on regional potential for trade in services, Planning Commission June 2013. http://ow.ly/lkdP301VCu6 accessed on 8 September 2016.

Ahmed, Vaqar and Batool, S., (2014), 'India-Pakistan Trade: A Case Study of the Pharmaceutical Sector.' *Working Paper 291*. Indian Council for Research on International Economic Relations. New Delhi.

Ahmed, Vaqar (2016) Social Enterprises and Development. The News, 30 October 2016.

Ali, L. and Akhtar, N., (2014), 'An Analysis of Gender Earning Differentials in Pakistan', *Research Journal of Applied Sciences, Engineering and Technology*, 7 (13): 2772–87.

Amen, U., (2014), 'Employer's Expectation Versus Performance of Fresh

Graduates: Business School', *Market Forces, College of Management Sciences*, Volume IX, No.2.

Aslam, M., (2009), 'Education Gender Gaps in Pakistan: Is the Labour Market to Blame?' *Economic Development and Cultural Change*, Vol. 57, No. 4, pp: 747–84.

Aslam, M., and Kingdon, G., (2009), 'Public-Private Sector Segmentation in the Pakistani Labour Market', *Journal of Asian Economics*, Volume 20, pp: 34–49.

Farooq, M., and Sulaiman, J., (2009), 'Gender Earnings Inequalities and Discrimination in the Pakistani Labour Market', *The Dialogue*, Volume IV, No. pp: 373–85.

Farooq, S., (2011), 'Mismatch between Education and Occupation: A Case Study of Pakistani Graduates', *The Pakistan Development Review*, 50 (4).

GIZ., (2012), 'The Labour Market Information System as an Instrument of Active Labour Market Policies', Internationale Zusammenarbeit (GIZ), 2012.

GOP., (2011), *Pakistan: Framework for Economic Growth*, Planning Commission Government of Pakistan.

GOP., (2014) *Pakistan 2025: One Nation, One Vision*, Planning Commission, Ministry of Planning, Development & Reform, Government of Pakistan.

Hassan, M, U., and Noreen, Z., (2013), 'Educational Mismatch between Graduates Possessed Skills and Market Demands in Pakistan', *International Education Studies*, Vol. 6, No. 11.

Husain, O. (2015) 13 startup incubators, accelerators, and co-working spaces in Pakistan. Tech-in-Asia, 25 October 2015.

Hou, X., (2011), 'Challenges for Youth Employment in Pakistan: Are They Youth-Specific?' *World Bank Policy Research Working Paper Series* 5544.

ILO (2001), *Reducing the decent work deficit—A global challenge*, Geneva: ILO.

ILO., (2013), *Pakistan Labour Market Update*, International Labour Organization, September.

Irfan, M., Anwar, S., Akram, W. and Waqar, I., (2013), 'Occupational Gender Segregation and its Determinants: An Analysis of Pakistan Labor Force Market', *American Journal of Economic Research*, 1 (7), pp: 221–4.

Jamali, S. and Ahmed, V., (2016), 'Tax Reforms in Sindh', *Sustainable Development Policy Institute, Policy Brief No. 54.*

Khan, A., Javed, A., Batool, S., Hussain, F., Mahmood, H. and Ahmad, V., (2016), 'The Role of Youth in Sustainable Development. Sustainable Development Policy Institute.

Maqsood, R., Zia, C. B. and Cheema, A., (2005), 'Problems of Employed Women at Faisalabad-Pakistan', *Journal of Agriculture & Social Sciences.*

Mazhar, Z, A., and Gill, J., (2014), 'Strengthening Labour Market Information System and Supporting Evidence Based Labour Policy Development in the Region', South Asia Labour Conference 2014: Lahore.

Mete, C. and Jamil, R. R., (2013), 'Enhancing Labour Market Conditions for Vulnerable Groups', *The World Bank, Pakistan Policy Note 7.*

Mirza, F. M., Jaffri, A. A., and Hashmi, M. S., (2014), 'An Assessment of Industrial Employment Skills Gaps among University Graduates in the Gujrat-Sialkot-Gujranwala Industrial Clusters-Pakistan', *USAID, Working Paper No. 017.*

Nazli, N., (2004), 'The Effect of Education, Experience and Occupation on Earnings: Evidence from Pakistan', *The Lahore Journal of Economics, Vol.9*, No. 2, pp: 1–30.

OPM, (2016), *Benazir Income Support Programme: Impact Evaluation Report 2016.* Oxford Policy Management.

PWC. (2015), 'European Union GSP Plus and Challenge of Labour Standards Compliance', *Pakistan Workers Confederation.*

Robalino, D., and Cho, Y., (2012), *Labour Market Policies under a Youth Bulge*, World Bank.

Sanchez, T. et al., *Revitalizing Industrial Growth in Pakistan: Trade, Infrastructure and Environmental Performance,* The World Bank, 2014.

SDPI, (2013), 'Social Protection in Pakistan', Sustainable Development Policy Institute.

Shaheen, S., (2008), 'National Internship Programme in Doldrums', Islamabad: *The Nation Newspaper*, 23 June 2008.

Webster, E., (2011), 'The Dilemma of Job Creation and Decent Work', *Corporate Strategy and Industrial Development, Number 73.*

Yaseen, F. and Ahmed, V., (2016), *Trade Wings of Change-Women*

Entrepreneurs on the Rise in South-Asia: Background Country Study-Pakistan, United Nation Development Programme (UNDP). Web link: http://sdpi.org/publications/externalpublications/Trade-Winds-of-change-Women-Entrepreneurs-on-the-Rise-in-South-asia-country-study-Pakistan.pdf.

Yasin, G., et al. (2010), 'The Determinants of Gender Wage Discrimination in Pakistan: Econometric Evidence from Punjab Province', *Asian Social Science*, Vol. 6, No. 11.

Notes

1. Details may be seen at: https://www.britishcouncil.gr/en/life-skills/about/what-are-life-skills.
2. We refer here to supply-side accountability measures which are designed and implemented by the state.
3. For a list and activities of major incubators in Pakistan, see Husain (2015).
4. For example, programmes by the federal government through Benazir Income Support Programme and programmes by rural support organizations administrated by provinces.
5. Also see Khan et al. (2016).

Index

A

Accountability 5, 8, 22–7, 37, 43–7, 49, 53, 57, 59, 67, 83–7, 92, 103, 141, 144, 146, 164–5, 167, 178, 183–4, 186, 190, 228, 306–7, 325, 336
ACT 129
ADB 53, 264
ADP 34
Advocacy 5–6
Afghanistan 2, 12, 70, 203, 206–9, 215, 219, 235, 256–8, 260–4, 268–9, 271–2, 276, 278, 280–3, 286–9
Agriculture 5–6, 22, 35, 41, 78, 87, 89, 117, 121–3, 126, 137–8, 219, 221, 235, 238, 242, 258, 294, 296–7, 316, 327, 332
ASEAN 223

B

Balochistan 3–4, 12, 51, 144, 156, 164–5, 174–6, 272–3, 277, 281, 288, 316, 324
Bangladesh 14–17, 38–9, 55, 98–103, 117, 200–1, 204, 209–10, 212, 256, 262, 265, 271, 276
Bank 2, 8, 22, 33, 35–6, 40, 55–6, 62, 71–2, 98–103, 109, 121, 139, 141, 164–5, 173, 177, 207–8, 212, 227, 231, 243, 265, 268, 278–80, 286, 317, 328
BBIN 262
Bed wear 206–8
BISP 303, 314–15, 326
Bonded labour 313
Brexit 222, 228
Budget deficit 15–17, 27, 41, 155, 157, 198

C

Capacity-building 74, 109, 139, 142, 156, 167, 185, 187–8, 218, 224–5, 232, 243–4, 306, 326, 329
CAREC 13, 230, 245, 259, 263, 268–71, 273, 284–6, 289
CASA-1000 3, 257, 263–4, 275, 278, 285
CDWP 35, 183
Ceramic goods 203
Chabahar Port 281

Chemicals 131, 134, 207–9
Child labour 295, 313, 324
China 2, 13, 38–9, 55, 98–103, 117, 133–4, 200–2, 205–10, 219, 221–3, 235, 239, 255–6, 258, 260–1, 265, 267–8, 270, 276–9, 289
Circular debt 3, 41, 44, 52, 81, 158–61, 174–6, 181, 274
Civil Service 11, 23–5, 36–40, 44–7, 57–60, 65, 71, 73, 80, 92, 101, 139, 145, 156, 167, 178, 185, 190, 213, 270
Civil society 5, 6, 18, 25–6, 37, 49, 86–7, 307, 318
Climate 26, 42, 48, 114, 168
Clothing 201–2, 204–5, 207, 208
Communications 113, 122, 226–7, 296–7
Communities 26, 59, 84–7, 111, 230–1, 260, 272, 307, 326
Community-based organizations 13, 326
Comparative advantage 201–3, 205, 232
Competition Commission of Pakistan 30, 216
Competitiveness 1, 2, 8, 11, 48, 62, 113, 117, 132, 141, 170, 196–7, 200–3, 205, 211–16, 218–19, 223–4, 227, 229, 242–4, 265–6, 278, 282
Corporate Tax 72, 128–9
Corruption 18, 22, 24–6, 37, 44, 83–4, 100, 139, 327

Cotton 10, 124, 146, 177, 197–8, 204, 206–9
Council of Common Interests 7, 35, 83, 164–5, 171, 199
CPEC 2–3, 11, 13, 221, 229, 245, 256–7, 259, 261, 268–9, 270–2, 283–4, 289–90
Credit 43, 76, 113, 175–6, 196, 234–5
Crowding-out 2
Culture 24
Customs 13, 40, 73, 75, 79, 116, 200, 212–13, 216, 236, 260–1, 266–7, 281–2
Customs duty 64, 115, 120, 132–3, 214, 223, 237

D

Debt 3, 10, 27, 32, 41, 44, 52, 57, 70, 81, 114, 157–61, 174–6, 181–2, 189–90, 197, 274–5
decent work 13, 293–4, 316, 318, 331
Decentralization 8, 23, 31, 38–40, 156, 164–5, 189
Development 1, 3–4, 6, 8, 10, 16–18, 23, 26, 29, 31–2, 34–5, 38–40, 48, 51, 56, 61–6, 71, 76–8, 92, 100–3, 105, 113–15, 152–3, 155–65, 167, 170–2, 175–7, 182–4, 186, 188–90, 198, 200, 202, 204, 216–18, 222, 227, 231, 236, 240, 243, 245, 262, 266, 268, 275–6, 278–80, 293,

298–9, 303, 305, 309–12, 315–18, 320–4, 326, 329, 330–1
Devolution 3, 23, 31, 41, 156, 164–5, 185, 189
DFID 139, 280
Diplomacy 69, 216, 218, 223, 231, 255, 260, 273, 286
Direct tax 9, 112, 115–17, 124, 127, 138, 145, 210–11, 238, 320
DISCOs 50, 81
discrimination 299–300, 304

E

EAD 69–70, 285
Earnings 264, 302
ECC 30, 33, 35, 64, 82
ECNEC 35, 183
ECO 133, 216, 261, 270, 285, 308
Economics 78, 302, 305
ECOTA 261, 284
EDF 76, 198, 224–25, 229–30, 243
Education 3, 13, 23–4, 26, 90, 114, 122, 142, 153–4, 156–7, 161–4, 166, 187–9, 244, 294, 301–4, 306, 311, 313–14, 316, 322–3, 329, 332
Efficiency 9–10, 23, 30, 32, 44, 48, 53, 111, 114, 123, 139, 143, 145, 152, 155–6, 159–61, 169–70, 188–9, 204, 267, 287–8, 293, 300
EFS 234–5
Electrical 130–1, 205

Electricity 27, 43, 49–50, 62, 80–1, 106–8, 113, 116, 121–3, 158–60, 172–4, 209–10, 218, 232, 257, 273–4, 276, 278–9
Energy 2, 3, 5, 8, 12–13, 36, 49, 51–2, 60, 79–81, 92, 131–2, 155–6, 174–6, 179, 181, 219–20, 234, 241, 257, 259–60, 263–4, 268–9, 273–9, 284, 289, 319, 327
Entrepreneurship 14, 29, 243, 307, 315, 327, 328, 332
Environment 2, 4, 24, 26–7, 36, 55, 66, 78, 117, 199–200, 210–13, 218–19, 277, 284, 313, 315, 319
European Union 1, 199, 231, 295, 317
Evaluation 12, 28, 58, 65–6, 70–2, 77, 91, 121, 139, 152, 180, 185–6, 205, 222–3, 226, 234, 239, 242, 245, 270, 288, 306, 310, 314, 316, 325, 333
Exchange rate 2, 113–14, 133, 175–6, 196–7, 202, 210, 212–14, 223–4, 274
Excise duty 115, 117, 136, 320
Export Development Surcharge 202
Export promotion 11, 64, 196–8, 202, 225–6, 228, 231
Exports 1, 15–17, 62–3, 76, 133–4, 196–8, 200–3, 206–13, 215, 217, 219, 221, 223, 225–8, 231, 235, 237–8, 240–2, 295

F

Federal Board of Revenue 8, 30, 116, 120, 199
Fertilizer 37, 52, 124, 130–1, 134, 158–60, 177, 207–9, 242
Finance Act 64, 113, 126
Fiscal policy 14, 27, 29, 33, 35, 42, 61, 68, 71, 124, 199, 319, 321–3, 332
Fiscal Responsibility and Debt Limitation Act 10, 32, 182
Fish and fish products 203
Foreign Direct Investment 129
FPCCI 243
FTA 77, 133, 204–5, 214, 223, 239, 262

G

GENCOs 81
General Sales Tax 40, 115
GIDC 51
GIZ 299, 300, 305, 316, 323
Governance 1, 3–8, 21, 22, 24, 28–30, 32, 34–9, 42–7, 53, 55–7, 60–3, 65, 72, 79–80, 83, 86–7, 91, 92, 114, 155, 159–60, 181, 213, 224, 240, 242, 245, 266, 270, 274, 279, 282, 284, 289
Grants 30, 32, 52, 53, 161–2, 172–3, 175–6, 189–90, 275, 307, 326
GSP 11, 76–7, 200, 214, 222, 224–5, 228–9, 245, 295
GSTS 120, 122, 136, 144

H

Health 3–4, 23–4, 50, 114, 125, 154, 156–7, 161–4, 166, 187–9, 215, 296–8, 303–4, 313, 314, 332
Human Resource 18, 20, 22, 58, 60, 65, 67–9, 73, 77, 92, 141, 152–3, 155–7, 170, 189–90, 312, 318, 329, 332
Hydropower 275–6

I

ILO 294–7, 316
IMF 1, 16, 17, 32–3, 36, 40–2, 52, 120–1, 126, 198, 222–3, 237
Import 133–4, 136, 159–60, 196, 199–200, 202, 204, 206–9, 212, 244, 264, 277
Income Tax 40, 74, 112, 117, 120–1, 127, 141
Income Tax Ordinance 112
Incubation 312, 315
India 2, 14–17, 38–9, 55, 98–103, 117, 133, 155, 198, 200–2, 204–6, 209–12, 216, 221–2, 233, 236, 255–8, 261–2, 264–7, 271–2, 276, 278, 281
Indian Ocean 268, 281
Indirect taxes 112, 115–17, 124, 138, 210–11, 238, 320
Industry 5, 50–1, 81, 117, 130, 199–200, 202, 207–10, 214, 219, 226, 230, 244, 258, 278,

286, 294, 305, 311, 313, 328–30, 332
Inequality 6, 22, 57, 111–12, 114, 151, 154, 169, 294, 298–300, 326
Infant mortality 3, 155
Infrastructure 2–3, 6, 12–13, 19, 21, 28, 51, 66, 122, 152–5, 157–60, 168, 174–6, 178, 180–1, 188, 202, 218, 220, 221, 238, 245, 259–60, 262–3, 265–8, 270–1, 273, 275, 277, 279, 281, 287–8, 327
Innovation 60, 89, 198, 212–13, 315, 332
Insurance 54, 77, 89, 122, 177, 225, 261, 280, 282, 303, 313–14
Interest payments 157, 159–60
Internship 305, 311, 313–15, 330
Intra-industry Trade 204
Iran 2, 13, 70, 202, 219, 221–2, 233, 236, 255–6, 258, 260–2, 270, 272, 276–7, 281–2, 284, 289

J

Job-creation 269
Jobs 14, 293, 299, 300, 304, 311, 314, 316–17, 319, 329, 330

K

Kazakhstan 13, 38–9, 55, 98–103, 261, 268, 270, 276, 281

Khyber Pakhtunkhwa 3, 12, 144, 156, 164, 210–11, 281, 288, 309, 311–12, 324

L

Labour 5–6, 13–14, 22, 55, 145, 155, 163–4, 196, 199–200, 215, 218–19, 239, 293–301, 303–5, 309–13, 315–18, 322–4, 329–32
Leather 198, 202, 207–8
Literacy 3, 164–5
LMIS 305, 322–3, 329
LPI 266–7
LTFF 234–5

M

Malaysia 204, 330
Management 1, 5, 8–11, 19, 24, 27–8, 31, 36–40, 43–4, 48, 52–3, 56–8, 60, 66, 69, 73, 75, 80, 82, 91–2, 121, 129, 137, 139, 141, 145, 151, 156, 167, 173–4, 178–9, 182–4, 186–7, 189, 197–8, 213, 215, 223, 232, 236, 243, 267, 270, 279, 284, 286–7, 300, 306–7, 321, 325, 327
MDGs 114, 167
Microfinance 89, 321
Middle East 202–3, 267–8
Ministry of Commerce 7–8, 56, 178–9, 198, 226, 228, 236, 269, 282, 328

Ministry of Finance 7–8, 53–4, 62–3, 130, 198, 229
Monitoring 10, 12, 28, 35, 38–40, 57, 65–6, 70, 121, 134, 152, 168, 171, 178, 183, 185–6, 189, 236, 238, 245, 282, 290, 306, 326
MoPDR 56, 67–8
MTBF 68–9, 73, 184

N

NADRA 9, 75, 146
National Accountability Bureau 8, 25, 83
National Economic Council 31, 35, 171, 180
National Finance Commission 31, 35, 120, 273
NATO 289
NAVTTC 310, 329
Nepal 256, 262, 271, 276
NEPRA 50–1, 79, 82, 87, 234, 241
Non-governmental organizations 49, 67, 225, 232, 259, 307, 323–6
Non-tariff Measures 215, 222, 224
Non-tax Revenues 115, 122, 319
NTB 310
Nutrition 114

O

OGDCL 51, 105, 175–6
OGRA 79, 82, 87, 241
Oil 2, 42, 52, 80, 130–1, 136, 158–60, 207–9, 241, 275–7, 279
Ombudsman 59, 74, 84, 142–3, 146
Outsourcing 212–13

P

Pakistan 1–2, 4–6, 8–20, 22–4, 26–30, 32, 34–41, 43–4, 48–53, 55, 62, 64, 71, 75–9, 82–4, 86–9, 92, 98–105, 108, 112–15, 117–19, 125–7, 129, 141–2, 144–5, 152–5, 158–60, 162, 167, 169, 174–7, 179–80, 188, 196–8, 201–10, 212–14, 216–17, 219, 221–5, 227, 228, 230–2, 235, 239–40, 243–5, 255–75, 277–89, 293, 295–302, 308–10, 317, 321, 328, 332
Participation rate 296–7, 299, 300–1
PEFA 164–5
PEPCO 50, 52
PFCs 35, 168, 186
pharmaceutical items 203
photographic products 203
PIA 104, 175–6
Planning Commission 8, 62–7, 77, 80, 171, 182–4, 221, 326
PML (N) 219
Port 220, 260, 265–6, 281, 289
Poverty 6, 22, 57, 111, 114–15, 151–5, 169, 171, 268, 288, 304, 312–13

PPP 81, 98–103, 326
PRAL 9, 144, 146
precious stones 203
private sector 2, 15–17, 26–7, 36, 42, 48–9, 52, 54–5, 59, 67, 81, 84–5, 98, 113–14, 124, 128, 141–3, 146, 153, 175–6, 182, 197–8, 201, 222, 225, 227, 229, 233, 245, 259, 260, 270, 274, 279, 287, 299–300, 302–3, 307–8, 310–12, 322–6, 329–30
Privatization 10, 27, 81, 177, 179
production 31, 62–3, 78, 89, 111, 136, 169, 175–6, 182, 196, 202–4, 213, 216, 228, 231, 234, 238, 278, 296–7
productive employment 13, 293, 312, 318, 325, 331–2
Productivity 145, 155, 197–8, 202–3, 212–13, 218, 226, 313, 322–3, 331
Provincial Government(s) 3, 7, 11, 14, 31–3, 35, 40–1, 62–3, 67, 76–7, 92, 108, 121, 123, 138, 159–60, 162–5, 167, 178, 185, 187, 189, 196, 198–9, 210–11, 217, 220, 224–6, 228–9, 231–2, 239, 241–2, 273, 281, 284, 293, 295, 308–10, 318, 321–4, 329–32
PTA 87, 262
Public Administration 4, 7, 10, 157, 170, 189
Public expenditure 1, 4–5, 10, 23, 28, 32, 114, 125, 151–3, 156–8, 164–5, 167, 169–71
public sector 1, 4, 6, 9–10, 13–15, 18, 20, 24, 27–8, 30, 32, 34–40, 44, 53, 58–9, 62–3, 66, 71, 79, 81–2, 92, 157, 161–2, 169–70, 175–6, 183–7, 190, 225, 231, 235, 270, 298–9, 302, 306–7, 309, 311, 314, 320, 326, 329
Public Sector Development Programme(s) 20, 32, 34–5, 62–3, 66, 186, 231
Public sector enterprise(s) 1, 10, 15, 27, 71, 161–2
public works 323–4, 329
Public-private Partnership 10, 81, 186, 284, 326
Punjab 3–4, 38–40, 122, 144, 146, 156, 164–5, 177, 210–11, 273, 300, 302, 309, 311–12, 315, 317

Q

QTTA 13, 270–1, 284, 289

R

RAFTAAR 155, 158, 173, 278
Rail 216, 220, 260–3, 266–7, 281, 284, 287–8
RBM 184
recreational services 205
regulation 5, 36, 53–6, 69, 79, 82, 86–90, 92, 108, 182, 242, 279, 299–300

research 5–7, 12, 28, 65–6, 71–2, 74, 77–8, 91, 114, 169, 171, 204, 218, 226, 233, 235, 242, 279, 288, 298–9, 318
Retail 120, 122, 146, 280–9
Revenue 1–2, 6, 8–9, 30, 37–9, 41, 57, 62, 64, 72–5, 105–7, 113–16, 120–1, 123, 128, 130, 133, 136–9, 141–6, 158–60, 168, 180, 182, 199, 222–3, 225, 234, 237, 288, 319–20
RIA 56, 88, 90, 220, 224, 242
Rice 177, 198, 202–3, 206–8, 219, 221
Road 155, 216, 220, 260–3, 266–8, 271–2, 281, 284, 287, 327

S

SAARC 216, 222, 233, 255–7, 261–2, 270, 308–9
safeguards 299–300
SAFTA 206, 223, 233, 261
Schools 136, 188, 230, 330
SDG-8 13, 331–2
SDPI 72, 115, 120, 125, 127, 139, 154, 283, 303, 320
Securities and Exchange Commission of Pakistan 8, 22, 141
Self-employment 13, 115, 318, 320, 322, 326
Services 5, 9, 16–17, 26, 36, 40, 44–7, 53–4, 58–9, 66, 76, 78, 84–5, 89–90, 101, 117, 120–2, 136, 145, 157, 162, 169, 171, 175–7, 180, 182, 205–6, 210–11, 217, 225, 232, 235, 239–40, 243, 258, 261–2, 267, 281, 294, 296–7, 308–9, 314, 327, 332
Sindh 4, 37–9, 122–3, 144, 156, 164–5, 210–11, 215, 273, 309, 312, 315–17
Singapore 204, 207–9
Skill(s) 18, 59, 74, 84–5, 114, 156, 214, 230, 239, 245, 293, 298–300, 302–8, 310–13, 315, 317, 322–4, 326, 329–31
SMEDA 224, 243, 321
SMEs 76, 89, 132, 216–17, 229–31, 233–4, 245
SNGPL 51, 174–6
Social accountability 5, 23, 26, 84–7, 146, 307, 325
Social capital 20, 26, 140
Social enterprise(s) 67, 326
Social entrepreneurship 307
Social protection 155, 298
Social safety net(s) 3, 14, 29, 170, 294–5, 314, 320, 325, 332
South Asia 3, 127, 154, 206–9, 222, 255–9, 261, 264, 270–1, 276, 305
South Asia Economic Summit 255, 259, 270
SPS 11, 215, 219, 228–9, 239, 245
SRO 30, 126, 180, 226
SSGC 51, 173–6
start-up 89, 320
State Bank of Pakistan 8, 22, 62, 141, 207–8, 227, 286

Strategic Trade Policy Framework 11, 133, 201, 240, 269
Subsidy 158–60, 173–4
Supply chain(s) 11, 28, 32, 186, 196, 199, 202, 221, 232, 238, 242, 245, 260, 265, 274, 288, 329
sustainable development 4, 26
Sustainable Development Goals 4, 114, 153, 293

T

Tajikistan 261, 263–4, 268–9, 271, 276, 278–9, 282–3
TAPI 3, 264, 275, 277, 285
Tariff(s) 64, 132–3, 159–61, 173–4, 181, 196, 202, 209–10, 215–18, 222, 224, 234, 236–9, 241, 260, 275, 287
TARP 72, 121, 139
Tax Administration 40–1, 72–3, 121, 129, 138–9, 145–6
Tax Gap 124–5
Tax Incidence 9, 64, 237
Tax Policy 9, 73–4, 111, 121, 124, 138, 141, 145
Taxation 5, 36, 41, 64, 74, 84, 105, 107–8, 111–12, 122–3, 125, 127, 136–7, 145–6, 210–11, 319
TBT 11, 215, 228–9, 245
TDAP 77, 222, 229, 240, 243
telecommunication 205
Think Tank(s) 6, 15–17, 65–7, 71, 233, 243, 286, 323–4

TIR 13, 269, 280, 283
Towels 206–8
Trade Facilitation 11, 260
transit 2, 5, 12–13, 156, 212, 216, 229, 232, 236–9, 245, 255, 258–9, 260–2, 265, 269–72, 277, 279–89
transport 12–13, 27, 60, 89, 120–2, 132, 177, 204–5, 212–13, 238, 260–1, 265–9, 280, 283, 285, 288–9, 296–7
TRTA 216–17
TTFA 261
TVET 294, 313, 316–18, 329–33

U

UAE 207–9
UFG 51, 82, 174–6
UIPT 138
Underemployment 14, 299–300, 312, 325, 330
Unemployment 14, 296–300, 303, 310, 312, 319, 322–3, 330
Unemployment rate 296–9
United States of America 1, 202
universities 305, 315
USAID 231, 280
Uzbekistan 261, 268, 276, 281

V

Value Addition 124, 202, 215, 218, 231, 234
value chain(s) 199, 204, 239–40, 258–60, 309, 321

VAT 130
venture capital 315
Vietnam 14–17, 38–9, 55, 98–103, 200, 209–10, 212
Vision 2025 62–3, 156, 171, 188, 221
Vocational training 163–4, 302, 311, 315, 317–18, 323–4, 330

W

Wagah 272, 282
Wage(s) 13, 115, 175–6, 189, 239, 300–2, 313, 322–3
WAPDA 159–60, 175–6
Warehousing 216, 219, 235, 280, 285, 289, 296–7
WEBOC 282
welfare 12, 23, 29, 72, 124, 136, 153, 182, 204, 304, 309, 330
Wheat 37, 52, 53, 158–60, 172–3, 206
WHTs 113, 127–8, 136
World Bank 56, 72, 98–103, 121, 127, 139, 164–5, 173, 210, 212, 231, 242–3, 265, 278–80, 317
WWF 304

Y

youth employment 306–8, 311, 325–6, 332